LOVING LEBUS

LOVING LEBUS

*Looking into
Lebus Furniture*

PAUL COLLIER

First published in 2022 by Green Frigate Books

Green Frigate Books is an imprint of Libri Publishing.

Copyright © Paul Collier

The right of Paul Collier to be identified as the author of this work has been asserted in accordance with the Copyright, Designs and Patents Act, 1988.

ISBN 978-1-911451-09-9

All rights reserved. No part of this publication may be reproduced, stored in any retrieval system or transmitted in any form or by any means, electronic, mechanical, photocopying, recording or otherwise, without the prior written permission of the copyright holder for which application should be addressed in the first instance to the publishers. No liability shall be attached to the author, the copyright holder or the publishers for loss or damage of any nature suffered as a result of reliance on the reproduction of any of the contents of this publication or any errors or omissions in its contents.

A CIP catalogue record for this book is available from The British Library

Cover and book design by Carnegie Book Prouction

Libri Publishing
Brunel House
Volunteer Way
Faringdon
Oxfordshire
SN7 7YR
Tel: +44 (0)845 873 3837

www.libripublishing.co.uk

Every effort has been made to trace the ownership of all copyrighted material. If any omission has been made, please bring this to the publisher's attention so that proper acknowledgement may be given in future editions.

Front cover: Sideboard courtesy of Adam Duxbury at Back from the Brink, Facebook. The Front cover: Sideboard courtesy of Adam Duxbury at Back from the Brink, Facebook. The sideboard was from the Guernsey or Airdrie dining-room suite pictured in 1966 (catalogue number 3401). From the Europa catalogue, 1970, Heidelberg was the name given to the chair and stool (catalogue numbers 9537 and 9539). Pictured in vinyl, the pair were also available upholstered in an alternative material (no further details were given). Both were on castors, and the chair could swivel. It was described as being 'not so much a chair, more of a single seat sofa. Lose yourself in its deep cushioning. Put your feet up on the matching stool. Enjoy it for what it is: a daring look into a brave and comfortable new world of armchair comfort. Plump loose cushions fit back and seat, the seat cushions – all in one with the arm cushions'.

Dedication

This book is dedicated to the memory of my beautiful friend

Pavlos Panayioti Mastihi

12 October 1956 – 23 October 2020

Pavlos, pictured in his home, Green Lanes, Haringey, N4, beside his prized vintage china cabinet. Photograph reproduced with kind permission of Athena Mandis.

Acknowledgements

I was fortunate enough to be afforded the enormous privilege of meeting with the closest descendants of Harris Lebus, including Harris's grandson Oliver, back in 2008 and working with his son Tim during my research.

Deborah Hedgecock and the staff team at Bruce Castle Museum (Haringey Archive and Museum Service).

David Dewing, Regional Furniture Society for his guidance and support.

Robin Pakes who shared some of his historic research on modernity and Bath.

Phillip Child, who in the course of his research into his own family's furniture business shared some of his relevant resources.

Harold Summers, who also shared some of his research while looking into his family connections with both Beautility and Summers furniture.

The team at Libri Publishing with a special mention to Steve Lane and Celia Cozens and to Lucy Frontani at Carnegie Book Production.

And finally, Karl Walker and the team at Lebus Upholstery for kindly sponsoring this book.

Paul Collier, 2021

A Word from Our Sponsors

We are extremely proud to sponsor this book, which looks into Lebus furniture of the past – both cabinet and upholstery. Whilst cabinet making ceased in 1970, Lebus Upholstery has continuously provided the nation with sofas and armchairs. Today we are one of the 'largest furniture manufacturers of UK produced upholstery'.

Whilst we operate from a modern, purpose-built factory of some 250,000 square feet in Scunthorpe, we have much affinity with our past and our origins. We are based close to where the story began in around 1840 with Louis Lebus arriving in Hull, and where his son Harris was born. Although the Lebus family connection with the business formally ended 40 years ago, we owe our existence to four generations of the Lebus family, and especially to Louis, Harris, and Sir Herman and Oliver.

Just as it was back then, we pride ourselves on manufacturing products to the highest possible standard in supplying independent retailers across the UK and Ireland. We make all our own frames from hardwood or composite materials, with all joints glued and pinned for triple strength and long-lasting rigidity. We have our own foam- and fibre-making facilities, and we invest in the latest computer technologies.

The designs which go to make Lebus upholstery today are exclusive to us. We could talk about these endlessly – and we do! But this book takes us back in time. It looks into the wealth of Lebus upholstered designs of the past and brings them to a new audience today. The ornate, carved, high-end sofas, easy chairs, armchairs, chaise longues, drawing-room suites and dining-room seating of the era before

From the Lebus catalogue, 1909, translated into French and German.

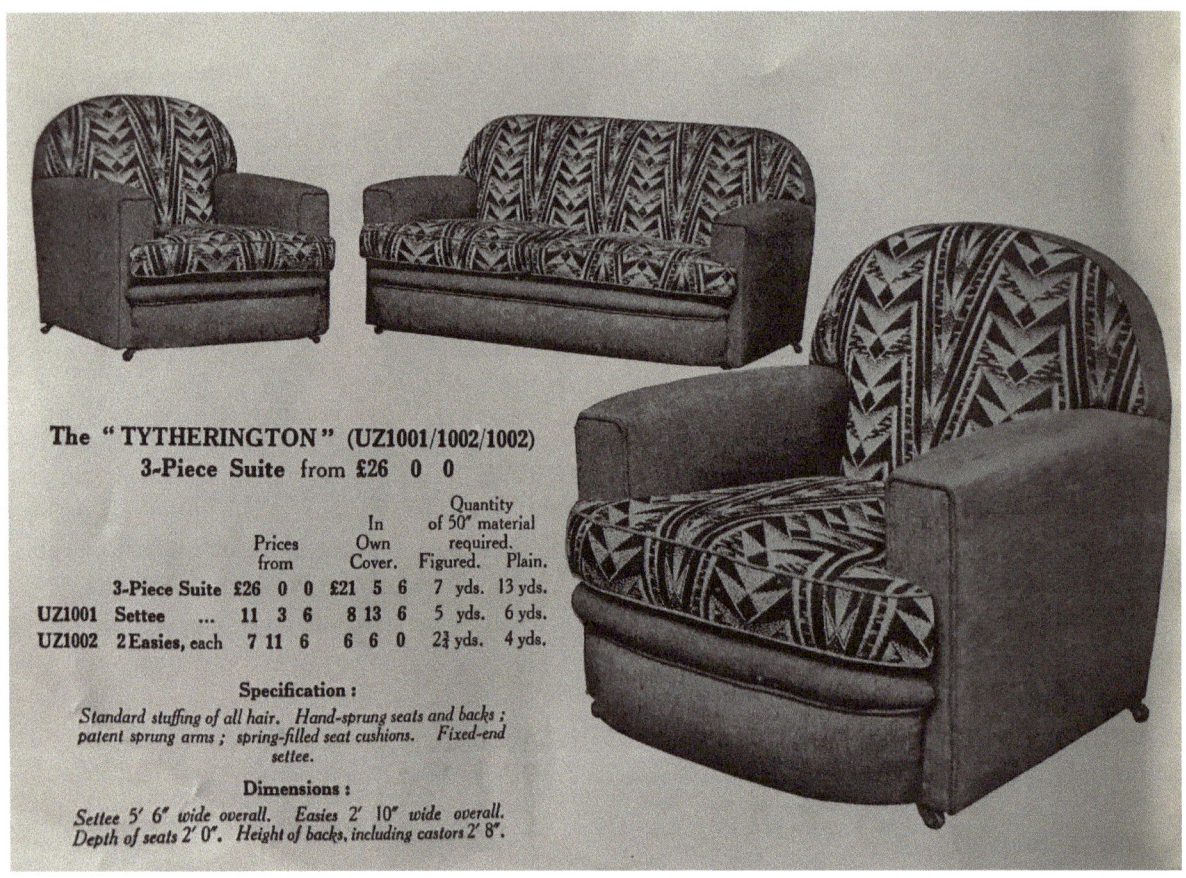

From the Lebus 1937 catalogue.

From the Lebus Europa catalogue, 1970.

World War One, covered with gorgeous fabrics, are truly quite a sight to behold. The graceful curves of the three-piece suites Lebus made in the Art Deco period and the soft furnishings of the mid-century modern period have all been brought to life in this book.

Paul has now told the story of Lebus furniture and Lebus upholstery, and the history behind it. Throughout this history we were struck by the loyalty of the workforce community and how they were considered an asset through the evolution of the business. That tradition and ethos is held just as passionately today. Lebus Upholstery is now entirely employee owned. (The technical description of the business is an Employee Owned Trust or EOT.) And we are grateful to Paul for his labour of love bringing the story of our past to a new audience of today.

Karl Walker, October 2021

Follow Lebus Furniture on Social Media

 Harris Lebus Book

Facebook group: Lebus Furniture

 harris_Lebus_book

 HarrisLebus@HLebusProject

The same sixties sideboard, different finishes: Libner Diaz (Etsy) has gone for a contemporary painted look while Dalena at Dalena Designs has used paint to frame the sanded and treated original walnut veneer.

This brings a smile to the face. Revive and Kicking brings bedtime fun with this Link cabinet decorated with this image of an oversized mid-century orange dial telephone.

Contents

Foreword ... xiii

Preface ... xv

Lebus and Me… ... 1

When We Loved Lebus ... 7
   Commercial success ... 7
   Enduring business model ... 8
   The four generations of Lebus – Louis, Harris, Herman, Oliver ... 13
   High-end furniture for the wealthiest households ... 14
   Affordable furniture for the many ... 17
   Moving to mid-century modernity ... 18
   Branching out – expanding the business with new products and services ... 21
   Could it really be we were *falling out of love with Lebus*? ... 21
   The Europa challenge – a gamble too far… ... 21
   Loving Lebus – all over again… ... 24

Looking into Lebus Furniture ... 31

From the Bedroom to the Office… and Every Room Between –
Art Nouveau/Arts and Crafts, 1873–1914 ... 33

Looking into 1907, 1909, 1912 and 1913 ... 40
   Bedrooms ... 44
   Sideboards and dining room ... 49
   Drawing room ... 55
   Miscellaneous ... 58
   Hall ... 59
   Library and office furniture (for commercial premises) ... 59

Affordable for All… Flats, Modest Terraces, Sizeable Semi-detached Houses –
Art Deco/'Modern Traditional', 1919–1939 ... 69

Looking into 1926, 1934, 1936, 1937 and 1939 ... 74
   Furnishing a modest terraced cottage or flat with three bedrooms and one reception room
      with small kitchen, making selections from the least expensive choices in the 1937 catalogue ... 84
   Bedrooms ... 84
   Living room ... 86
   Furnishing a suburban four-bedroom (one a box room) detached house with the more expensive
      choices in the 1937 catalogue ... 89
   Bedrooms ... 89
   Dining room ... 91
   Sitting room ... 94
   Hall ... 96

Candy-floss Colours Morphed into Neon Bold: Utility Furniture and Mid-century Modern, 1943–1970   **99**

Looking into 1953 and 1954   103
- Bedrooms   103
- Dining furniture   112
- Three-piece suites   116
- Kitchen free-standing units   118
- Hall   122
- Miscellaneous furniture   123

Looking into 1956 – Link   124

Looking into 1965   138
- Bedroom suites   141
- Sideboards and dining furniture   148
- Lounge   154
- Kitchens   162
- Looking briefly into Lebus's main competitors   165

Looking into 1967 – Europa   167

Still Loving Lebus: Lebus Upholstery   **177**
- Silver Anniversary at the Woodley plant in 1975   177
- What might be lurking behind the sofa…?   177
- The twilight years, 1979–2005   180
- Saved by a customer, 2005–2012   180
- One of the largest upholstered furniture manufacturers in the UK, 2012–2021   180
- Employee Ownership Trust – Lebus Upholstery   181

List of Main Sources   183

Foreword

The story of Lebus Furniture is a key to the history of British furniture manufacture in the 20th century, a history which is not yet fully researched, analysed and understood. Lebus was, by their own definition (and never doubted) 'the largest furniture factory in the world' from the 1920s to the 1960s and its sheer size and output place it at the heart of the British industry. From its beginnings in the Edwardian period as a maker of quality reproduction furniture, through its rapid growth in the interwar period as volume producer of middle quality domestic and office furniture, to its efforts in the 50s and 60s to appeal to a younger market with more affordable ranges, Lebus was in many ways a litmus paper for the wider industry. In the end, the very size of the organisation made it harder to adapt to a rapidly changing consumer market and the volatile economic conditions of the post-war era. Perhaps it had to collapse in the 1970s in order to be re-born and it is heartening now to see the brand revived and a thriving trade in restoring and up-cycling the mid-century models.

Loving Lebus is the companion volume to *Harris Lebus: A Romance with the Furniture Trade* (2020) in which Collier unravelled the intricate history of the family and the fascinating development of the company. This volume shows us the products, using images from the catalogues and marketing material in the extensive Lebus archive now held by Haringey Archive and Museum Service, and of surviving examples of the furniture. Identifying the furniture is one the difficulties encountered by the author as well by collectors and dealers, because almost all sales went through independent retailers and much of the furniture, at least until the 1950s, was marked not by Lebus but by the retailer. This publication will be a significant aid in matching furniture to documentary evidence and in revealing whether or not there is a recognisable Lebus style, when compared to similar models made by other manufacturers.

In any study of furniture, understanding the context is essential. Domestic furniture, for example, is best studied in the context of the home and family life, as Collier has shown here. The design, layout and functions of rooms has evolved over time, reflecting changes in family routines and ways of living, and this creates the impulse for change in furniture design and function, as well as its appearance and style. The Sheraton style drawing room of the Edwardian period illustrated here was intended for the formal lifestyle of a middle class family in a house with large rooms and no doubt one or two servants. By comparison, the 1950s living room featuring Lebus's new Link furniture was aimed at a young family in a relatively small house on a tight budget, where living was less formal and the furniture was more adaptable. Marketing materials provide a valuable source for researching the history of the home as well as furniture.

Comparing Lebus to other manufacturers is work in progress. We need more publications like this, examining the fortunes of other companies, before we can really see how the industry as a whole coped with the social and economic changes of the 20th century, and in particular the post-war period when so many companies struggled to keep their share of the market. The author makes a brief reference to this in the chapter 'Looking into 1965', and it is to be hoped that Loving Lebus will inspire similar studies of those companies which have yet to be researched.

David Dewing, President of the Regional Furniture Society and former Director of the Geffrye Museum (now Museum of the Home).

A Sheraton-style drawing room from before World War One.

Front cover of a catalogue for Lebus Link furniture launched in Autumn 1956.

Preface

The brand name Lebus was not one that was familiar to me when I moved into my current home in 2007. The simple mention of the former furniture factory in a newsletter from our residents' association was the springboard for my journey of discovery into all things Lebus. I became captivated by this history, and it became clear that the business initially bearing the name of Harris Lebus was more than simply a manufacturer of furniture. The story of a life, a business, a family and a workforce community is, for me, a ready-made screen drama. The book *Harris Lebus: A Romance with the Furniture Trade* (Libri Publishing, March 2020), encapsulating this narrative, is a product of my fascination and research.

Of course, in writing this history I included Lebus furniture. I provided an overview of the influences for Lebus designs and focused on how they were made and by whom. However, I felt there was more that could be said about the furniture itself. Many Lebus products were not branded until the 1950s. This begs the question: how can once-*loved* Lebus-made furniture be confidently attributed to the firm? Is there something 'typical' about Lebus? As I continued looking into Lebus furniture I became aware, through social media, of an appetite for knowledge. And the question I get asked most is: 'When was this piece of Lebus furniture made?'

My private collection of catalogues – which has grown to 13 – yielded answers to many questions. Just how many individual Lebus furniture designs might there have been? Were there overlaps between each catalogue or were designs completely new with each

The author's private collection of Lebus catalogues.

subsequent issue? Was it the case that the same number of designs were on offer each year or did this vary? How did Lebus adapt its products to changes in the way we used our homes through the twentieth century? Did these reflect changes in consumer tastes? Were significant price increases evident over time? How much furniture was produced by Lebus and how much of this are we still living with today? I have looked into four distinct periods of furniture manufacture at Lebus: leading up to World War One; the interwar years; after World War Two; and that which followed the company's reinvention in 1966 to facilitate the production of the Europa furniture brand. I have increased my knowledge about Lebus furniture and discovered much to tell. This companion book has enabled me to build on the history and to share my passion for Lebus furniture. *Loving Lebus: Looking into Lebus Furniture* now completes the story.

So, look into Lebus furniture. I hope that by the end of the book, you too will be *loving* Lebus.

Paul Collier, 2021

Early to mid-sixties oak interchangeable four-drawer chest, up-cycled by Anita Quintana at Quintana ReDesign (Facebook). A copy of Harris Lebus: A Romance with the Furniture Trade sits on top.

Lebus and Me...

When Lebus named one of its dining-room suites after a Scottish town in 1937, no one could have imagined that years later, where once stood the main production plant for Lebus furniture, people would live in homes on a street sharing the name Armadale. I am proud to say I am one of those residents living in Armadale Close, on what was once the site of the Lebus veneer workshop.

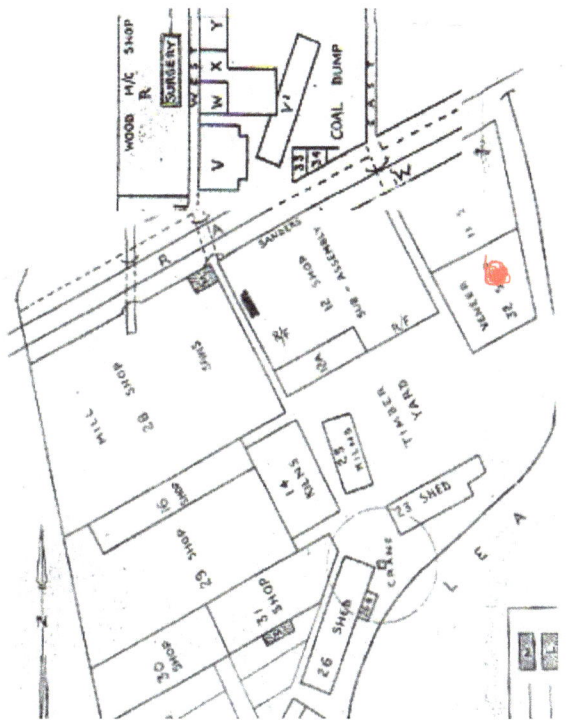

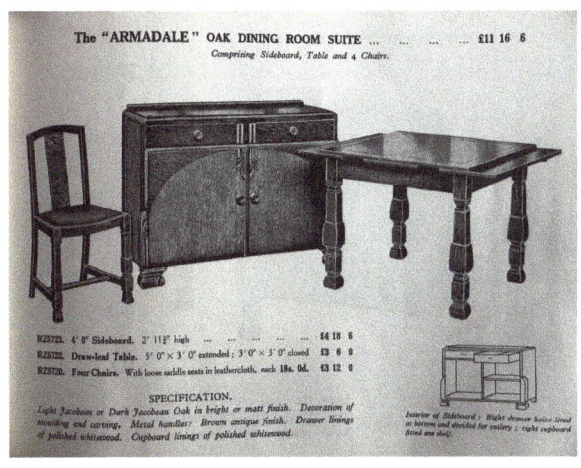

Armadale dining-room suite from the Lebus catalogue, July 1937.

Sketch map of the factory indicating where the veneer shop was and where Armadale Close is now.

Photograph of the same area (original print acquired on eBay).

Lebus consistently made the claim to be the 'largest furniture factory in the world'. It was featured in the firm's advertising throughout. This claim appears to have gone unchallenged – even in the United States of America. It made headline news in the *Michigan Artisan*, on 25 February 1907, when Harris's son Herman publicly made the assertion on a visit to Grand Rapids, Michigan (then America's leading furniture-producing region).

The complete factory at Tottenham Hale as pictured in the 1965 catalogue.

Imagery used in a post-World War Two advertisement in the *Cabinet Maker and Complete House Furnisher* in 1947, which associated Lebus with the world.

It follows, then, that due consideration must be given to the notion that to justify its claim and to warrant such eminence, Lebus manufactured and sold furniture in enormous volumes. With the application of logic, the business should have supplied more furniture than any other contemporaneous furniture manufacture in the twentieth century – if only to gain maximum returns on its capital investment in its plant and infrastructure. Its furniture wended its way to the nation's homes such that it can be said that a considerable proportion of households were furnished with Lebus. The conclusion can be drawn that, as a nation, we have lived with and *loved* Lebus furniture.

Inevitably, I asked myself this question: had I lived with Lebus furniture without knowing it? Perhaps I had stayed in an hotel room containing Lebus furniture? Or maybe it was the student bedsits that I lived in during the mid-1980s?

Number 81, Pepys Road, south London was a typical, late-nineteenth-century Victorian villa with 12 or more rooms over three floors. I had what had been the master bedroom, which came furnished with dark, shiny furniture – surely some of this was Lebus?

I looked back at family photographs taken when I was still a baby at 77 High Street, Weston (once a separate village on the fringes of Bath). This nineteenth-century cottage was rented from a private landlord by my parents with a young family. By all accounts it was in

An art piece I completed sometime during the early 1980s to capture the feel of my student accommodation: fireside chair, dining table, dressing table. Were any of these pieces in my rented furnished bedsit made by Lebus?

a bad state of repair. It had no semblance of a fitted kitchen – was the painted blue-and-white free-standing kitchen larder cabinet in the background Lebus made?

Within a few years we had moved and my memory of the home I grew up in and how it was furnished is clearer. Number 2, Odins Road was one of 360 houses built in the

77 High Street, Weston, Bath, birthplace of the author. The original drawing is by Peter Coard and is from his book *Vanishing Bath*. Image courtesy of Bath Preservation Trust.

The author as a baby in nan's arms – was our kitchen larder cupboard made by Lebus?

early 1930s on the Fosse Way estate at Odd Down as part of Bath City Council's response to the rising demand for affordable social housing and for tenants displaced by inner-city slum clearance programmes. We had

Were our kitchen table and chairs Lebus made? The Gayday breakfast set was described thus: tabletop covered in blue or yellow patterned plastic material with brass and white plastic edge trim and white enamelled under-frame. Chairs with upholstered seats and backs in blue or yellow patterned plastic material and gold-colour edge trims on backs and white enamelled frames.

one of those metal-laminated plastic-topped kitchen tables – mid-blue speckled with black star-like shapes and legs of white, enamelled aluminium with matching chairs. It was the kind of mid-century furniture that Lebus manufactured. This was placed at the end of the scullery in front of the full-height coal cupboard, which was next to a walk-in pantry with marble slab shelf to keep perishables cool. The other end of the room had a butler sink with wooden draining board and space for a free-standing cooker and the twin-tub. In the living room we had a mid-blue wing-backed three piece with ebonised legs. Surely this was Lebus made? There were picture and dado rails, and a cast-iron fireplace, as well as open fires in the three bedrooms. And despite the fitted, gloss-painted pine dresser, we had a dark-stained veneered wooden sideboard and an oak extending dining table that had sizeable carved acorns as part of the table's two sturdy legs. These pieces *had* to be Lebus.

My parents subsequently bought the house in Odins Road for the princely sum of £4,000 – a lot of money for a manual engineer. Dad put his skills to use in the age of 'do it yourself' (DIY) and modernisation, ripping out many of the original features of the house, including the coal cupboard and walk-in larder. Replacing these with a designated family dining space, his self-designed, self-built, self-assembled kitchen units from floor to ceiling in mid-blue (which jarred somewhat with the neon orange walls) made it difficult for anyone to stand tall in front of the stove without hitting their head on a wall-mounted double cupboard. With central heating, the focal point of the living room with its bright and bold 'flower power' wallpaper in shades of mauve and blue was no longer the crackling fire, but the TV unit.

An interest in interiors, interior design and a liking for vintage go back as far as I can remember. As a young boy I used to play at rearranging the furniture of the lounge at Odins Road. My mum would often have a nap in the afternoon or simply go to her bedroom to have some time to herself. She knew what I was going to do. I used to call this game 'Mr. Shifter'! With no one else in the house at the time I could happily unleash my creativity and keep myself amused for hours. There were things I genuinely didn't like about the way furniture and accessories at home were arranged. I disliked symmetry – and still do! An example might be a fireplace with matching vases at each end and a clock in the middle. I wanted the clock to be on one side and the vases grouped on the other. This desire to rearrange has stayed with me. Not just content with regularly rearranging my own home, inspired by magazines and books, I am invariably thinking about how I can rearrange when I visit the homes of friends and other people. Some friends, such as Pavlos, even appreciated this and would call on me for help and advice. Going back to my play at Odins Road, when I had finished rearranging accessories and furniture pieces, I would proudly show it to mum when she re-emerged. The disappointing part was that, although mum said she liked my new arrangements, she still wanted it all put back the way it was.

My grandparents' house used to intrigue me as a child. They lived in an Edwardian terraced house: 38 Avondale Road, Bath. It had a very basic scullery kitchen. There was no bathroom and my grandparents and dad often told stories about bath-time in a galvanised tub in front of the coal fire. But the house had been 'modernised' – a cast-iron bath had been installed and disguised under a removable makeshift kitchen work top. Even then, imagine the palaver of taking a bath! The house always seemed a bit impractical to me. With the front room and its comfy, cosy co-ordinated three-piece kept for high days and holidays (you had to plan its use in advance and light the coal fire), everything was crammed into their rear living room. This was dominated by an extendable dining table and chairs, mid-century walnut-veneered sideboard, two easy chairs, a settee (my sister and I used to laugh because the side arm rests could be pushed downwards to make it longer) and a TV set perched atop a tall occasional table with barley-twist legs. Mismatched, not mixed-matched, retrospectively I have wondered, could it be that any of these furniture pieces were Lebus made?

The significance of my anecdotes may now become apparent: perhaps there are those who live with Lebus furniture without realising they do? Lebus was a prolific manufacturer, and from the time it was made, Lebus furniture, with its range of functions, was to be found in a variety of homes and settings across the nation and the globe. Many of these furniture items have survived.

My Lebus tallboy bedroom chest of drawers manufactured in the early sixties, accessorised and with a backdrop of my art.

From the outset, I experienced a sense of familiarity about Lebus furniture. The more I have looked into it, the more I have grown to love Lebus. My own tastes have changed with time. Back when my current home on the Ferry Lane Estate was completed in 1978, I was content with a teenage bedroom furnished with an MFI[1] white melamine flat-packed wardrobe and desk. Today, however, I am the proud owner of both a Lebus mid-century high chest of drawers and a Lebus oak-framed desk. (Made in 1956 as part of a commission for the War Office, the desk has removable legs as it was designed to be taken on manoeuvres.) Passing through the company's manufacturing process in the fifties and sixties, I have, quite literally, brought these furniture pieces home.

My Lebus desk, dated 1956 and part of a commission for the War Office. The detachable legs can be stored in brackets under the desk top in order to be easily transported for use on manoeuvres.

---

1 MFI (Mullard Furniture Industries) was a furniture chain selling inexpensive, mass-produced, flat-packed, self-build furniture items, manufactured cheaply abroad, in stores run like furniture supermarkets.

When We Loved Lebus

Commercial success

There is no doubting the commercial success of the furniture-making business of Lebus, which was often considered by its contemporaries to be one step ahead. The fact that it influenced and played a role in shaping Britain's furniture industry itself must surely be undeniable.

But the path for Lebus was not always a smooth one. The two world wars each caused furniture production to cease completely at Lebus. And such was the impact of war on design decisions, type of products, raw materials, methods of manufacture and target market that we can identify the furniture within three distinct manufacturing periods – each of these with its own chief designer.

Lebus made high-end furniture for the wealthiest households during the Art Nouveau and Arts and Crafts period leading up to the advent of World War One in 1914. This was the first period. It produced affordable furniture for the many during the 'Modern Classical' or Art Deco era between the two world wars, 1919–1939, in the second period.

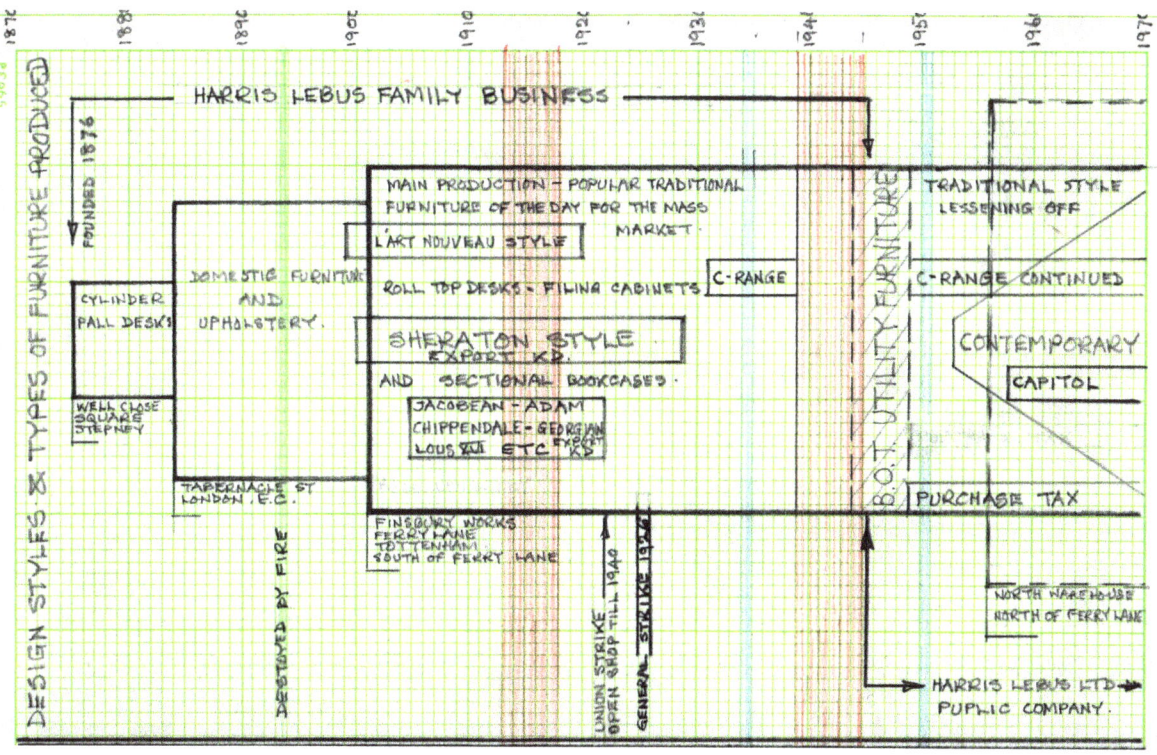

Spanning 100 years – furniture styles adopted by Lebus, with a reference to where manufacturing took place. This was found amongst the personal archives of Oliver Lebus.

Whole-page advertisement from the *Cabinet Maker and Complete House Furnisher*, 10 October 1931, intended for independent retailers and using the imagery of Lebus furniture as a magnet to draw in customers.

The move to mid-century modernity after World War Two was the third. During this production period from 1945 onwards, the family partnership was dissolved with the formation of the public limited company in 1947. This period spanned the regulated and controlled Utility furniture years to the idiosyncrasies of the fifties and sixties.

The Europa challenge – a gamble too far – can be considered to be a fourth period (still with the same chief designer, in post since 1951), when the business was forced to reinvent itself in 1966.

Enduring business model

One factor that remained stable throughout was the Lebus business model. This was built around a simple concept: a travelling sales force armed with regularly updated catalogues of current Lebus furniture ranges. Sales representatives would continuously travel around their designated area encouraging individual furniture shops and outlets to buy, stock and retail Lebus-made furniture on a wholesale basis.

This business model worked for retailers since they were usually sole traders and could make sales by acting as an agent, selling Lebus-made products from the catalogue without having to stock every single piece. A retailer paid Lebus only when they sold an item to one of their local customers.

An advertisement for Ward Stores Ltd, an independent retailer based near the Lebus factory on Seven Sisters Corner, N15, from the *Tottenham and Edmonton Weekly Herald*, 8 November 1946. (Source: Bruce Castle Museum, Haringey Archive and Museum Service)

Here, Ward Stores has a window display with Lebus furniture alongside posters for the Festival of Britain in 1951.
(Source: Bruce Castle Museum, Haringey Archive and Museum Service)

A double-page spread from a supplement in the *Cabinet Maker and Complete House Furnisher*, 5 March 1932, listing three permanent showrooms outside of London (Tabernacle Street) – in Manchester, Birmingham and Glasgow – with a temporary exhibition at Olympia, London.

Clockwise from top left: Northampton Co-op label found on the back of a mid-sixties Lebus wardrobe; a trademark badge for Lloyd Williams, Connah's Quay, Wales underneath Lebus's own trademark badge from the early to mid-fifties (from around 1950 onwards Lebus began to trademark furniture); a trademark badge for Meenan & co, Belfast, Northern Ireland underneath Lebus's own trademark from the late fifties; a Maple and Co trademark badge on Lebus made furniture.

To the buying public, Lebus's business model provided choice and flexibility as they could see all its available products pictured in a catalogue along with full details about them, including price, with the final cost dependent upon their chosen finish (material for upholstered products and veneer for cabinet pieces). The notion of interchangeability or 'mix and match' increasingly became a promotional feature – a customer could furnish their home over time, when personal finances allowed, safe in the knowledge that there would always be new Lebus designs that would blend.

The firm had one premier UK showroom in London and for many years this was the Tabernacle Street premises in London's East End. At Tabernacle Street, Harris Lebus also stocked and sold what were known as 'factored' (or bought-in) goods. By supplementing its own furniture pieces, Harris Lebus was able to sell a diverse range of products, thereby acting as wholesaler for other smaller firms and giving its customer base the potential to find every possible type of furniture piece under the one roof. Tabernacle Street was relinquished in March 1954 for a new building on a bombed site at 17–19 Maddox Street (just off Regent Street) in London's West End. There were seven floors with 12,000 square feet of display area. Individual floors were divided into bays by the use of curtains and showrooms decorated in different wallpapers and paints to display furniture.

The firm's only international showroom was in Paris, in a wholesale furniture district: 21 Faubourg St. Antoine opened in 1909. This replaced a previous premises at 2 Rue de la Roquette, opened in 1900 when Lebus sent a sales representative to France. Just like London, Paris had its furniture-making district and there was a significant market for the high-end, hand-made furniture that Lebus made. This showroom was closed with the advent of World War One.

After World War One, four regional showrooms were established in Manchester, Birmingham, Glasgow and Liverpool. They were invitation-only spaces. The 1939 catalogue reads: 'Retailer's customers may visit [a showroom] accompanied by a retailer or unaccompanied if in possession of an "Introduction Card" issued by a retailer (available on application).'

Since these had all been closed down at the start of World War Two, the company embarked on a process to re-establish a network of regional showrooms, beginning in 1952 with Glasgow (the third-largest city in Britain by the start of the fifties) then Liverpool two years later. A showroom opened in Plymouth in 1955 was a short-lived venture. Showrooms established in Leicester and Hull were also subsequently closed as they were deemed too small, with no capacity to develop. With plans for a Birmingham showroom shelved, the list also included Manchester, Bristol and Edinburgh. All were decorated in the firm's corporate colours – red, sky blue and grey.

In commercial terms alone, despite different target markets, both periods either side of World War One were lucrative. The mid-century period proved to be the most commercially challenging and design-wise had the potential to be the most exciting, free and radical; but it was also this period that presented mixed fortunes for Lebus.

The four generations of Lebus – Louis, Harris, Herman, Oliver

The success of this furniture business – with origins that can be traced back to 1840 – is testament to the dedication of successive generations of the Lebus family. There were four, and in each of these generations emerged one clear driving force.

Harris was the driving force of the business bearing his name for a period lasting 34 years – from when he set up as a sole trader on 25 September 1873, until he died prematurely in September 1907, though he did invite his younger brother Sol to join him as a partner on 19 September 1892. Their father, Louis, had been a cabinet maker. As a single man in his early twenties, he emigrated around 1840 from what is now Wroclaw in Poland and settled in Hull where he married, later moving his family to London's East End furniture district in 1857. After an argument with his father and a year during which they did not communicate, Harris returned. Though they were reconciled in late summer 1873, it was at this juncture that Harris became an entrepreneur. Harris achieved phenomenal success and a reputation for the manufacture of high-end, quality furniture.

When Harris died, his two sons Herman and Louis Harris (known as Louis) were made partners alongside their uncle Sol and a fourth partner, Harris's widow, Sarah, who was a silent partner. It was Herman who would emerge as the driving force of the business for the next 50 years.

In 1946, Herman's two son's Anthony and Oliver joined the business, just at the point where the family partnership was dissolved and replaced by a public company. Herman was elected by shareholders as chairman and managing director, a post he held until his death in 1957. After serving for several years as joint deputy chairman, Oliver was elected to the role of chairman in January 1961; he held the post for the remainder of the company's existence.

The achievements and legacy of the Lebus family are truly remarkable and should not be underestimated. Furniture aside, many consider the phenomenal contribution the firm made to both world wars to be attributable to one man: Herman, who received a CBE for his contribution to World War One and a knighthood for the role he played during World War Two. Harris deserves credit for the success and legacy of the business in the pre-World War One era because today, Lebus products are noteworthy in the antique furniture trade. Despite the absence of branding, Lebus furniture is distinguishable for its quality.

High-end furniture for the wealthiest households

The period of Arts and Crafts and Art Nouveau is distinct for two reasons: Harris Lebus produced beautiful high-end furniture for

Advertisement which appeared in the *Cabinet Maker and Art Furnisher*, February 1892, which shows Lebus-produced bedroom suites and office furniture at this point in time. The text mentions the 'latest and most improved machinery'. (Image courtesy of Phillip Child)

One of the most expensive upholstered suites was catalogue number 2955, mahogany or satinwood inlaid, D-grade stuffing covered in silk for either £20 2s 9d or £25 10s 9d in 1912 and £21 4s or £26 17s in 1913. The settee and chairs were individually priced and so were available to buy separately. For the sofa in the choice of finishes, the price in 1913 was £9 7s or £11 14s and the chair £5 18s 6d or £7 11s 6d each.

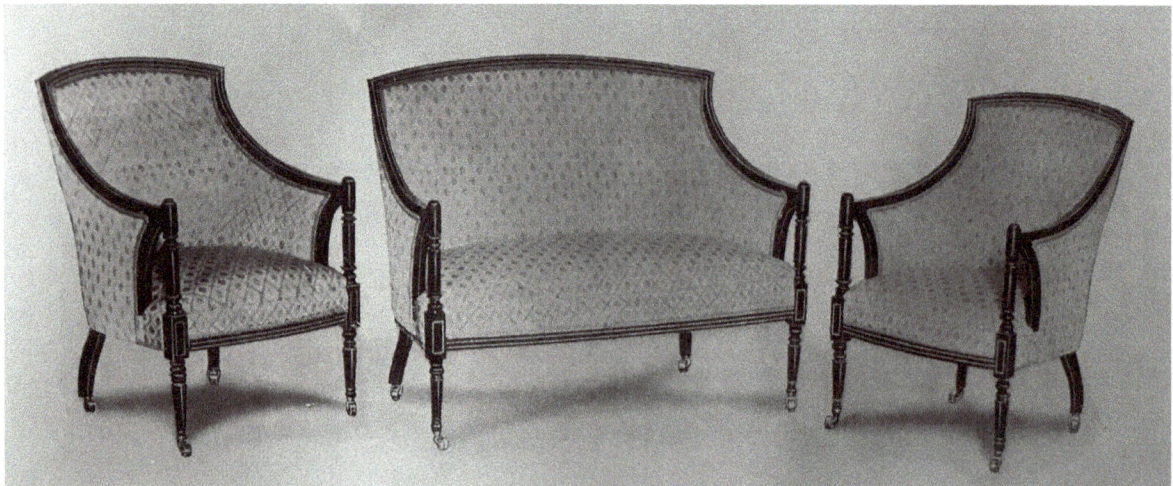

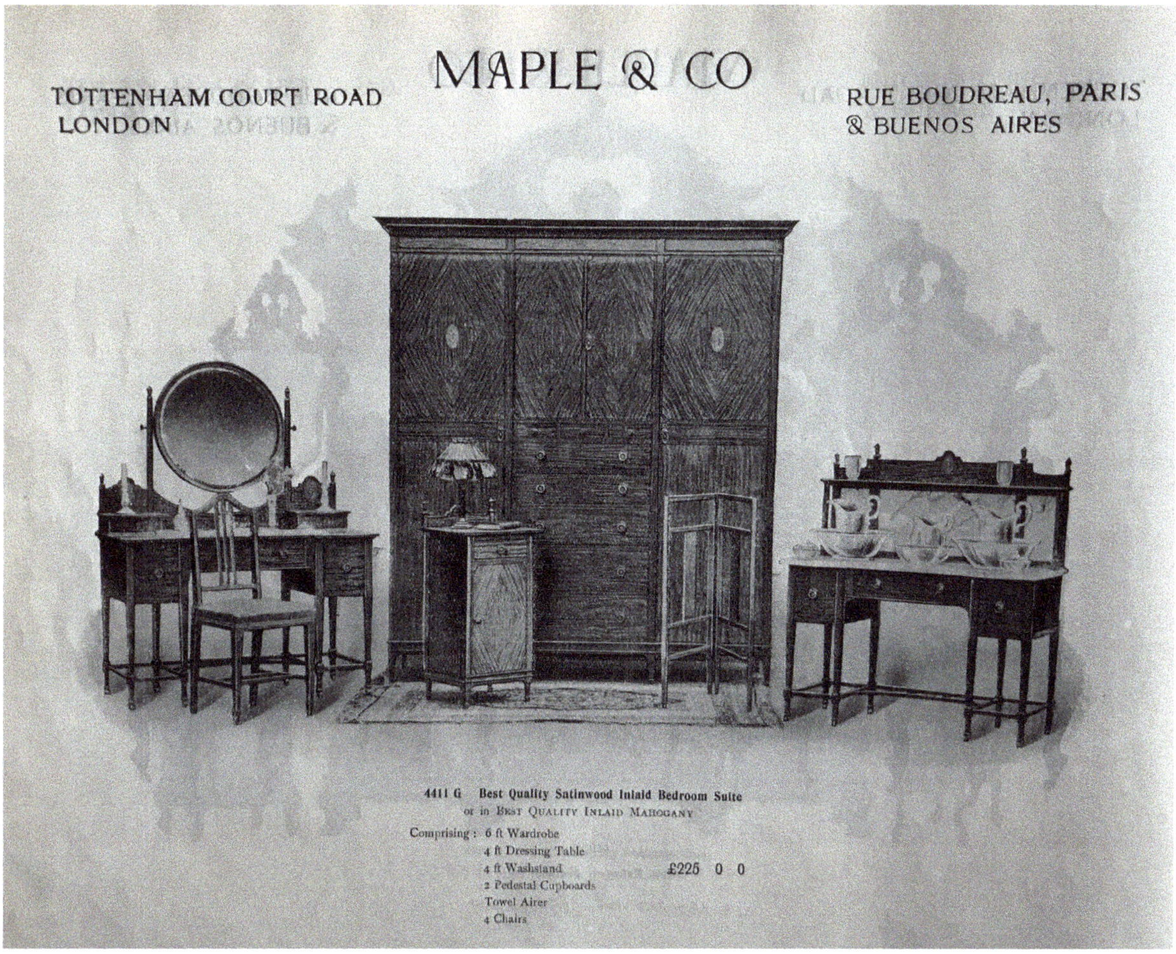

A 1912 catalogue produced by retailer Maple and Co. which was exactly the same size and format as that of the Lebus catalogue that year had this identical bedroom design from the Lebus catalogue.

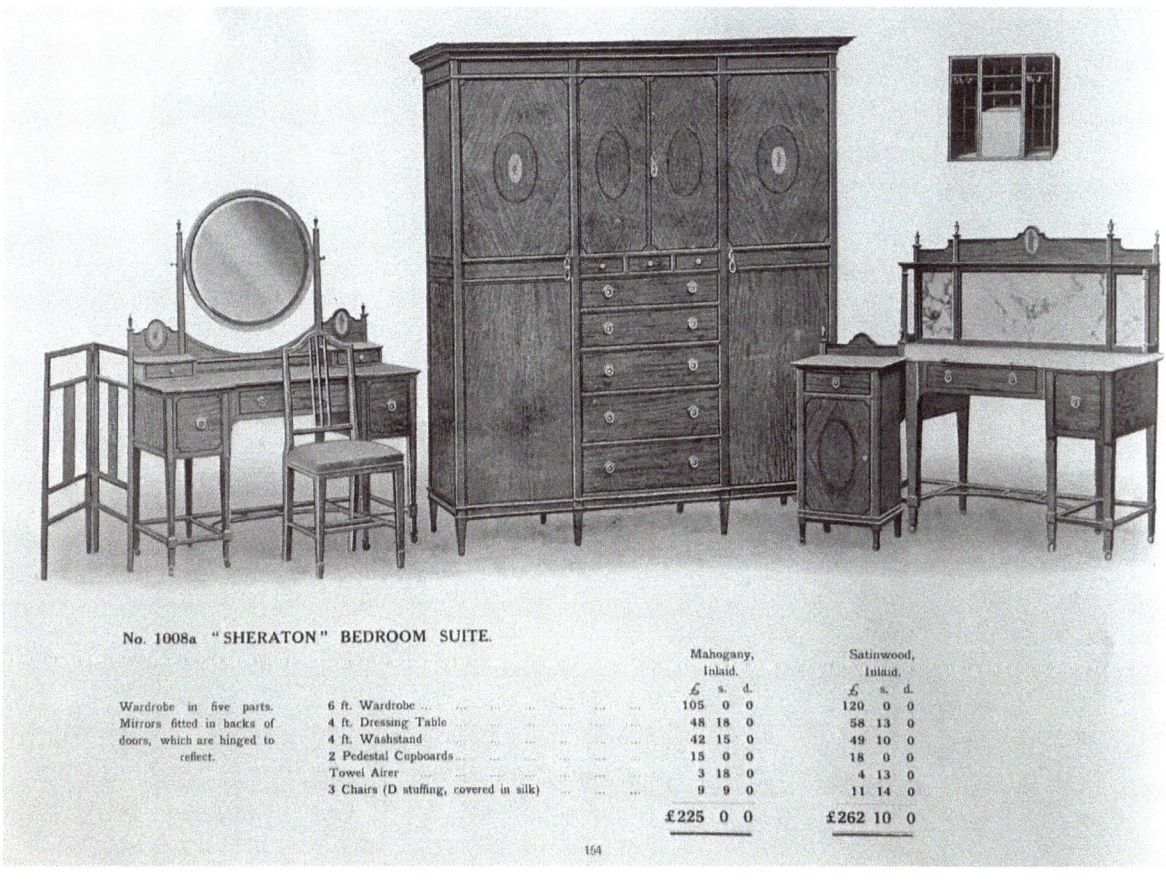

customers in the upper income bracket at this time, and the firm built up a reputation for delivery of large-scale contracts including hospital and hotel refurbishments and ship interiors.

Harris initially focussed on decorative bedroom suites and practical furniture for commercial office premises. As the twentieth century beckoned, he extended the scope and range of his domestic furniture products to include dining- and drawing-room suites and other miscellaneous items. He oversaw an expansion in both cabinet and upholstered furniture.

Quality furniture manufacture and contracts work demanded highly skilled individuals, who were to be found amongst the Lebus workforce, and the best machinery on the market. Harris had been influenced by American production methods. To state that Harris Lebus propelled not just his own factory but Britain's furniture industry into machine-assisted manufacturing production and 'engineering in wood' would not be unreasonable. This was a time when British furniture was still made by the hands of skilled craftsmen with very little input from machines. Woodworking machines – such as those that sawed and carved – were initially accommodated in the firm's Tabernacle Street premises in East London during the latter decades of the nineteenth century and then, from 1901, at its cabinet-making works at Tottenham Hale, North London. These were sourced from America, because they were not available in Britain. Decades before the National Grid was rolled out in the 1920s, these machines were driven by a system of belts and shafts by a powerful coal-driven stationary steam engine. Made by Marshall, Sons and Company of Gainsborough, the 350-horsepower reciprocating engine with its huge flywheel (which had first been used in Tabernacle Street) drove all the woodworking machines in Tottenham Hale's cabinet-making mill and machine shop at an average speed of 4,500 rpm.

Lebus products would have found their way into the grandest of houses and settings. Houses contained many rooms that were intended to be used differently, whilst sharing the fact that they were adorned, as much as anything else, to be aesthetically pleasing. There were houses with space for furniture pieces that might be seldom used, or at least not for any great length of time. Whilst furniture pieces were designed for function and use (as well as beauty), such was the opulence of the period that in many instances, furniture could be bought for its inherent beauty and decoration, which transcended any function that it may have performed in the home.

Maple and Company in London's West End was the firm's largest single domestic customer in the years leading up to World War One, accounting for an annual average of 13 percent of the firm's gross turnover.

Harris Lebus also capitalised on an export market for British-made furniture. Italian by origin, Mr. Nazzari was the international sales representative covering South Africa, Australia, New Zealand, India, America and South America. He produced an enormous amount of business with a firm called Thompson in Buenos Aires, as well as a smaller amount of business with the Wanamaker department store on New York's Broadway. Interestingly, turnover from exports to Europe when totalled were relatively small, with France and Italy the main markets. As World War One loomed, the firm's export market almost doubled in size from just over 11 percent of turnover in 1908 to 20 percent the following year, and by 1913 the export market generated a quarter of the firm's total turnover.

Contract work constituted a large part of Lebus's business; it was both prestigious and lucrative. Contracts ranged from commissions for the production of specific furniture pieces as well as large-scale projects. The firm made thousands of bookcases for the Educational Book Company and the Encyclopaedia Britannica, large numbers of gramophone cabinets for HMV and an enormous number of towel cabinets for the Initial Towel Company. Some contract work was also done for Waring and Gillow of Lancaster, who specialised in ships' furniture. One of the most prestigious contracts of this era was for fine inlaid mahogany furniture for staterooms of an entire deck of the Cunard ocean liner *Aquitania* (which was later put to military use in World War One as a hospital ship). The Midland Railway Company's Adelphi Hotel, Liverpool on its opening in 1914 was described as 'the world's most palatial hotel', and it was Harris Lebus who furnished all four hundred bedrooms in French walnut. The Sefton Suite was, at one time, rumoured to be a replica of the first-class smoking lounge of the *Titanic*.

Looking into Lebus furniture, the catalogues of Office and Library Furniture 1907, Dessins D'Ameublements / Mobel-Vorlagen 1909, and those of 1912 and 1913 serve to show that Lebus was at its zenith during this period.

Affordable furniture for the many

After World War One there were decisions to be made. At a meeting on 23 July 1920 the partners reached a decision which would ultimately determine the destiny of the firm – they agreed to fundamentally shift manufacturing policy to affordable furniture for the lower ends of the market

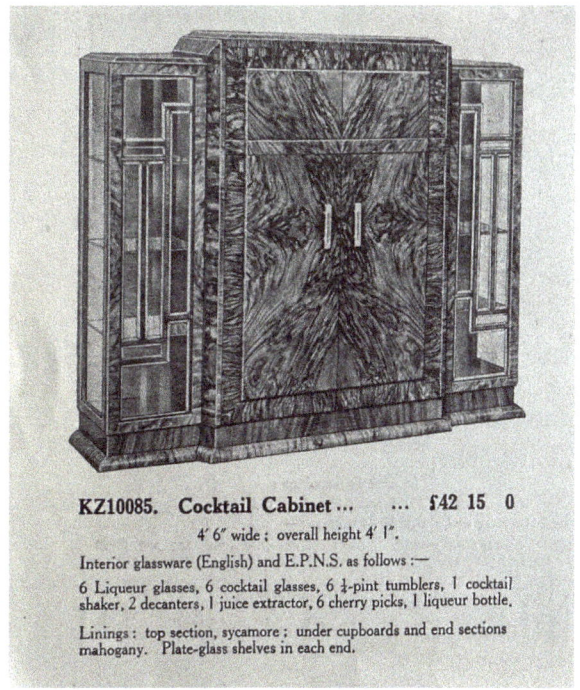

This cocktail cabinet from 1936 would have looked stunning with its walnut veneer.

The UZ74/5 Burrington three-piece suite from 1939. Note the inset image showing the springs inside the upholstery.

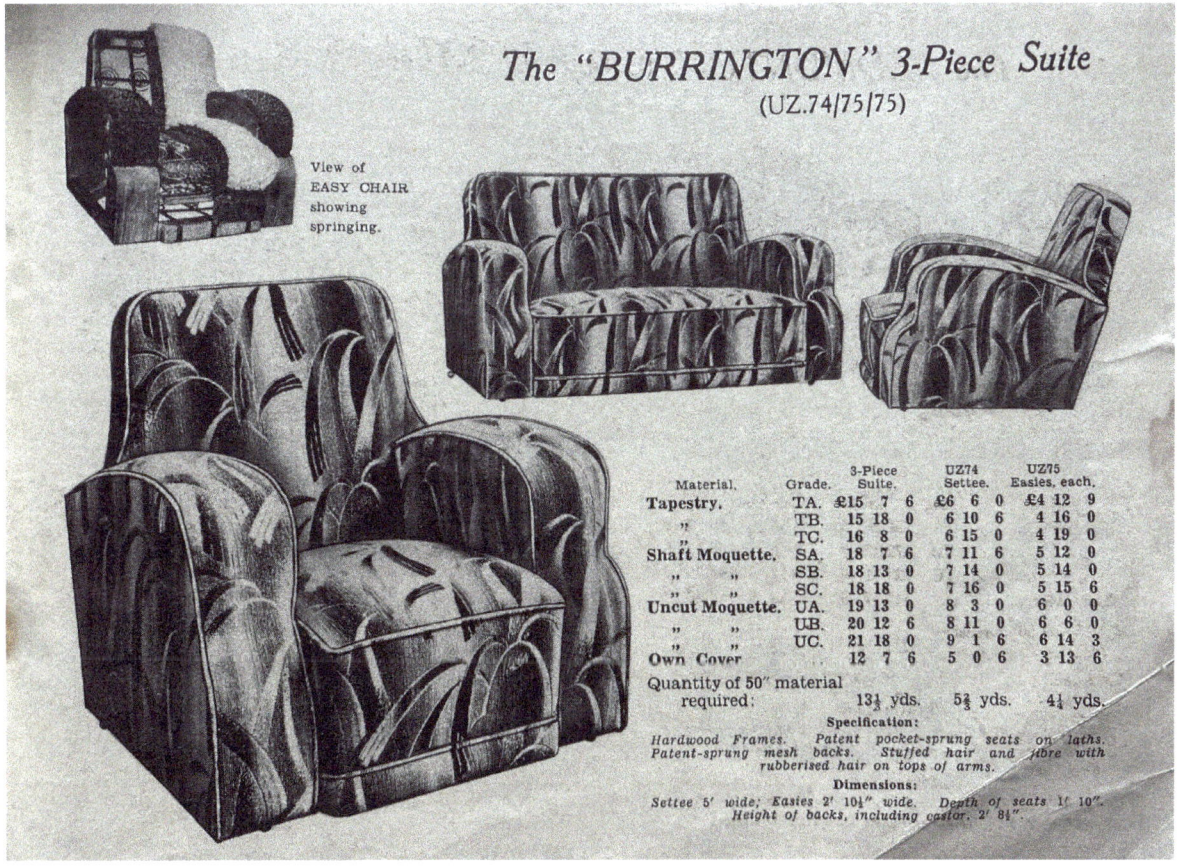

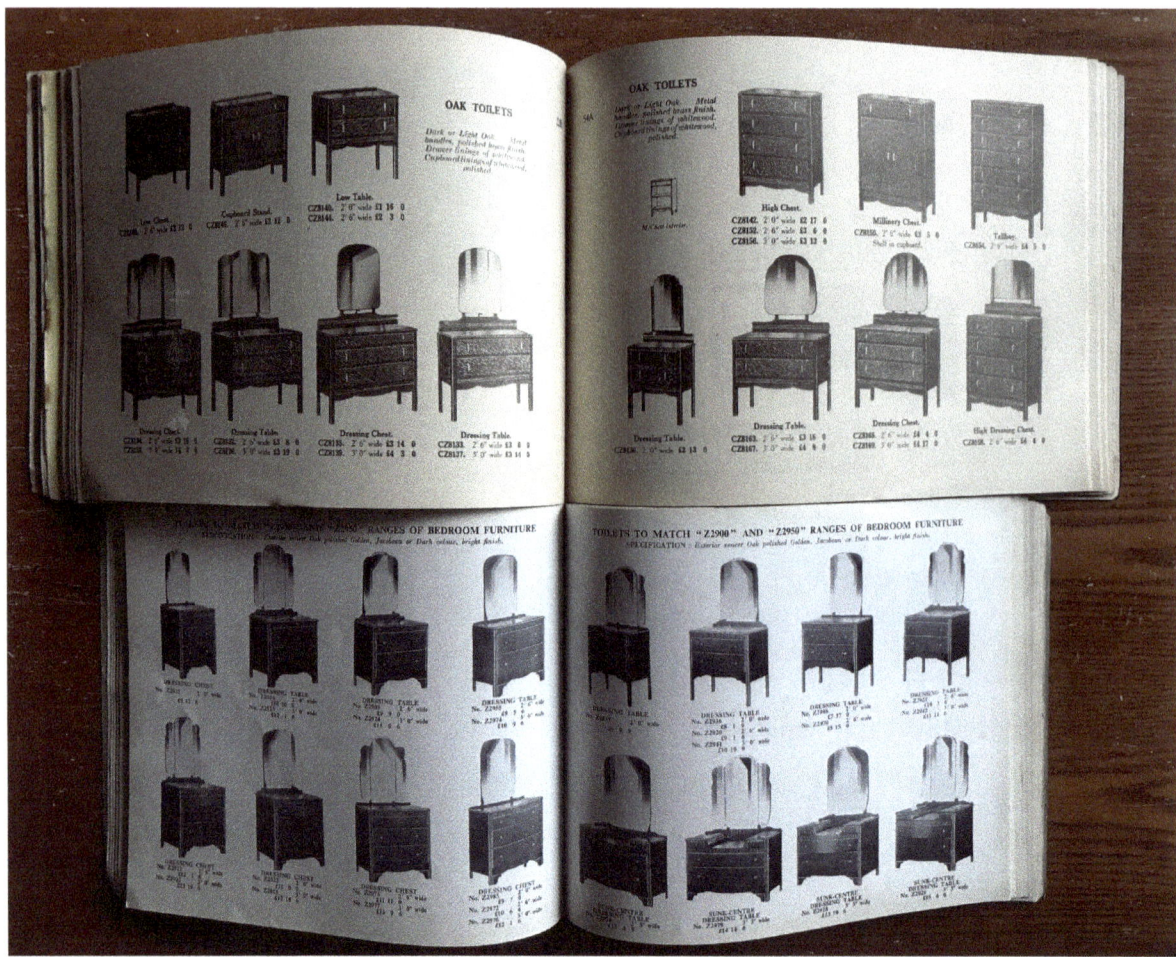

Dating Lebus furniture is not always easy. The 1954 catalogue is pictured below that of 1939 for a similar range of bedroom furniture. It is hard to tell the difference at first glance. However, the legs on the furniture are different. The price differential over this 13-year period is noteworthy: a two-drawer chest with mirror of the same width (catalogue number CZ8133) is £3 6s in 1939, and the equivalent in 1953 (catalogue number Z2955) is £9 5s 6d.

and the majority buying public. Although this evolution of the business required considerable investment in plant and machinery, the interwar period proved extremely lucrative, helped along by a boom in post-war house building.

Lebus was catering to a huge market with a wide spectrum of disposable income and appears indeed to have understood the mass market for furniture during the interwar years perfectly. The Lebus catalogue of 1937 provides a point of anchorage with a wide variation in pricing evident across the board. Using this to furnish a modest, inner-city terraced cottage or flat with the lowest-priced furniture at one end, and a four-bedroom detached or semi-detached suburban house at the other, the difference in expenditure is quite staggering: the former could be done for as little as £25, whilst choices made for the latter could have racked up to around £540.

Moving to mid-century modernity

The relationship between Lebus and its customer base after World War Two was a rockier affair. As time elapsed, it became apparent the business was conflicted between allowing itself to be adventurous with design and keeping an established customer base happy. Standing between the ultimate consumer of Lebus furniture and the decision-making management in the Lebus business model was the interface between the Lebus sales team and the individual furniture retailers. Whilst a conduit to the success of the business, this relationship was also, paradoxically, a hindrance to it – the balance of power, it seems, was with the individual retailer, with their guidance as to what customers would ultimately buy taken as read. This misguidance became all too clear to Lebus management with erratic sales figures during the early years of the swinging sixties.

Immediately after World War Two, Lebus embraced the challenges and the uncertainties surrounding Utility furniture production and sales. The public company was formed in 1947, which raised significant finances for reinvestment. The furniture industry itself became more organised through the formation of the British Furniture Manufacturers trade association, with annual shows held at Earls Court, London.

On 26 June 1950, upholstery production moved from Tottenham Hale (where it had been located since moving from Tabernacle Street in 1943) to Woodley, near Reading. By the mid-sixties upholstery employed 450 people. This move to Woodley cemented a permanent separation of production from cabinet making. This would prove over time to have been a wise choice.

The year 1955 saw major expansion plans at Tottenham Hale in the form of a huge new warehouse extension, which when completed, brought the factory to three times its original size – from 13.5 acres (54,228 square metres) to 45 acres (just under 183,000 square metres). The original land purchase, layout and building design at Tottenham Hale in 1901 had resulted from the vision and energy of a relatively young city architect, Samuel Clifford Tee, and had been meticulously planned to enable the delivery and unloading of wood from the River Lea in the south-east corner through the processes of manufacture to warehousing and distribution by rail in the north-west corner at Ferry Lane. The new warehouse was designed by Clifford Tee and Leslie Gale.[2] Built on the company's landholdings north of Ferry Lane, the new warehouse was linked to the main factory by an automated conveyor running through a bridge under the road. The factory was now a conglomeration of original brick buildings squeezed amidst brick and concrete additions, with concreted floor and virtually all under one continuous roof. Furniture production was a mixture of batch and flow production zigzagging across the complex, a direct consequence of piecemeal expansion.

As the fifties drew to a close and the sixties beckoned, the company's greatest challenges were yet to come. Perhaps the sight of quality guarantee tickets attached to products leaving the warehouse swinging in the breeze could have been an omen for the swinging fortunes that Lebus would experience in this decade.

---

2 The firm grew out of the original business established by Samuel Clifford Tee who had teamed up with his nephew Leslie Gale. CTG Consultancy celebrates 125 years in 2020.

The Gaycourt three-piece suite from 1965.

This Link advertisement for the slick new Link furniture launched in 1956 was targeted at younger people. It began with the statement: 'We had young people very much in mind when we planned "Link" furniture. Displayed is a bedroom set-up in a finish of sable oak.'

Branching out – expanding the business with new products and services

The company embarked on a programme to diversify operations both at home and abroad. New subsidiaries included Bentwood Chair Supply; Moorgate Trading Company (for timber importing); Eventide (Bedding) Limited; investment in a Nigerian furniture-making business, C.F.C. Furniture Company (Lagos and Port Harcourt, Nigeria); Record Mill, Great Harwood, Lancashire (with plans afoot to increase floor space for upholstery production alongside Woodley); Merchandise Transport, operating a fleet of lorries licensed to carry other firms' products as well as Lebus's own;[3] White Hart Lane Garages Ltd at Tottenham (to service the Merchandise Transport fleet and raise revenue from car sales and repairs); and Merchandise Funds, to manage hire-purchase credit (for both motor cars as well as furniture).

The sales team was sizeable by the early sixties – it had grown to 67 sales representatives and five area sales managers. Each sales representative was expected to maximise orders daily and forward 'call sheet', so the sales department knew 'exactly where they had been, who they had seen and how much business they generated'. In addition, they performed the role of customer care, accepted complaints on all aspects of quality and service, listened to customers' particular problems, and gave out advice on many and varied things affecting business. In other words, they were tasked with customer care and maintaining the company image.

At the beginning of the sixties about 40 percent of all sales of furniture in Britain were made through the various forms of instalment credit.[4] Hire purchase increased costs for firms – administration and payment collection as well as risks associated with payment default. Hire purchase worked on a simple principle whereby an item could be acquired at the point of an initial down-payment with the remainder of the cost, with added interest on the balance, payable in instalments spread over a period of choice – 12, 24 or 36 equal monthly payments. (In 1966, the Board of Trade reduced the maximum repayment period to 30 months.) In 1958 all hire-purchase restrictions on furniture had been temporarily removed, which led to a sudden and unforeseen increase in demand for the company's products and higher than expected turnover figures. The pattern was to repeat itself in 1964 but between 1960 and 1963 sales of cabinet furniture, such as for the interchangeable oak bedroom range were on a continuous spiral of decline.

Could it really be we were *falling out of love with Lebus?*

Despite huge strides being made in marketing methods and media, the company's relentless marketing and sales-driven strategy covering the whole of the UK, could it really be the case that its customer base was falling out of love with (some) Lebus furniture?

Lebus furniture catalogues of 1953, 1954 and 1965, its leaflets and pamphlets accompanying new ranges (such as Link, launched in 1956), press and magazine advertisements, as well as press commentary on Lebus products show the progression of design in the mid-century modern period at Lebus.

The Europa challenge – a gamble too far…

Lebus looked to some of its UK rivals and came to the realisation that they were making revolutionary changes to feed a market looking for something different, something innovative, something to excite; furniture that was lightweight and easy to move around; furniture that, whilst being functional, was beautiful by design, and – importantly – affordable. Lebus had the potential to compete; it took up the Europa challenge – to thrust the company into the modern age with a different product, produced in a different way, for a different target market, and… ultimately (to be) located in a different location. A strategic plan to reinvent Lebus, had it come to fruition, would have seen the company operating from

---

3 The commodities carried had ranged from antiques to biscuits, tyres to feathers, gymnastics equipment to waxed paper tubes – 18 feet long and four feet in diameter – for moulds for the concrete pillars of the construction of the St Albans bypass.

4 J.L. Oliver, *The Development and Structure of the Furniture Industry.*

Lebus's marketing included advertisements which were either aimed at the fifties housewife or which used the allure of women to sell its products: Here we have the front cover of the Europa furniture catalogue 1970, a magazine advertisement for the Link range in *Ideal Home* in March 1957 and promotional material for Eventide Bedding from the mid-sixties.

Lebus used plastic veneers with wood-grain effect for some of its dining and bedroom furniture ranges during the fifties and sixties. This sixties sideboard in original condition (image courtesy of Richard at Mid-century Retrotique) has teak-wood-veneered drawer fronts and a door with plastic burr 'walnut' wood effect veneer. The intent was to simulate burr walnut veneers used on this bedroom suite catalogue number 432 from 1909. Burr (or burl) walnut refers to parts of the tree where smaller branches or roots have sprouted, creating additional pattern and decoration. Given that there is less of such parts in the timber cut from a tree and that they are thus harder to source, burl cost more. And its use as veneer on a furniture piece required skilful blending.

Andy enjoys a modern seventies Lebus sofa in the Hiscock household, way back in 1981. (Photo courtesy of Andy's mum, Shirley Hiscock, who was a seamstress at Lebus Upholstery in Woodley, Reading.)

a purpose-built hub in a new-town location outside London.

The short-term brought significant changes at Tottenham Hale – to the plant, to the employees and to the end product. What didn't help was the 'credit squeeze' of 1966 and 1968; these were the government's way of addressing the devaluation of the pound sterling, but the measures dissuaded spending on anything other than essential goods. The launch of the Europa furniture range would be a gamble too far and the cabinet-making side of the business collapsed in the spring of 1970 under the weight of financial obligations the company had to settle. This was a huge blow: to the firm's employees, to the individual retailers who stocked Lebus furniture and to the industry as a whole.

Lebus had categorised its furniture into two main groupings for convenience: cabinet pieces and upholstered. This separation had been formalised in the restructuring of the company in 1966 when Lebus Upholstery was made a subsidiary of the parent company. When the cabinet-making side of the business effectively ceased in 1970, upholstery production was on a sound footing to continue at its established plant at Woodley, Reading. With some adjustments to the plant, a small amount of cabinet furniture for the bedroom and lounge continued to be manufactured alongside upholstery under the brand name 'Europa'.

Loving Lebus – all over again…

And what of surviving original Lebus furniture today?

Antique furniture has always been popular. Mid-century style is trending and vintage items, whether furniture or ceramics, textiles or glassware, are highly sought after. The market for vintage is booming, driven by glossy magazines and social media – Facebook, Pinterest, Instagram. And the way we think about and use consumer durables has changed – we are now, more than ever, conscious of the effect waste can have on the planet. Furniture recycling, up-cycling, repurposing (a terminology debate exists) fits with an ethos of re-use and reducing waste and landfill.

Lebus furniture is a popular choice. This raises the question: is Lebus furniture re-entering the nation's consciousness as it did mine and arousing a sleeping appreciation? And are we now, years later, falling in *love* with Lebus furniture all over again?

The Lebus furniture pieces most favoured for up-cycling are china cabinets, sideboards, bureaus, tallboy chests of drawers and millinery (linen) cupboards. With the exception of wardrobes, up-cycling and repurposing invariably involve displaying and serving alcoholic refreshments. Whilst many collectors or customers looking for that

Lebus sideboard in a state of disrepair. (Image courtesy of Beverly Ingham)

Zander Campbell von Benzon shares this image of the veneer restoration process on a chest of drawers.

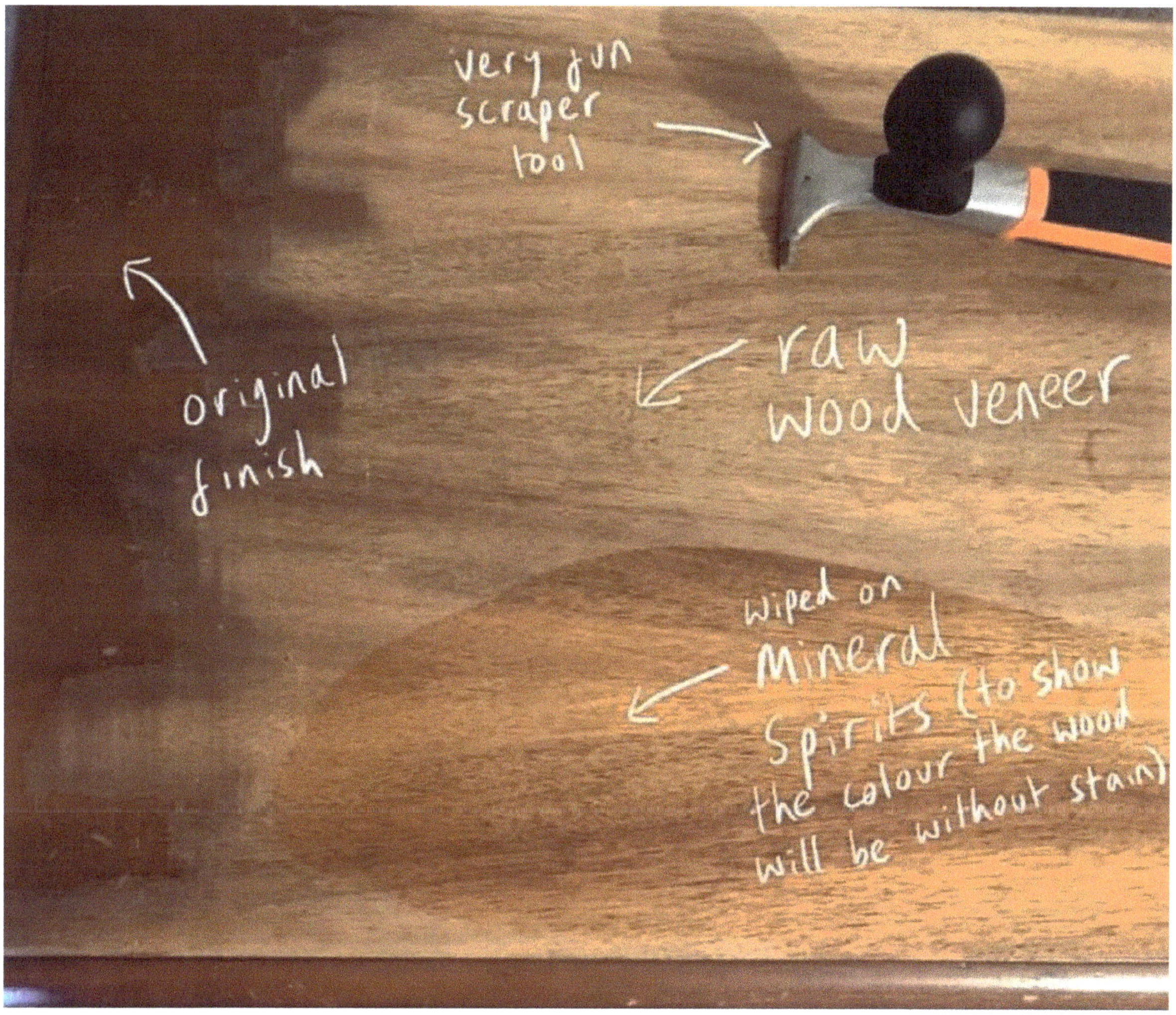

very fun scraper tool

original finish

raw wood veneer

wiped on Mineral Spirits (to show the colour the wood will be without stain)

WHEN WE LOVED LEBUS   25

Europa
Como

Seeing is believing. And here it is.
One of the most sophisticated ranges of bedroom furniture you're ever likely to see.
There are fifteen matching pieces to choose from. Each one finished inside and out with tough, hardwearing melamine.
All wardrobes are fitted with castors, and a special storage unit allows dressing tables and chests of drawers to be built around the corner of the room.
Finished in a warm, subtle magnolia, with dark brown contrast and stylish brass handles, the Como range is simply magnificent.

Lebus used materials other than wood. This 1970s Como bedroom suite made by Lebus in Woodley is made of melamine.

Lebus sideboard in a state of disrepair.
(Image courtesy of Beverly Ingham)

Zander Campbell von Benzon shares this image of the veneer restoration process on a chest of drawers.

Nigel T. Wybrow shares his labour-of-love restoration of a chest of drawers from the mid-sixties. Nigel's granddad Charlie worked in the Lebus machine shop – he's pictured here in 1956 (on the right of the photograph).

'something different' prefer to keep their finds as true to the original as possible, a raft of others like to repurpose or decorate, expressing themselves through the application of paint. And not simply 'one coat all over', but through playful experimentation or carefully considered patchwork and lines, skilfully executed and perhaps accompanied by the application of patterned wallpapers. Such treatment produces a blend of the new with the old, as original wood finishes and veneers are buffed up to shine forth once again.

The story comes full circle as the nation continues to love… or rediscovers and falls in love with Lebus all over again.

Starting its life as a millinery (linen) chest and hidden away in a 1930s bedroom, this is now a stunning cocktail cabinet. It has been lovingly rejuvenated to showcase its Art Deco characteristics by Lee O'Gorman at Lee O'Gorman Home. The walnut veneer on the cabinet's doors is truly gorgeous. Its beauty can now be admired by the many guests who stay at the Royal an Lochan Hotel, Tighnabruaich, Argyll, Scotland.

Looking into Lebus Furniture

From the Bedroom to the Office… and Every Room Between

Art Nouveau/Arts and Crafts, 1873–1914

The chief designer in this period was Basil Archer (until his retirement in 1919).

Between 1892 and 1900, Lebus expanded its range of furniture – which had been limited to bedroom suites and commercial office furniture – to cater for every room in the home. Archer's creative scope was considerably widened. This was the period of Art Nouveau and Arts and Crafts – though in practice, the influences on Archer's designs were wide and varied. He appears to have taken inspiration from seventeenth-century Jacobean style (the name was derived from King James I) with ornate carvings a characteristic of Lebus's oak furniture – sideboards, hallstands and so forth. Archer's elegant frames, slender column legs, inlaid wood and veneer patterning on furniture could have been influenced by Thomas Sheraton's style. He had a fondness for elegant styles incorporating shield backs, fluted legs, blends of gothic, rococo and Chinese influences which could also have stemmed from his awareness of Sheraton's eighteenth-century cabinet-making contemporaries – George Hepplewhite and Thomas Chippendale. His designs which favoured motifs drawn from classical Rome, such as vases, urns, arabesque vine scrolls and framed medallions, bear a passing resemblance to the furniture designs of Robert Adam (an architect by profession). Archer's designs with cabriole legs and little ornamentation he attributed to Queen Anne, whilst some elegant, asymmetrical pieces, decorated with seashell-like curved forms and delicate carvings, hark back to French country chic. He indicated that these were inspired by the Louis style (King Louis XV and his son King Louis XVI reigned in France in the eighteenth century). With a Harris Lebus showroom in Paris, it is not surprising to see some French influence in Archer's designs.

Chippendale style: china cabinet from 1909.

It is important to note that Archer's designs were only loosely based on these influences. Notwithstanding this, his designs are truly quite extraordinary.

This expansion into furniture making for every room in the home initiated the move to a purpose-built manufacturing plant at Tottenham Hale in 1901. This was exclusively for cabinet pieces, while upholstery production remained at Tabernacle Street.

Lebus furniture was made by hand with some machine assistance for specific tasks, such as sawing. Cabinet furniture orders moved around the various workshops at Tottenham Hale in batches of up to half a dozen of the same item at a time. Many furniture pieces had carved decoration; carvings were either hand-made or produced with the aid of a machine such as that which enabled two matching carvings to be made simultaneously.

Sample makers hand-made very small quantities of the highest grade six-foot and

William and Mary style: Sofa from 1912.

Queen Anne style: drawing-room suite from 1912, catalogue number 139.

Hepplewhite style: sideboard from 1912.

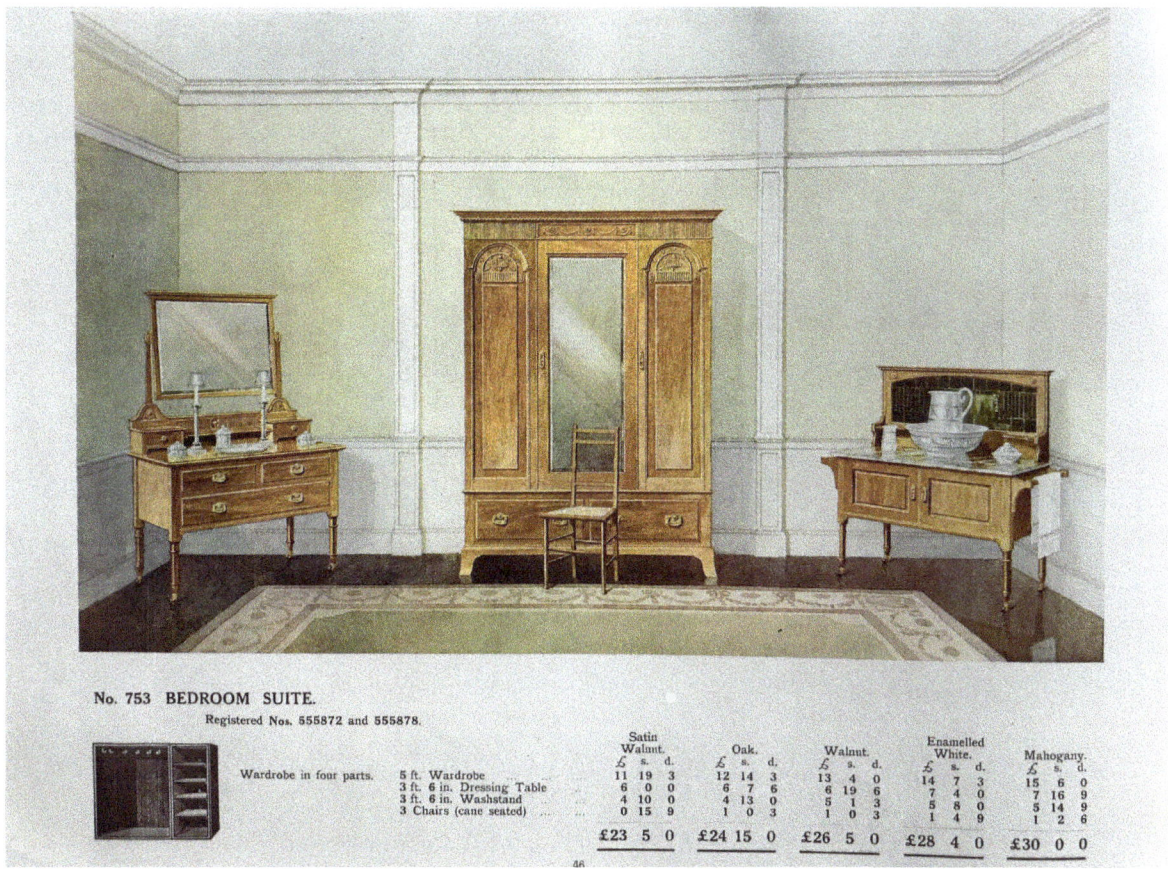

Bedroom suite catalogue number 753 was offered in the widest choice of finishes in 1912.

Bedroom suite in fumed oak with inlaid pewter from 1909 catalogue.

FROM THE BEDROOM TO THE OFFICE... AND EVERY ROOM BETWEEN

Wardrobe originally sold new by Maple and Co., now with Driscoll's Antiques. It is thought by the author to be made by Lebus.
(Photograph courtesy of James Driscoll)

The Lebus bedroom suite catalogue number 295 from 1909 is all but identical to the one opposite.

seven-foot bedroom suites – the Sheraton style, and those made from mahogany, satinwood and walnut.

Hardwood was the main component for all furniture, with softwood used only for drawer runners and some interior work. Basswood imported from America was favoured for its creamy white colour and because it is soft and light. It was used as an alternative for some dining tabletops because it offered a less expensive choice to customers.

Furniture was offered in different finishes. French polishing produced a high gloss finish to hardwoods such as mahogany and it served to 'fill' wood grain, producing a smooth finish. The polish was produced by diluting shellac (a resin secreted by the female lac bug) with methylated spirit, and Harris Lebus was licensed to produce this at the cabinet-making factory. Gentle application using an oil-lubricated cloth was a labour-intensive and slow process, with many thin coats necessary, one layer at a time. The final coat needed some time to harden completely.

Oak pieces were generally treated with water-based stains, though some were fumed (or smoked). Fuming was a relatively new process, still at an experimental stage. The process involved placing the furniture item in a chamber next to a heated vessel of ammonium hydroxide solution for 24 hours, causing the tannins in the wood to darken. It worked best on white oak with a high tannin content.

The backs of cheaper furniture would be painted in greenish yellow ochre, as was customary in the trade, while the more expensive ranges were left white (untouched).

One of the finishes offered by Lebus for its furniture was 'enamelled white'. In fact, this choice of finish was one of the most expensive. How this was achieved is a mystery, so it is assumed that some form of white paint (probably oil based and with some lead content) was applied to seal, finish and protect the wood. The concept of white-painted furniture emanates from the eighteenth century. Charles Rennie Mackintosh (1868–1928) had been offering some of his furniture designs painted white from around 1895.

A few designs were offered hand painted all over, and with decoration to mimic stylised plaster relief, or romanticised paintings of a country scene or people at leisure.

With upholstered furniture, many of the made-up frames were sourced from specialist manufacturers located near Tabernacle Street,

Chest of drawers in satin walnut. (Images courtesy of Mathew)

An enamelled white suite from 1912.

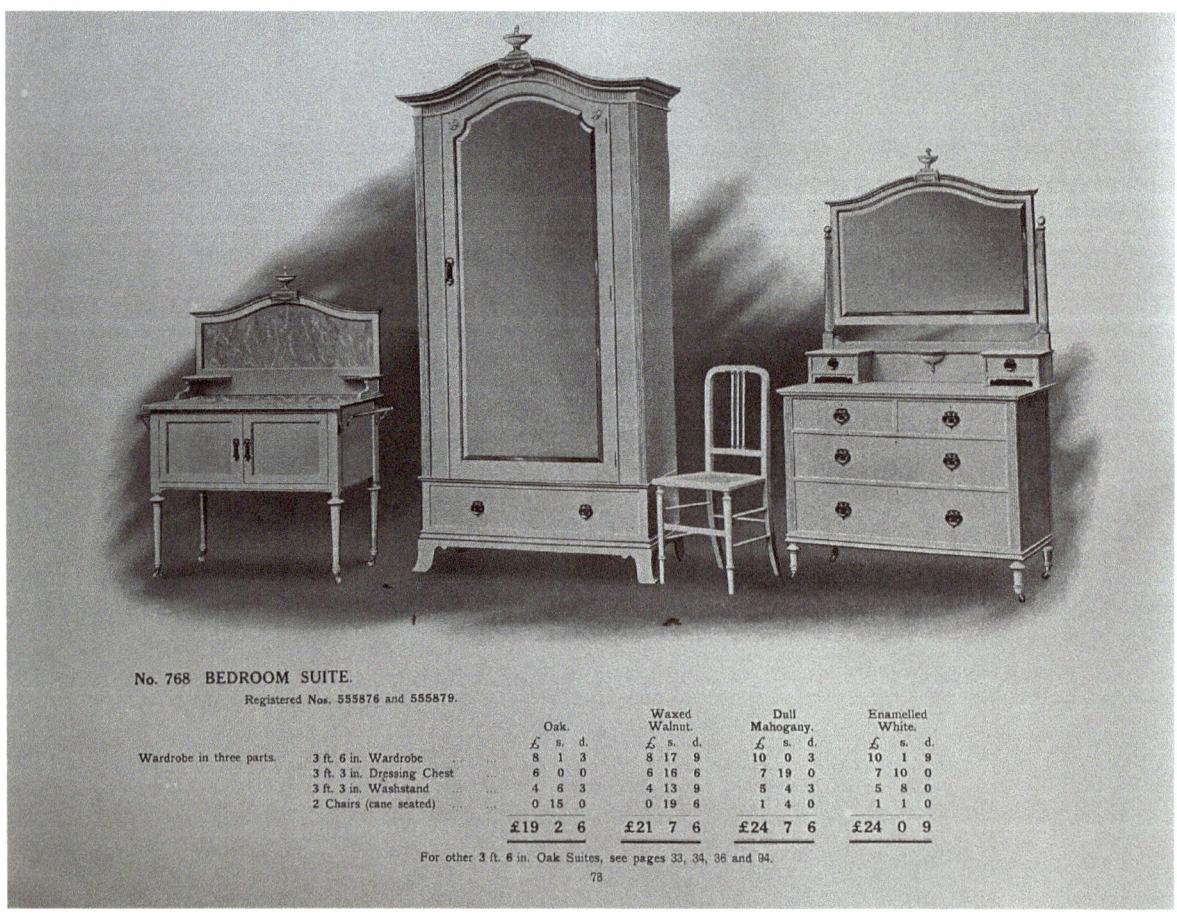

38 LOVING LEBUS

to be upholstered in-house using traditional methods. Soft furnishings were covered in various luxurious, expensive fabrics including those described as tapestry, cretonne (a patterned, heavy cotton fabric) and silk. Moroccan leather and Rexine (a trademarked name for faux leather) was favoured for chairs – especially for dining suites.

There was no trademark on much of the Lebus-made furniture during this period because retailers, such as Maple and Company, sold items as their own. Identifying Lebus pieces from this period is by design, quality of product, and patent plates. Some wardrobe and chest-of-drawer locks displayed face plates engraved with the small initials 'H.L.L.' – Harris Lebus London. Roll-top desks were often trademarked with 'Lebus Desk' engraved on the escutcheon plate.

Traditionally and exclusively, Lebus supplied wealthy, upper-class households who occupied large houses, with various rooms of differing functions that could accommodate large, elaborate furniture suites and a range of individual pieces. Throughout both the Victorian and Edwardian periods, an emerging and aspiring middle class was also in the market for furniture.

The entrepreneurial Harris had himself joined the wealthy, upper middle class in the course of developing his furniture-manufacturing business. From 1894, 11 Netherhall Gardens, Hampstead NW3, was the home of Harris, Sarah and their large family of nine children. It was a larger than average Victorian villa in a wealthy suburb. With reference to the 1901 census, eight live-in servants also shared their home – a cook/housekeeper, domestic maid, parlour maid, two under-parlour maids, two housemaids and a nurse. I like to think the home was furnished with the best of the furniture from the business bearing his name.

The period from the turn of the century to the advent of World War One saw a boom in house building as suburbia grew around big towns and cities. Typically, new-builds were terraced, two-storey houses, with bathroom, master bedroom, medium- and smaller-sized bedrooms, and a back addition scullery and kitchen. There were plenty of homes ready to be supplied by Lebus.

Whilst Lebus continued to produce high-end furniture catering for the highest earners in society, an article by Ardern Holt (possibly a pen name) in the *Lady's Realm*[5] of April 1905 suggested that a young couple setting up home would need a little over £100 and possibly up to around £150 when choosing furniture at the least expensive end of the market. Holt indicated that around half this sum would furnish the bedroom and drawing room, with a further £20 for the dining room. In the absence of fitted kitchens, she suggested that a minimum spend of a further £15 could set up a working kitchen. Holt goes on to suggest that an expectant bride and bridegroom should have at least another £50 in hand to settle themselves thoroughly comfortably, but even without this they would be much better off than their grandparents, who would have had to spend double and treble the sums involved in furnishing a house.

Holt acknowledged that rooms were becoming smaller and so making choices on which furniture pieces to buy was influenced not just by expense, but also by space. Many of Lebus's furniture items were large and bulky since most rooms and houses of the higher-income earners were large. This is the case for bedroom suites – some wardrobes had to be made as four or five separate pieces for ease of transportation and then placed and secured together in situ in the home. Holt pointed out the virtues of combination furniture pieces and advocated, as examples: the dressing table, chest of drawers and looking glass should be all in one; the wardrobe should have a pier glass (full-length mirror); and a boot cupboard should find a place under the washing stand. In the hall, one piece of furniture should represent a hall table, umbrella stand and looking glass, the sides having big hooks on which to hang coats.

---

5 The *Lady's Realm* was an illustrated monthly women's magazine published in London in the nineteenth century, initially edited by W.H. Wilkins. It was published in 36 volumes between 1896 and 1914.

Lebus was at this stage conscious of combination furniture. It was not necessarily a new phenomenon – the concept of a nest of tables, space saving and versatile, can be traced back to the Regency period and attributed to Thomas Sheraton. As the Edwardian era progressed, Lebus offered combination furniture for the bedroom and hall, albeit high-end items for the upper end of the market. These were stylish and pleasing to the eye. As demand for combination furniture grew, in discussing the needs of those on lower wages with less disposable income, Holt suggests that the look of a furniture piece took second place to cost with consumers, and further, that manufacturers aiming for such custom were becoming more aware of this.

Looking into 1907, 1909, 1912 and 1913

Lebus catalogues were expressly produced for independent retailers to select stock they determined would meet with the approval of their own customers. Bound in hard, grey covers, this perhaps explains why they seem drab by today's standards. The earliest catalogues were produced and issued at least annually in the years preceding World War One. They contained images seemingly printed from original drawings, nearly all of them in black and white. The inclusion of some coloured plates is a welcome relief. A number of images appear more like drawings or paintings; they are artworks in their own right. The development of photography improved the quality of catalogues. An unnamed driver with the firm with a keen interest in photography produced the early prints in a studio at Tabernacle Street.

The printing of catalogues was outsourced. The 1909 catalogue was printed by Culross and Sprotson Ltd, Leeds and London; the 1912 catalogue was printed by Harrow and Sons, 'Printers in ordinary to his majesty', in St. Martin's Lane, W1; and the 1913 catalogue was

A price increase has been made to this Sheraton style suite in the 1913 catalogue.

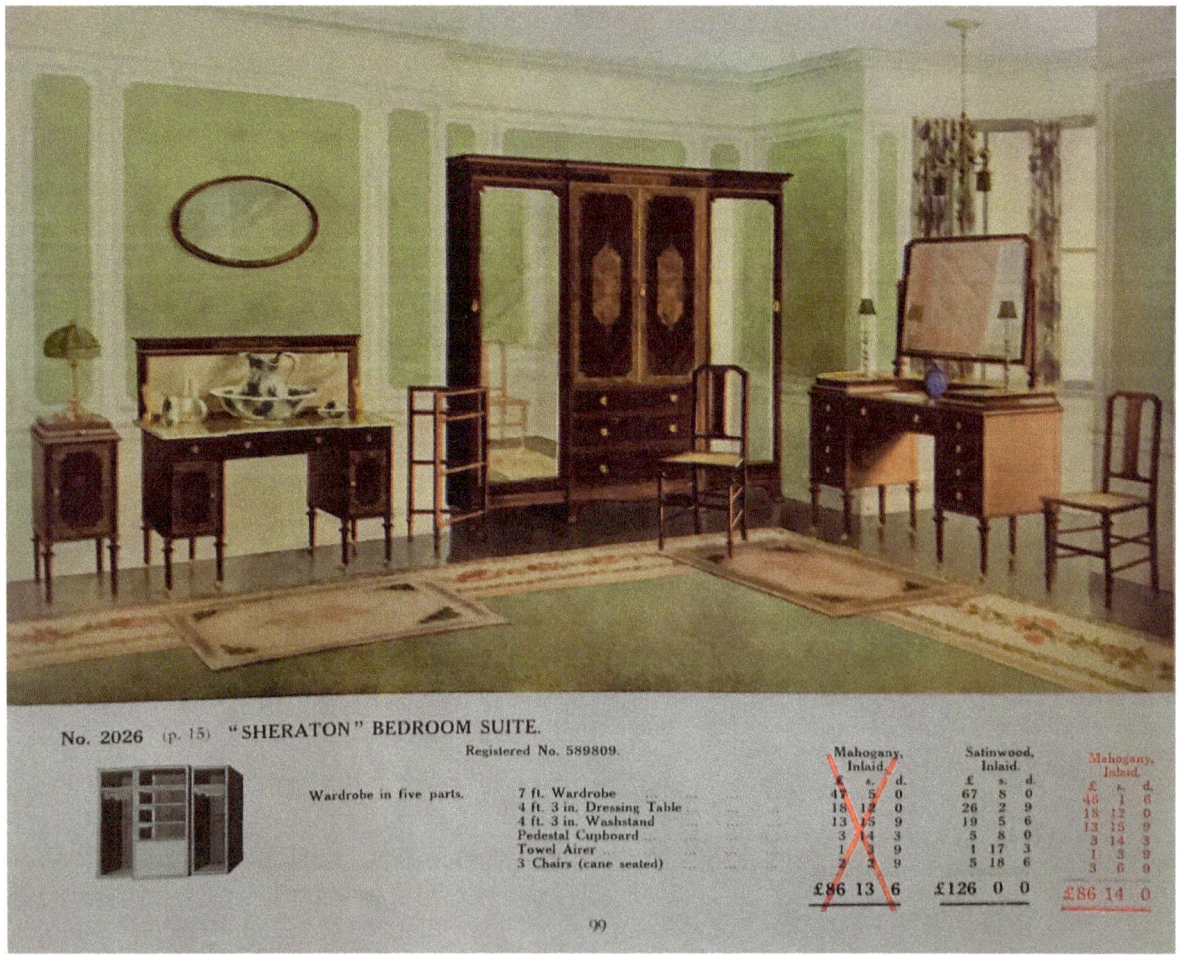

Round-edged lock plate patented by Lebus in 1904 with the initials 'HLL'.

An Arts and Crafts bureau, catalogue number 901b. It appeared in the 1910, 1912 and 1913 catalogues, which indicates it was a popular item. It is an example of space-saving furniture and an indication that homes were becoming smaller.

printed by Hanbury, Thomsett and Company, Kensal Rise, North West London. This suggests Lebus was keen to use a printer giving the most competitive rates for the job.

As World War One loomed, these catalogues arguably formed the pinnacle of this era. The front cover of my copy of the 1912 catalogue has the stamp of John Barker and Company, Kensington,[6] indicating it was once used by that business for purchasing Lebus products. Viewed alongside a Maple and Company catalogue from the same period, and amongst its other suppliers, Lebus stock on sale by the store can be identified (even though these are not attributed to Lebus).

---

6 Barkers was a prestigious department store on Kensington High Street sharing its postal district with Harrods.

INDEX.

BEDROOM FURNITURE.

	Pages
Bedroom Suites, see pages IV-V.	
Bedside Tables	104
Bedsteads	103
Box Ottomans	113
Chairs	104
Chests of Drawers	108-109
Cheval Mirrors	106
Combination Dressing Chests and Washstands	111
Commodes	105
Corner Washstands	110
Dressing Chests	110
Dressing Tables	110
Dress Stands	105
Gentlemen's Wardrobes	107-108
Linen Cupboards	107
Lounges	112
Luggage Stands	105
Pedestal Cupboards	104
Shaving Stands	112
Toilet Glasses	106
" Tables	106

DINING ROOM FURNITURE.

	Pages
Argentieres	154, 144, 146, 149
Chairs	165-174, 115-149
" Easy	175-184, 257-265
Dining Room Suites	156-164, 115-149
Dining Tables	150-153, 115-149
Dinner Wagons	154-155
Overmantels	289-295
Settees	176-185, 266-274
Sideboards and Complete Dining Rooms, see page V.	
Trays, Butler's	300
" Sandwich	300
" Sets of	300

DRAWING ROOM FURNITURE.

	Pages
Cabinets, China	186-212, 214-226
" Corner	194
" Curio and Showcase	304
" Drawing Room	211, 219, 221, 222, 226
" Music	285-286
Cake Stands	301
Chairs, Arm	256
" Easy	257-265
" Occasional	246-255
Complete Drawing Rooms	214-226
Davenports	331
Drawing Room Suites	227-245, 214-226
Music Ottomans	284
Overmantels	289-295
Piano Stools	280-283
Settees	266-274
Tables, Card	305-307
" Curio and Show Case	304
" Occasional	308-322
" Sutherland	321
" Tea	302-303
" Work	213
" Writing	323-331
Urn Stands	300

HALL FURNITURE.

	Pages
Carved Oak Furniture	378-383
Chairs	376-377, 383
Cupboards	378-379
Hall Stands	369-376, 380-382
Seats	377, 383
Tables	376
Umbrella Stands	369

OFFICE & LIBRARY FURNITURE.

	Pages
Bookcases, Bureau	339-343
" Library	346-347
" Revolving	344-345
" Secretary	348
" Sectional	349-350
Bookstands	344
Bureaux	334-338
Chairs	363-368
Complete Libraries	332-333
Desks, Clerk's	358
" Flat Top	352-353
" High Roll Top	355-357
" Low Roll Top	354
" Typewriter	352
Filing Cabinets, Drawer	361-363
" Vertical	359-360
Tables, Typewriter	352
" Writing	351-352

MISCELLANEOUS.

	Pages
Coal Boxes and Cabinets	287-288
Footstools	212
Lavatory Glasses	105
Palm Stands and Pedestals	296-299
Photo Frames	212
Screens	212
Tables, Gate Leg	316
" Liqueur	302
" Nests of	322
Three Piece Suites	275-279
Washstands, Corner	110
" Lavatory	110

All previous Lists cancelled. Subject to alterations without notice.

The index page from the 1912 catalogue, which indicates the range and breadth of Lebus furniture for sale in this period.

There was a staggering number of individual furniture pieces on offer from Lebus during the Edwardian era. The range of products offered were indexed under 'Bedroom', 'Dining Room', 'Drawing Room', 'Hall', 'Office and Library' and 'Miscellaneous'. Many individual furniture pieces were allocated a design/catalogue number, or alternatively, these numbers applied to a complete suite of furniture – bedroom, dining room or drawing room. Some suites had an additional patent registration number (though these are not recorded in the 1909 catalogue). Whilst a significant amount of the content in 1913 compared with 1912 is new designs, there are also many of the same suites and individual pieces on offer again in 1913. The 1907 catalogue is devoted to office furniture only.

In each section, furniture is arranged in ascending order of price. Each piece is individually priced (indicating the purchaser could buy one item at a time) and the total outlay for a complete suite is provided as an end total. There are no prices given in the 1909 catalogue – this could reflect the fact that it was aimed for French and German readers. Prices quoted in catalogues are assumed to be retail price – in essence, a (flexible or rigid) recommended retail price (RRP) for the eventual consumer. This would fit with a note in the front of the 1913 catalogue which reads: 'The numbers in parentheses after the identification numbers of the goods give the page numbers where net prices may be found in the Net Price List.'

A statement at the beginning of the 1913 catalogue indicates a structured approach, with a pricing formula applied according to the desired finish. Oak bedroom furniture could be supplied as was or enamelled white at an extra

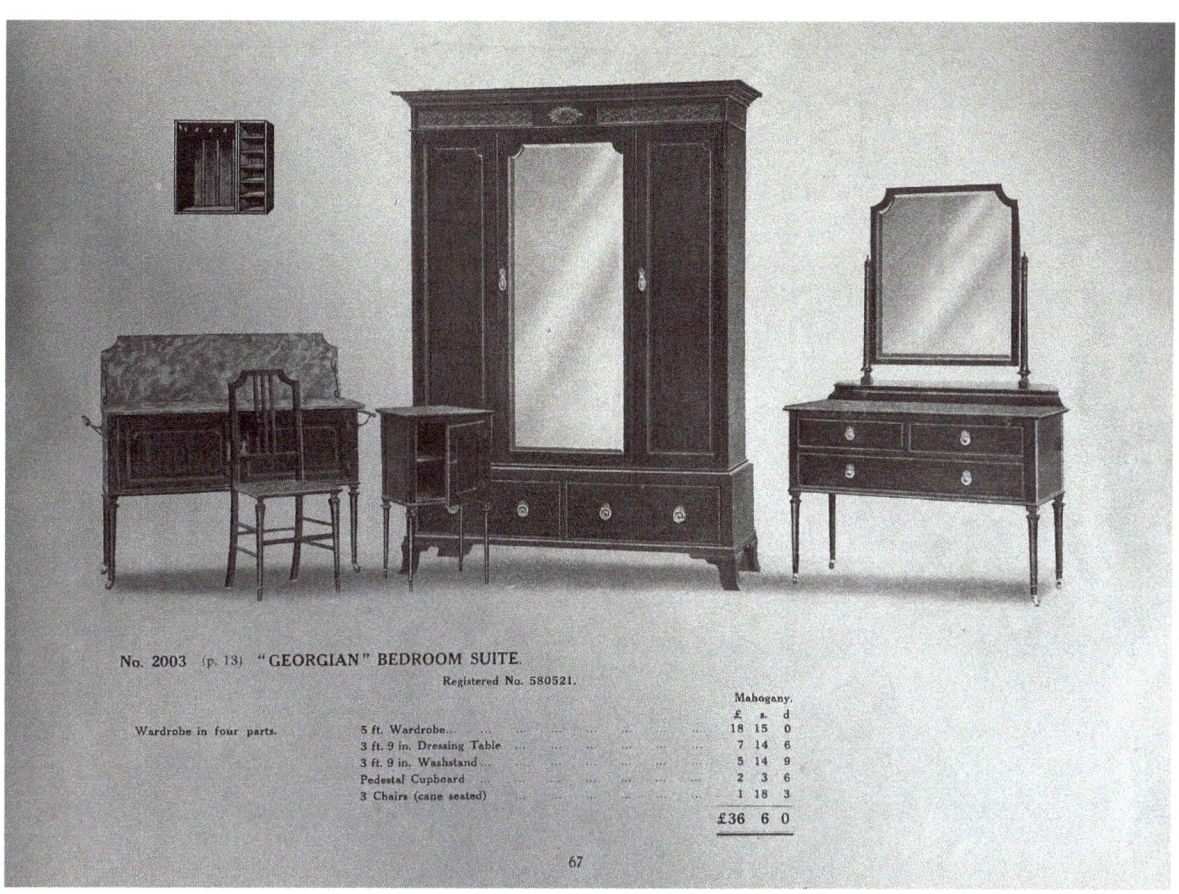

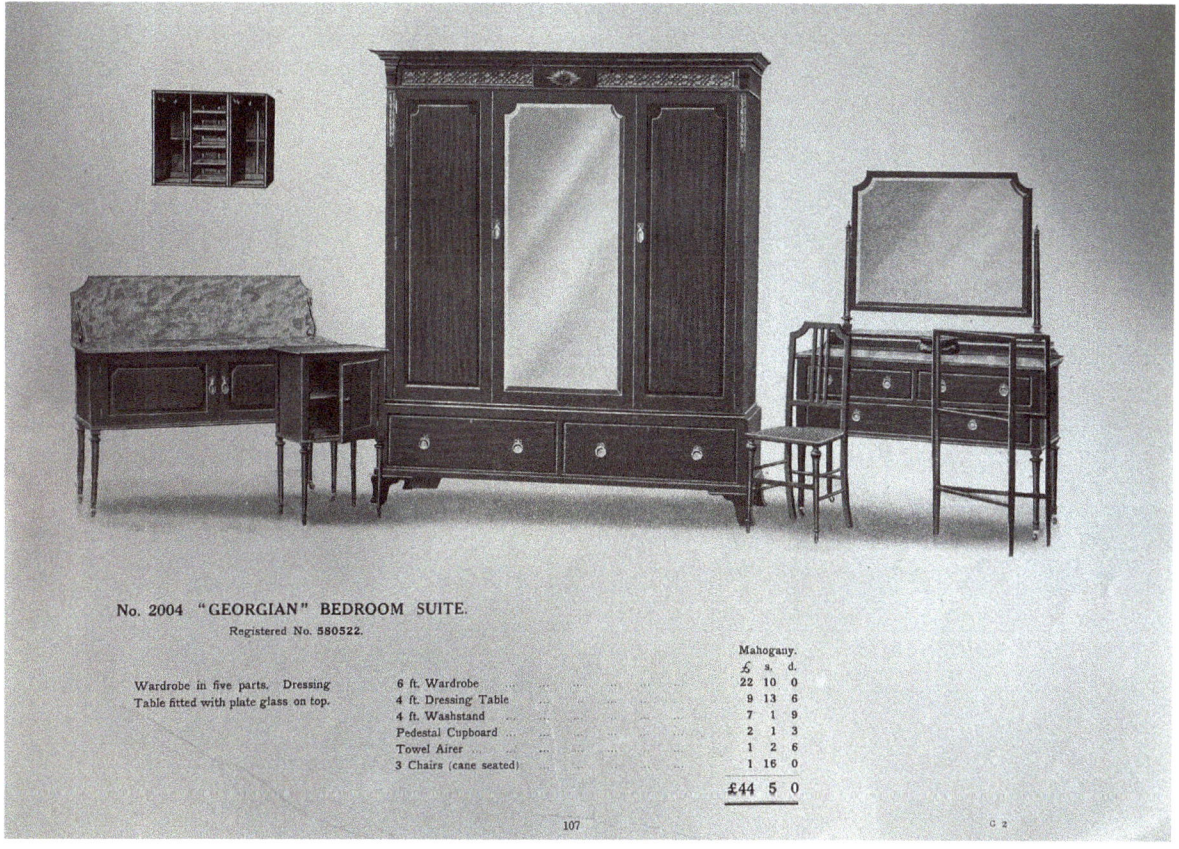

Georgian style: These bedroom suites were designed at the same time. From 1913 is the 580521 with catalogue number 2003, and from 1912 design registration number 580522, catalogue number 2004. This tells us how close to the last design a new one could be, perhaps with just a few tweaks.

FROM THE BEDROOM TO THE OFFICE... AND EVERY ROOM BETWEEN 43

charge of 25 percent; satin walnut bedroom furniture could be supplied as was or finished in mahogany or walnut wood dye and French polished at an extra charge of 7.5 percent (the catalogue of 1912 states that walnut suites are supplied waxed finished without extra charge) or enamelled white at an extra charge of 20 percent. Soft-furnishing stuffing materials were assigned a letter – 'A', 'B' and 'D' appear frequently. It is not known exactly what the differences were between them, except that the more expensive sofas and lounge furniture appear to be stuffed with D.

Bedrooms

Described as a 'pair of toilets', a simple bedroom suite consisted of a chest of drawers (with or without mirror) and a matching washstand. In the era before bathrooms with running water, washstands with their marble tops and tiled splash back were commonplace and were an essential bedroom furniture piece, being used with china sets consisting of water jug, bowl and soap dish. These furniture pieces were offered in a range of widths.

No. 303 4 ft. Combination Dressing Chest and Washstand
Manufactured in Satin Walnut, Walnut, Oak, Mahogany, and Enamelled White

No. 303 Commode-coiffeuse et Lavabo combines, 1 m 22
Fabriquée en Noyer Anglais, Noyer, Chêne, Acajou et laqué blanc

No. 303 Toiletten-Kommode und Waschtisch zusammengestellt, 1 m 22
Angefertigt in Satin Nussbaum, Nussbaum, Eiche, Mahagoni und weiss lackirt

A combination unit – washstand and chest of drawers – was a compact alternative to having two separate pieces. The merging of two traditionally separate furniture pieces reflects a demand for flexible furniture in smaller rooms. Perhaps these were destined for servants' bed chambers. There was a choice of three designs offered in 1913: 303, 317 and 327. They were a repeat of those offered the previous year. Two were available in six finishes – ash, satin walnut, walnut, oak, mahogany or enamelled white. The only difference with the third piece was that it was not available in ash. Prices in 1913 ranged from £4 13s 9d for the smaller piece (three feet six inches) in ash to £7 0s 3d for one of the larger pieces (four feet wide) in enamelled white. In 1909 these pieces included a fourth, the 316.

A bedroom chest of drawers. Identifying Lebus furniture from the pre-World War One era is made more difficult because much of it is not trademarked. This chest of drawers has the series of horizontal parallel indents across the drawers which is a characteristic of Lebus furniture. It also has the lock plate with round edges. This chest of drawers has been lovingly rejuvenated by Jayson at Whisper and Echo UK.

An Adams-inspired bedroom suite, 1031a was the most expensive in the 1913 catalogue. It consisted of eight items with a 'framed medallion motif' and was offered with a choice of inlays – mahogany (price listed first) or satin wood (price listed second) at £393 15s or £472 10s 6d. (These prices in 1912 had been £375 and £450 respectively.) Each item was individually priced, indicating they could be bought separately: the seven-foot wardrobe, in five parts was £170 2s or £201 6s; the four-foot-six-inch dressing table, with bevelled mirror, was £95 6s or £115 14s 6d; the four-foot-six-inch washstand was £75 6s or £92 2s; a pair of bedside cabinets was £21 5s or £24 12s; a free-standing towel rail fitted with sliding tray was £9 15s or £12 6s; and finally a set of four chairs with cane seats and loose cushions covered in 'lining' and with D-grade stuffing was £22 1s or £26 10s.

Within the Sheraton-influenced bedroom range in 1913 were 30 different suite choices. The most expensive of these was 1009a, consisting of a seven-foot-wide wardrobe in five parts, dressing table and washstand, each of four feet three inches, a pedestal (bedside) cupboard, towel rail and four chairs (with D-grade stuffing, covered in lining). The suite came with inlaid decoration in either mahogany at £180 in 1912 and £189 in 1913 or satin wood at £219 in 1912 and £230 in 1913.

This Sheraton-style wardrobe recently came up for sale on the vintage market. It appears to match the bedroom suite in mahogany finish with inlay that was catalogue number 45 in 1909. Whilst the 1909 catalogue does not have the design registration numbers, this wardrobe has the registration number 447063 embossed in the top edge of the wardrobe's bottom drawer. (This number applied to the whole suite.) There were bedsteads to match this suite and which could be used with any of the inlaid Sheraton-style suites.
(Images of the wardrobe courtesy of Lloyd)

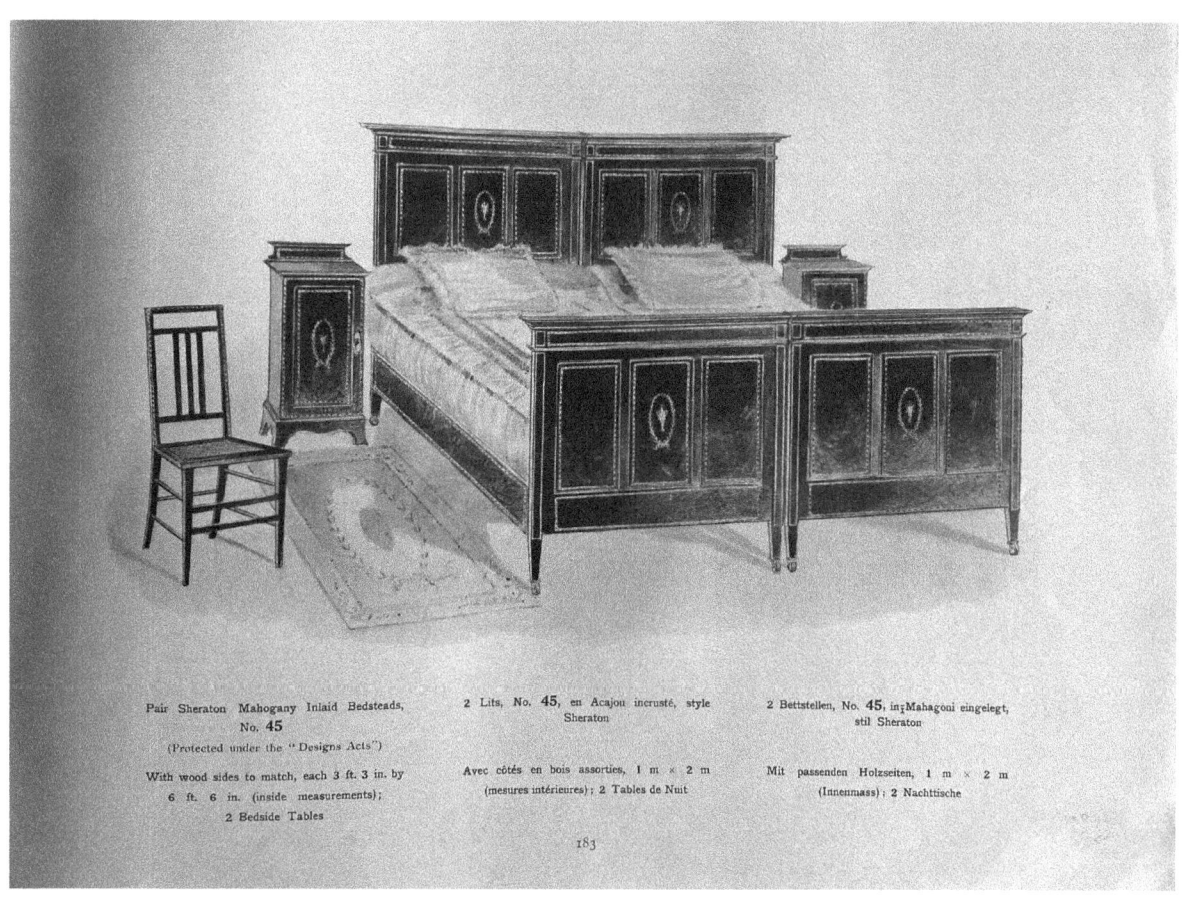

Sheraton Bedroom Suite, No. 45
(Protected under the "Designs Acts")
Comprising :—
6 ft. Wardrobe, made in 5 parts, loose plinth and cornice, centre carcase fitted with 5 drawers and 2 shelves, the left and right-hand wings all hanging, with shelf at top ; 4 ft. Dressing Chest ; 4 ft. Washstand, Rouge marble top and back, with Pedestal Cupboard attached ; Towel Airer ; 3 cane seat Chairs
Manufactured in Mahogany, Inlaid

Chambre à coucher, No. 45, en Acajou, style Sheraton
Comprenant :—
Armoire à vêtements, 1 m 83, faite en 5 divisions, avec corniche et plinthe démontables, corps du milieu avec 5 tiroirs et 2 tablettes, partie droite et gauche en penderie avec tablette en haut ; Commode-coiffeuse, 1 m 22 ; Lavabo, 1 m 22, avec dessus et dos en marbre rouge, Table de nuit attachés ; Porte-serviettes ; 3 Chaises à siège canné
Fabriquée en Acajou incrusté

Schlafzimmer-Einrichtung, No. 45, in Mahagoni, stil Sheraton
Bestehend aus :—
Kleiderschrank, 1 m 83, in 5 Abteilungen, mit losem Karniess und Sockel ; mittlerer Teil mit 5 Schubladen und 2 Fächern, rechte und linke Seite mit Hängevorrichtung und Fach im oberen Teil ; Toiletten-Kommode, 1 m 22 ; Waschtisch, 1 m 22, mit Platte und Rückwand in rotem Marmor, mit Nachttisch ; Handtuchhalter ; 3 Stühle mit geflochtenem Sitz
Angefertigt in Mahagoni eingelegt

Pair Sheraton Mahogany Inlaid Bedsteads, No. 45
(Protected under the "Designs Acts")
With wood sides to match, each 3 ft. 3 in. by 6 ft. 6 in. (inside measurements) ;
2 Bedside Tables

2 Lits, No. 45, en Acajou incrusté, style Sheraton
Avec côtés en bois assorties, 1 m × 2 m (mesures intérieures) ; 2 Tables de Nuit

2 Bettstellen, No. 45, in Mahagoni eingelegt, stil Sheraton
Mit passenden Holzseiten, 1 m × 2 m (Innenmass) ; 2 Nachttische

Thereafter, bedroom suites are indexed according to the ascending widths of their wardrobes. A choice of ten different sizes were available, the more expensive suites having the larger sizes.

For the bed itself, there was a choice of bedsteads as singles or doubles in four different basic designs in 1913. They were available in a choice of seven finishes. In addition, bedside cabinets, free-standing towel rails and chairs (either with cane seats or upholstered) could be added. To complete the bedroom, a choice of five upholstered furniture pieces for reclined relaxation were on offer.

Table: Bedroom furniture pieces and choice of sizes

Size	Furniture piece		
	Wardrobe	Chest of drawers (with or without mirror)	Washstands
Two feet six inches	√	√	√
Two feet nine inches	√	√	√
Three feet	√	√	√
Three feet three inches	√	√	√
Three feet six inches	√	√	√
Four feet	√	√	√
Four feet three inches	√	√	√
Four feet six inches	√	√	√
Five feet	√	√	√
Six feet	√		
Six feet six inches	√		
Seven feet	√		
Seven feet six inches	√		

No. 2087a (p. 22)
LOUNGE. C stuffing, covered in tapestry.
£8 6 0

There was a choice of box ottomans available for the bedroom along with an elongated chair, which has the appearance of an armchair with combined footrest, described as a 'lounge'. Catalogue number 2087a came with C stuffing covered in tapestry and was priced at £8 6s in 1913 (£7 17s 6d in 1912).

Sideboards and dining room

Since this section is headed 'sideboards and dining room', it suggests the sideboard was the first consideration for the room alongside the table and seating. Sideboards are listed in ascending price order. A correlation between price and style influence emerges.

There was an extensive range of furniture to adorn a dining room. These included:

- Argentieres (usually with plate-glass shelves and mirrored back; often hard to distinguish from a china cabinet)
- Dinner wagons (trolleys) and various trays (butler's, sandwich and sets of)
- Over-mantels (with mirrors designed to sit above a fireplace).

Dining-room set from the 1909 catalogue. With the over-mantle, sideboard, table, two carvers and four dining chairs there are nine individual pieces of furniture.

ARGENTIERE (made to match any sideboard). Prices on application.
No. 126 (p. 28)

FROM THE BEDROOM TO THE OFFICE... AND EVERY ROOM BETWEEN   49

To navigate the selection of dining tables, a Lebus sales representative would have been a necessity. There were 14 individual designs listed in the dining tables section, numbers 500 to 519 inclusive (501, 502, 504, 506, 512 and 516 were no longer available). A choice of different widths and extending lengths could be made, as well as the final finish. Solid-top tables were more expensive than bass-top tables and a note in the catalogue states that bass tops were 'always left in the white'; in other words, they were left without being wood-dyed and French polished so that the customer could choose their preferred colour and polish finish. Where the letter 'a', 'b' or 'c' came after a design number, further incremental savings could be made when using less-expensive raw materials: oak, birch legs and bass tops were cheaper.

Further, the catalogue described four additional options available with each design:

- D ends[7] on a square frame (extending tables were the screw expander type)
- Oval tops on either an oval or square frame
- Circular tops with circular frames.

---

7 It is thought that 'D ends' refers to two halves of a tabletop which, when parted, could accommodate an additional tabletop piece in the middle.

D ends cost an extra 8s 6d regardless of table size, and the most expensive choice was the circular top, costing an additional £3 11s 6d.

One of the least expensive dining-table options was the 500c, with an 'as it comes' angled corner, with oak bass top and birch legs. Selecting the smallest size at three-foot-six-inches wide and five-foot long, it was priced at £1 16s 9d in 1912 and £1 19s in 1913.

One of the most expensive choices would be the 519, with solid, circular top on a circular frame, at the largest width of four feet six inches and an extending length of ten feet (the maximum length with the circular top) and finished in the more expensive walnut or mahogany. There was an add-on charge of £3 7s 6d and £3 11s 6d in 1912 and 1913 respectively for circular tops and frames. Making this selection would cost £20 14s in 1912 (£17 6s 6d + £3 7s 6d) and £21 15s 6d in 1913 (£18 4s + £3 11s 6d).

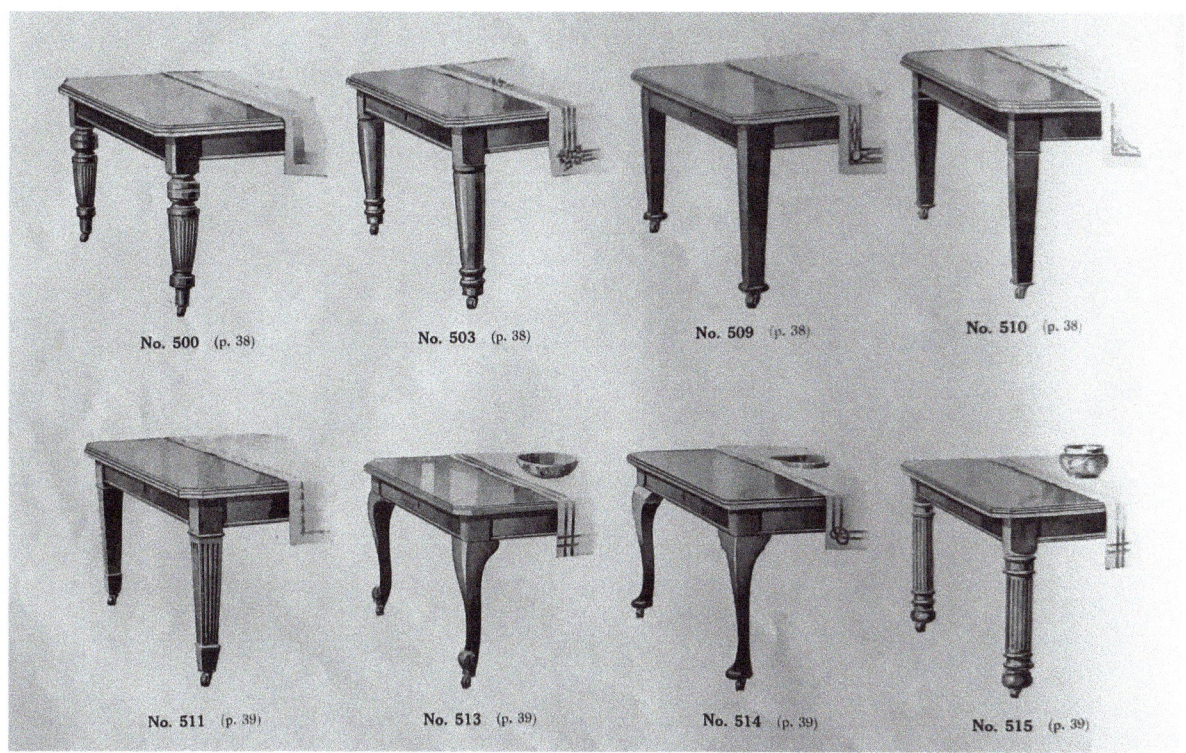

The complete range of dining tables available in 1912 and 1913.

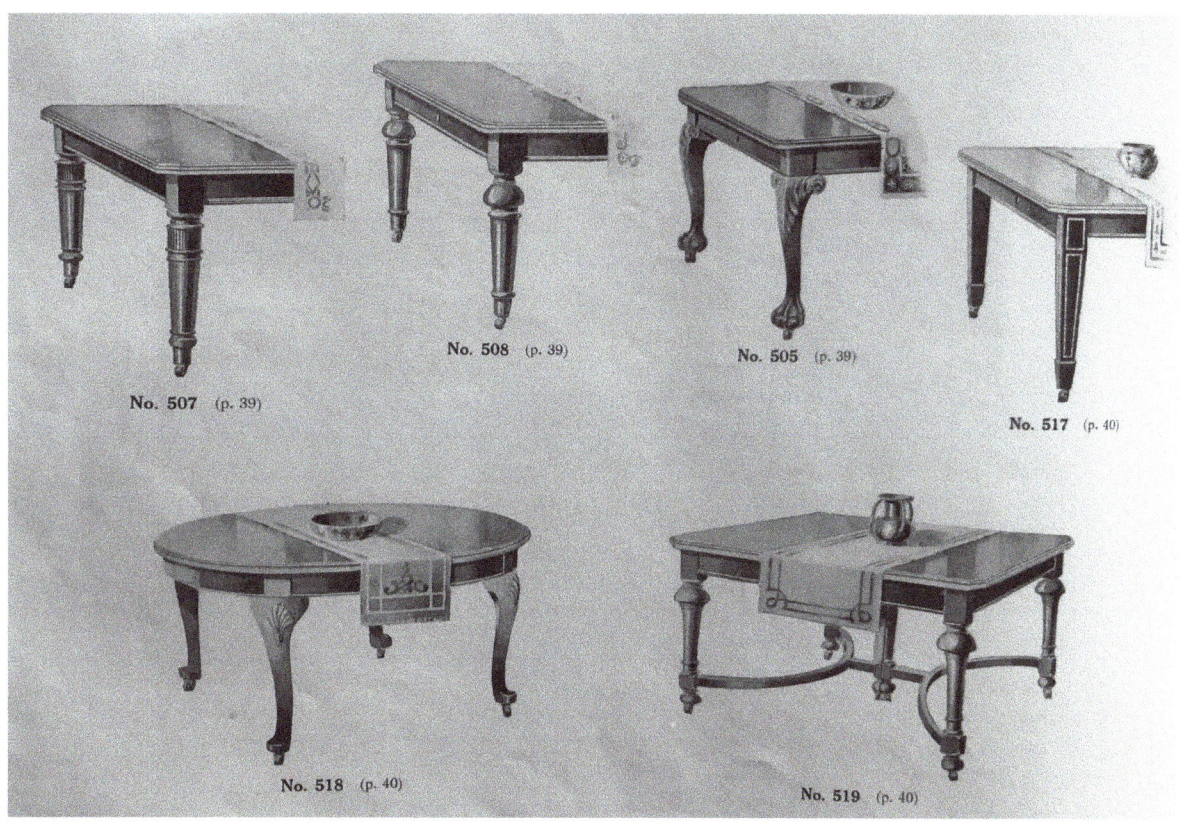

FROM THE BEDROOM TO THE OFFICE... AND EVERY ROOM BETWEEN

Table: Dining tables and choices

Cat. no.	Finish		Dimensions: Widths x extendable lengths						
		Width 3ft 6in			Width 4ft		Width 4ft 6in		
	Oak	Walnut/Mahogany	5ft	6ft	7ft	6ft	8ft	10ft	12ft
500	√	√	√	√	√	√	√	√	√
500a	√		√	√	√	√	√	√	√
500b & c	√	√	√	√	√	√	√		
503	√	√	√	√	√	√	√	√	√
503a	y	√	√	√	√	√	√	√	√
505		√	√	√	√	√	√	√	√
507	√	√	√	√	√	√	√	√	√
507a	√		√	√	√	√	√	√	√
508	√	√	√	√	√	√	√	√	√
508a	√		√	√	√	√	√	√	√
509	√	√	√	√	√	√	√	√	√
509a	√		√	√	√	√	√	√	√
510	√	√	√	√	√	√	√	√	√
510a	√	√	√	√	√	√	√	√	√
511	√	√	√	√	√	√	√	√	√
511a	√		√	√	√	√	√	√	√
513	√	√	√	√	√	√	√	√	√
513a	√	√	√	√	√	√	√	√	√
514	√	√	√	√	√	√	√	√	√
514a	√		√	√	√	√	√	√	√
515	√	√	√	√	√	√	√	√	√
515a	√		√	√	√	√	√	√	√
517	√		√	√	√	√	√	√	√
518	√	√	√	√	√	√	√	√	√
519	√	√	√	√	√	√	√	√	√

Tops available in solid or bass except 500b and 500c, which were bass only. These were also available with birch legs.

Available as Sheraton inlaid 517.

A dining-chair set was considered as four dining chairs (minimum) with two additional carver chairs. The more luxurious dining-room suites, as well as the dining chairs and carvers, included more comfortable upholstered seating for relaxation. Some settees (sofas) are indexed under both dining room and drawing room, suggesting they were intended for use in either setting, and a further choice of settees was indexed under only the dining room, indicating that this was the intended destination for these specific designs.

The least expensive dining-room suite in both 1912 and 1913 was catalogue number 141, design registration 53796. With a four-foot sideboard and a three-foot-six-inch-wide round dining table, two armchairs upholstered in Victoria cloth and four small chairs, it was priced in 1913 at £14 4s 6d in oak and £16 9s 6d in walnut.

The most expensive dining-room suite in both 1912 and 1913 was catalogue number 0108.

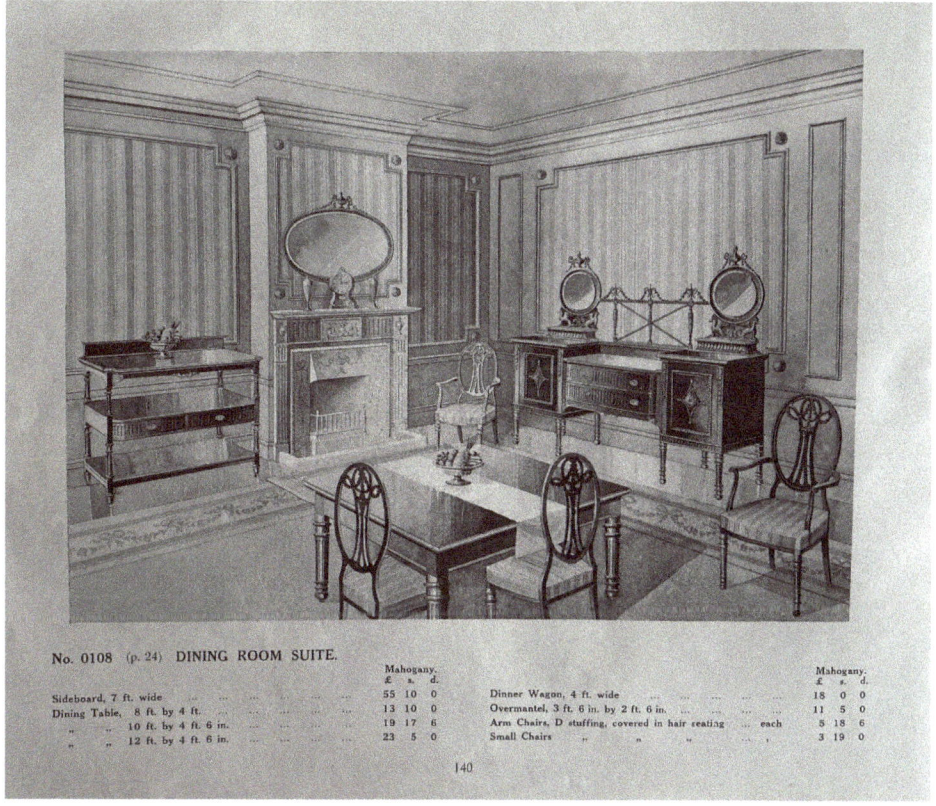

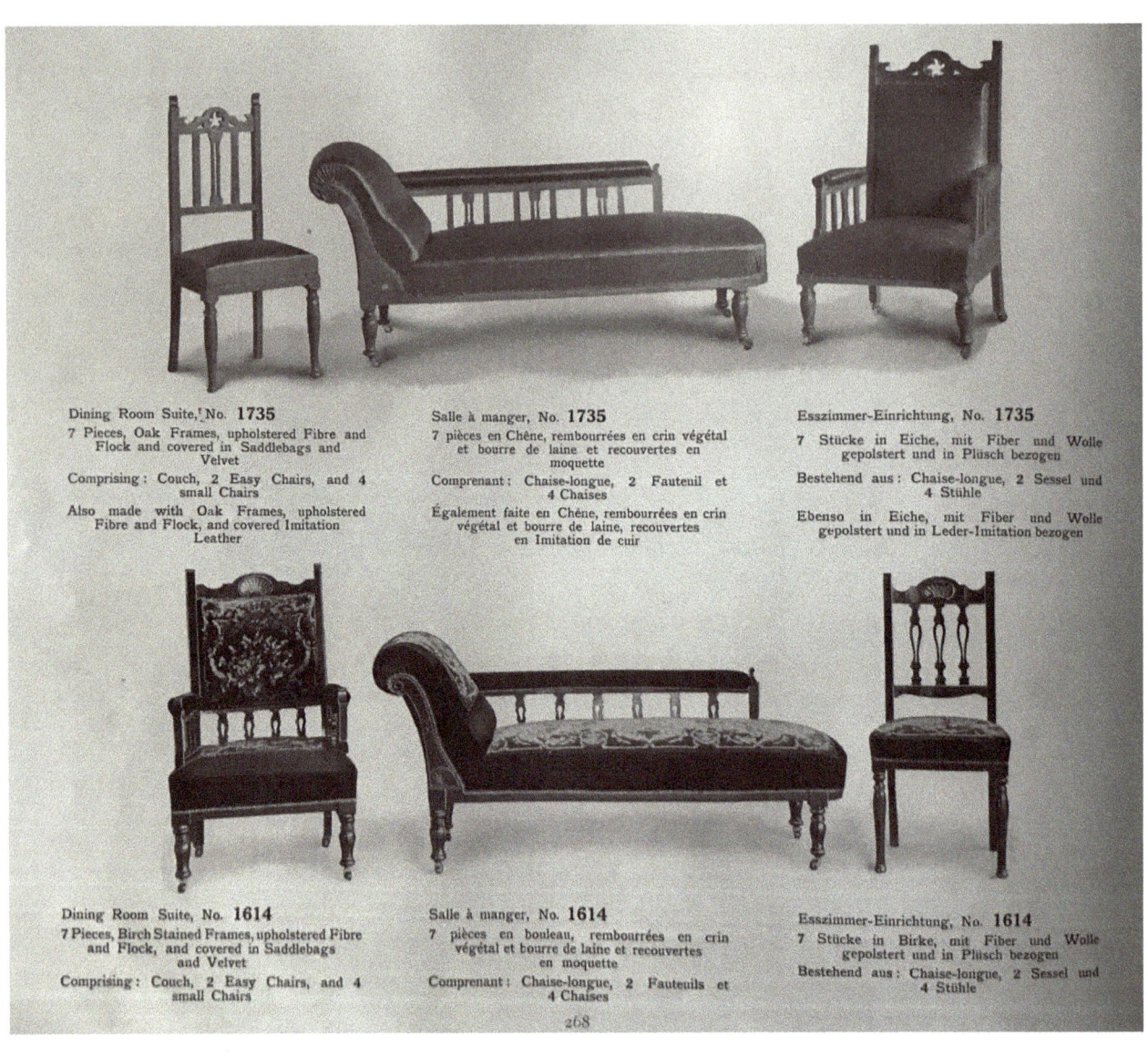

Pictured in the 1909 catalogue, both these dining-room suites were amongst a number still available in 1912 and 1913, which indicates they were popular with customers.

Drawing room

The drawing room during this period was for relaxed seating, as well as entertaining guests. Upholstered furniture was an important consideration for this room and Lebus offered a multitude of choices, including settees, armchairs, easy chairs and occasional chairs, as well as three-piece suites and complete drawing-room suites.

The least expensive drawing-room suites in 1913. The price compares favourably to the most expensive suite, catalogue number 3196 upholstered in silk at a cost of £35 9s 6d mahogany inlaid and £41 15s satinwood inlaid.

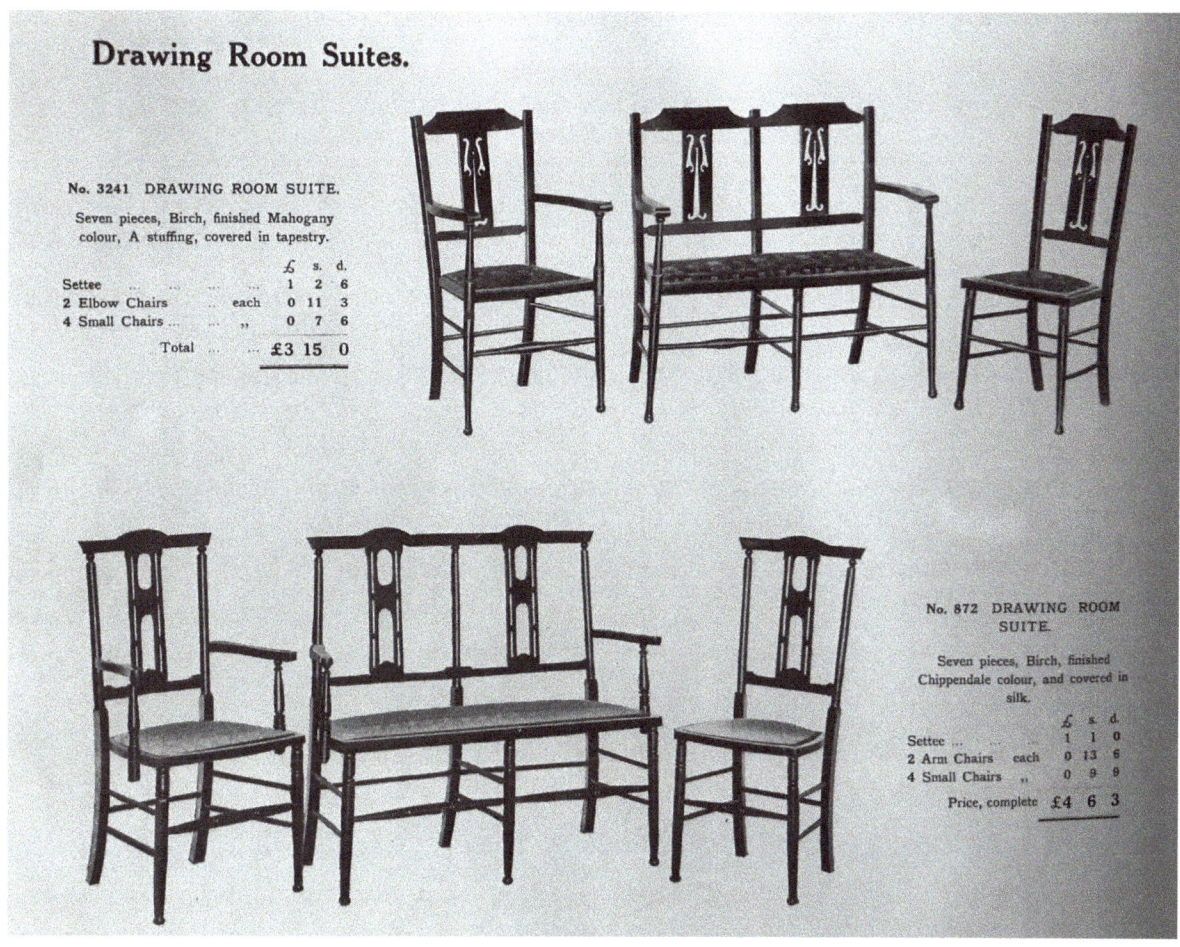

This drawing-room suite from the 1909 catalogue is just exquisite.

Drawing-room suites were, to all intents and purposes, the same as dining-room (upholstered) suites. They consisted of seven furniture items: a settee (sofa), two easy (arm) chairs and four (dining-style) chairs. A choice of 38 of these suites were offered in the 1913 catalogue.

Complete drawing-room suite, catalogue number 0111 in 1913, with china cabinet, writing desk, music cabinet and card table.

Whereas today we tend to associate lounge seating with the three-piece suite, these are indexed only under miscellaneous furniture. There were only ten complete three-piece suites (sofa and two chairs, all with matched upholstery and usually, but not always, with the chairs being of the same shape or design). There was a choice of 12 three-piece suites available for the drawing room in 1912. This figure was reduced to ten the following year.

56   LOVING LEBUS

Three-piece suites. The least expensive of the three-piece suites was 1750, with oak under-frames, B-grade stuffing covered in tapestry for £10 17s 6d in 1912 and £11 9s in 1913. The settee and chairs were individually priced, suggesting they were available to buy separately.

The most expensive was the 3268 made of satinwood, with cane seats and backs with hand-painted decoration to solid wood – romanticised scenes of angelic figures in heavenly skies. Combined, the suite was £45 14s 6d in 1913 (£43 10s in 1912). Individually, the sofa was £23 5s, the carver was £14 3s 6d and the dining chair £8 6s in 1913.

China cabinets were one of the most popular furniture items of the period. The 1912 catalogue contains 117 designs. Thirty are inspired by Louis style, 17 by Sheraton and six by Adams.

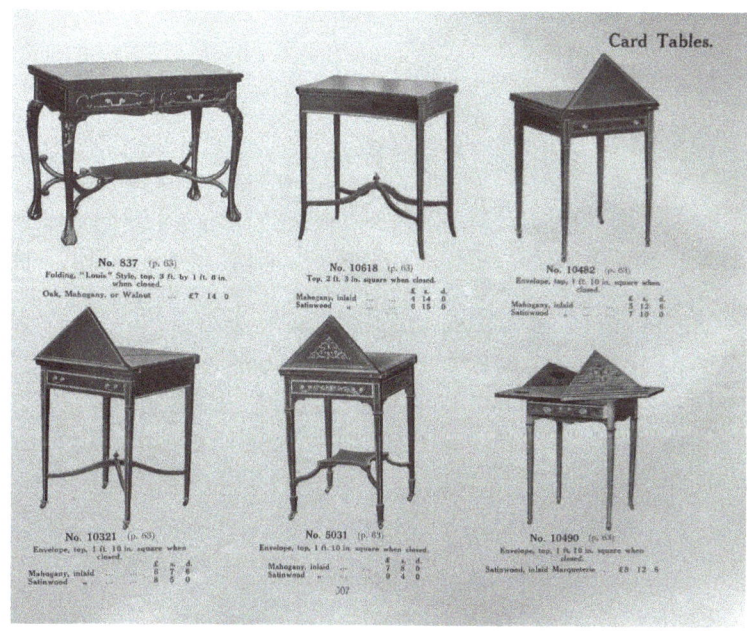

Some of the card tables on offer in 1913.

FROM THE BEDROOM TO THE OFFICE... AND EVERY ROOM BETWEEN   57

Miscellaneous

The smaller furniture pieces such as urn stands (for large vases of flowers or ornaments) tended to be those listed under miscellaneous items. Included were: music cabinets and ottomans (piano stool with under-seat storage), small tables intended for different uses including serving tea, playing cards, as well as occasional tables, Sutherlands (with fold-down leaves) and nests of tables.

A screen (to go in front of fireplaces when not in use) was a little under £7. Palm stands and pedestals (for displaying plants at different heights) cost anywhere between £1 and £3. Coal boxes (to store coal for keeping open fires supplied) could be purchased for a little under £1. Some were more than £3. Footstools were a little over £1. A lavatory glass (wall-mounted mirror with towel rail) would have set you back £1 1s. And there was one photo frame on sale, catalogue number 0412, measuring 10.5-inches high by 7.5-inches wide, made of satinwood with hand-painted decoration that was priced at 16s.

A modest Sheraton inlaid corner cabinet with fabric back and a similar cabinet top with Driscoll Antiques. (Photograph courtesy of James Driscoll)

Hall

The hall section included: hallstands for hats, coats and umbrellas; chairs, cupboards and seating. The most expensive furniture piece for a hall was the 8159 intricately carved oak cupboard standing six-foot-ten-inches high, four-foot wide, stained dark at £20 5s.

The hall was the place in which visitors were welcomed into a home and it was the first room they saw. Hall furniture ranged from simple umbrella stands to elaborate cupboards. One of the most expensive hall cupboards was oak carved, catalogue number 8159. In 1912 it was priced at a little over £20.

Library and office furniture (for commercial premises)

This section of both the 1912 and 1913 catalogues was an amalgam of furniture for the home library and commercial office.

In the 1913 catalogue, for the home library there were bookcases of various sizes: revolving bookcases and glass-fronted cabinet bookcases, bureaux and writing tables in styles derivative of Louis, Sheraton and Carlton (based around late Georgian style). There were half-a-dozen Davenports, two of which were attributed to Chippendale style.

Library suite from 1913, catalogue number 0165.

FROM THE BEDROOM TO THE OFFICE... AND EVERY ROOM BETWEEN

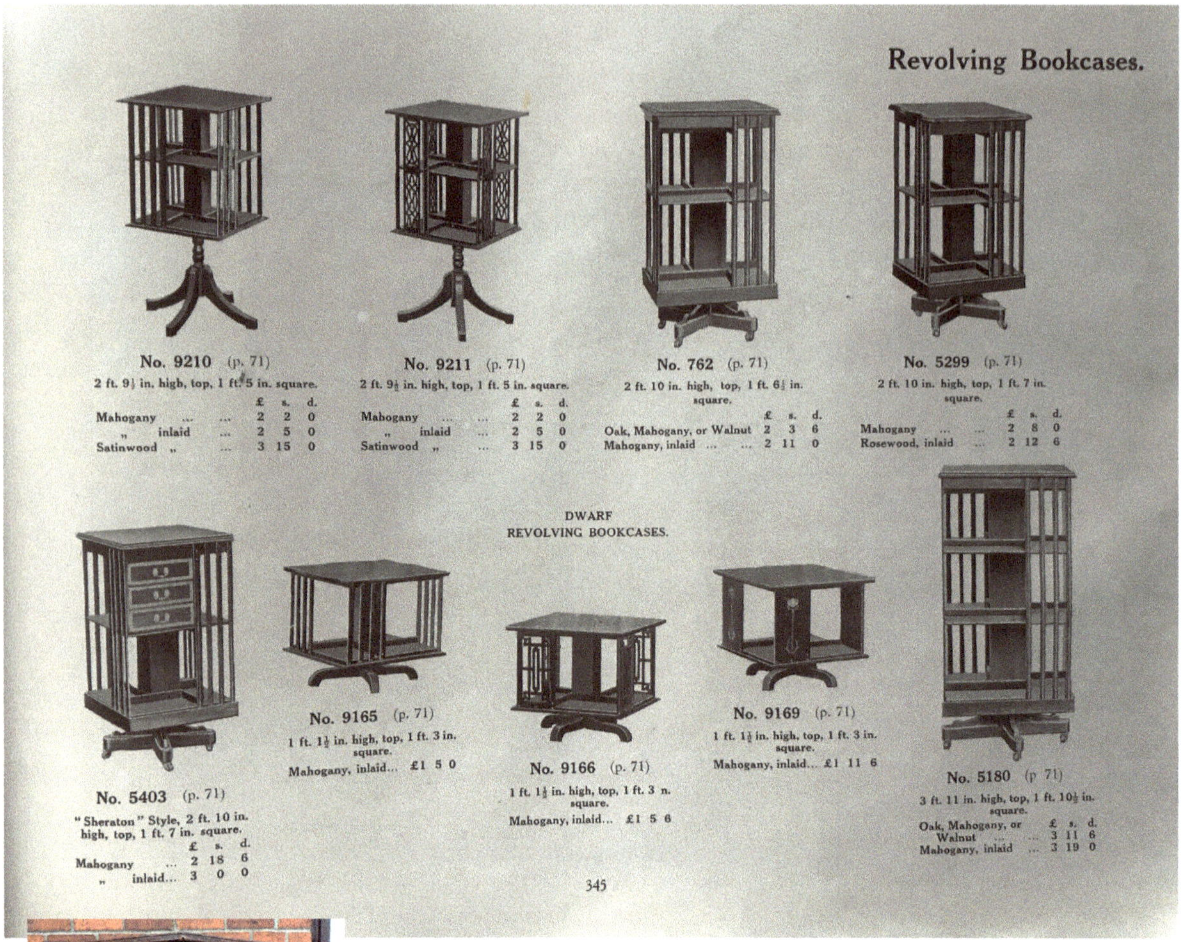

Revolving Bookcases.

No. 9210 (p. 71)	No. 9211 (p. 71)	No. 762 (p. 71)	No. 5299 (p. 71)
2 ft. 9½ in. high, top, 1 ft. 5 in. square.	2 ft. 9½ in. high, top, 1 ft. 5 in. square.	2 ft. 10 in. high, top, 1 ft. 6½ in. square.	2 ft. 10 in. high, top, 1 ft. 7 in. square.
£ s. d.	£ s. d.	£ s. d.	£ s. d.
Mahogany ... 2 2 0	Mahogany ... 2 2 0	Oak, Mahogany, or Walnut 2 3 6	Mahogany ... 2 8 0
" inlaid ... 2 5 0	" inlaid ... 2 5 0	Mahogany, inlaid ... 2 11 0	Rosewood, inlaid ... 2 12 6
Satinwood " ... 3 15 0	Satinwood " ... 3 15 0		

DWARF REVOLVING BOOKCASES.

No. 5403 (p. 71)	No. 9165 (p. 71)	No. 9166 (p. 71)	No. 9169 (p. 71)	No. 5180 (p. 71)
"Sheraton" Style, 2 ft. 10 in. high, top, 1 ft. 7 in. square.	1 ft. 1½ in. high, top, 1 ft. 3 in. square.	1 ft. 1½ in. high, top, 1 ft. 3 in. square.	1 ft. 1½ in. high, top, 1 ft. 3 in. square.	3 ft. 11 in. high, top, 1 ft. 10½ in. square.
£ s. d.	Mahogany, inlaid... £1 5 0	Mahogany, inlaid... £1 5 6	Mahogany, inlaid... £1 11 6	Oak, Mahogany, or Walnut ... 3 11 6
Mahogany ... 2 18 6				Mahogany, inlaid ... 3 19 0
" inlaid ... 3 0 0				

345

Some revolving bookcases from the 1913 catalogue and one that recently came up on the antiques market.

Desks for the library came in a range of sizes and styles. Some were traditional like this Chippendale-style Davenport from 1913. Sheraton-style compact bureaux, the type with which many may be familiar today, were being produced. This example from the 1913 catalogue is an indication that homes were getting smaller – this piece of furniture could slot into any room in the home.

No. 806 (p. 54)
1 ft. 10 in. wide, 3 ft. 1 in. high.
"Chippendale" ... £8 5 0

No. 9192 (p. 72)
"Sheraton" Style, Mahogany, inlaid.
	£ s. d.
2 ft. wide	4 7 0
2 ft. 6 in. wide	4 14 6
3 ft. wide	5 15 0

This elaborate writing table from the 1909 catalogue is very similar to one recently available at Driscoll's Antiques. (Photographs courtesy of James Driscoll)

Lebus had made the manufacture of office furniture a specialism and was much experienced in this area. The 1907 *Lebus Catalogue of English-made Office and Library Furniture* (A5 landscape) contains 63 pages of, essentially, commercial office furniture. There are 40 pages of roll-top desks (one model for each page), 12 pages of filing cabinets and five pages of sectional bookcases. There is also one page for bookstands and even an office wardrobe. Of 40 desks, 25 are high roll top, five are low roll top and ten are the more common flat top. The desks are indexed according to grades one to four. (It is assumed these pertain to quality.) All desks were available in a choice of either fumed oak or satin walnut finished as walnut or stained mahogany, except models 21, 22, 23, 27, 28 and 29, which were described as 'good figured oak or walnut', and 24, 25 and 26, which were made of 'fine Cuban mahogany highly polished'. Desk number 5, a four-foot-wide roll-top desk, was one of the most popular and sold well.

In the 1909 catalogue, alongside models 1 to 40, are a further seven desks numbered 41 to 48 (45 is absent). Models 41, 42, 43 and 44 are roll tops. Models 46, 47 and 48 are typewriter desks, with 46 having a roll top. There is another desk listed: catalogue number 930b is a Davenport.

Table: Desks 1–40

Desk catalogue number	Quality/Grade 1	2	3	4	Type Roll top	Flat top	Width in inches 30	36	42	48	50	54/55	60
1		√			√			√					
2		√			√						√		
3		√			√							√	
4		√			√								√
5	√				√					√			
6		√				√		√					
7		√				√					√		
8		√				√						√	
9		√				√							√
10	√				√					√			
11	√				√			√					
12	√				√				√				
13	√				√							√	
14	√					√		√					
15	√					√			√				
16	√					√						√	
17		√			√		√						
18*	√					√	√						
19	√				√				√				
20	√					√			√				
21				√	√						√		
22				√	√							√	
23				√	√								√
24				√	√						√		
25				√	√							√	
26				√	√								√
27			√		√						√		
28			√		√							√	
29			√		√								√
30	√				√						√		
31	√				√							√	
32	√				√								√
33	√				√					√			
34		√			√						√		
35		√			√							√	
36		√			√								√
37	√				√					√			
38		√			√						√		
39		√			√							√	
40		√			√								√

* Typewriter desk

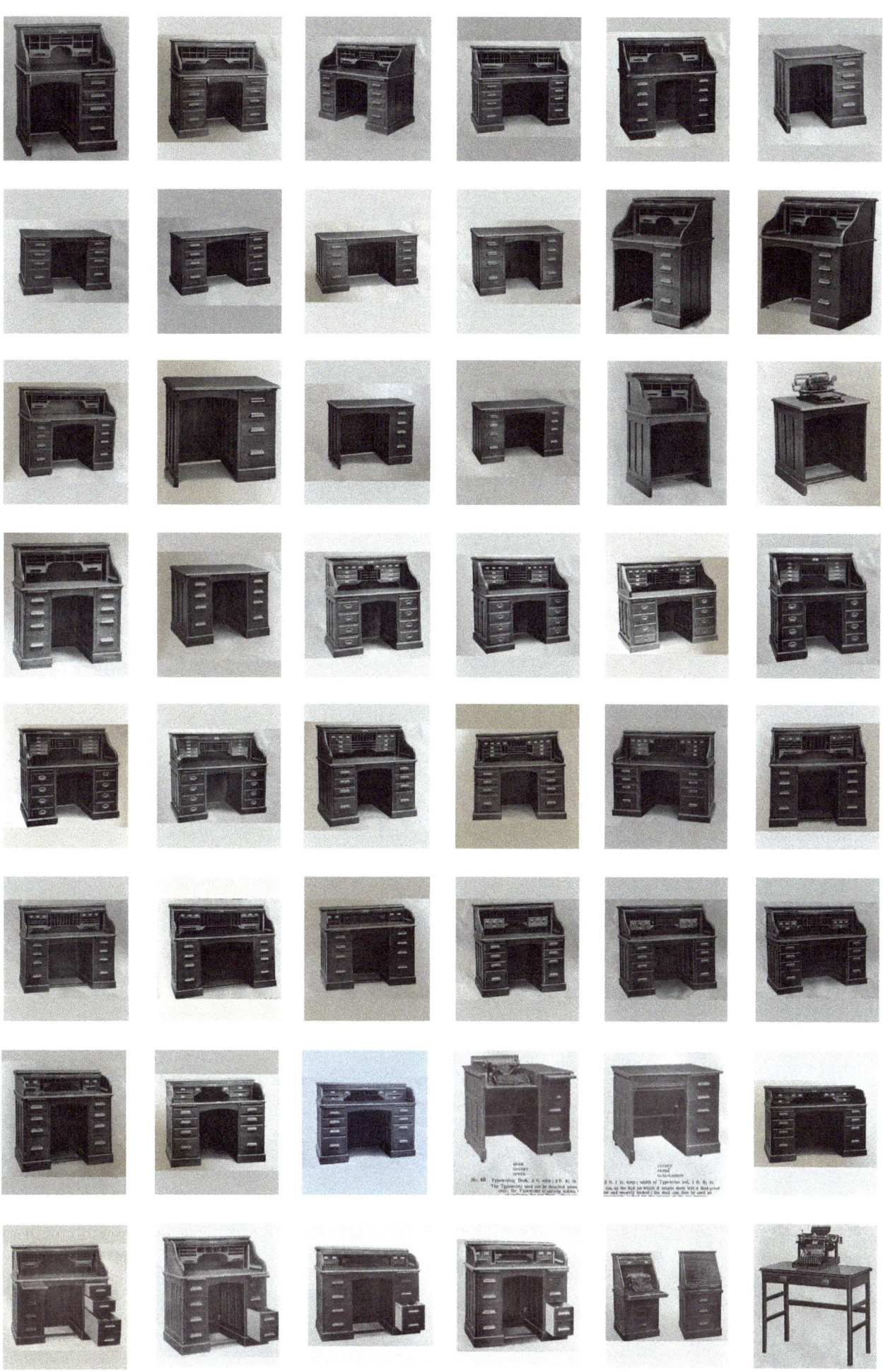

FROM THE BEDROOM TO THE OFFICE... AND EVERY ROOM BETWEEN

Desk number 5. (Photographs courtesy of Linda)

By 1913, just 18 of the original desks numbered 1 to 40 are listed. It is not known if the omitted 22 designs had been withdrawn.

The Lebus sectional bookcases were a popular addition to both homes and offices at the turn of the century. To match the desks there was a choice between oak with a fumed finish or satin walnut in either walnut or mahogany. Between a standard base section and a top section to finish, as many self-contained, standard-sized compartments from a choice of two – glass fronted or open shelved – could be added. Each standard glass-fronted section was self-contained and fitted with a lock and key. This bookcase system is an early example of modular furniture because it could be extended horizontally along a wall as well as being stacked vertically. By 1913 there were corner units available too. In addition, there was a bureau section (along with its specific base section) which could be added to an office or room configuration.

Sectional bookcase components and how they fitted together. These pages from the back of the 1907 catalogue display their age.

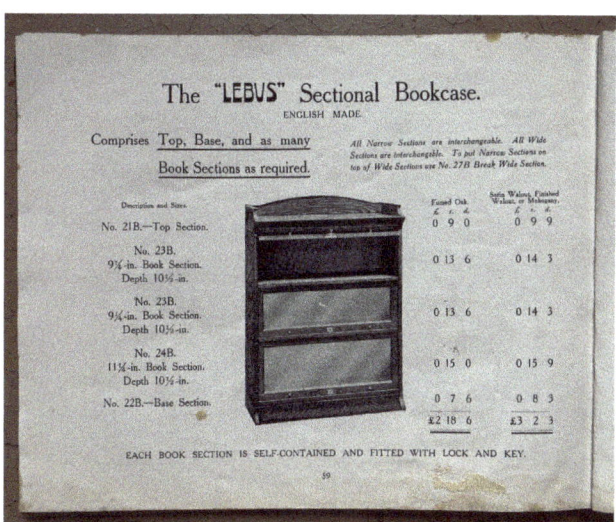
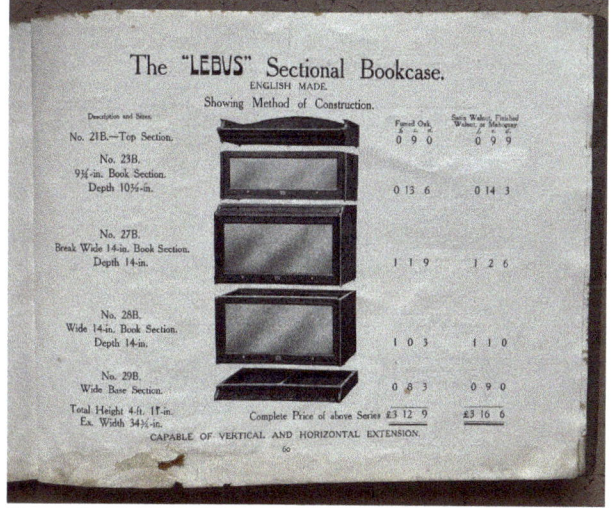
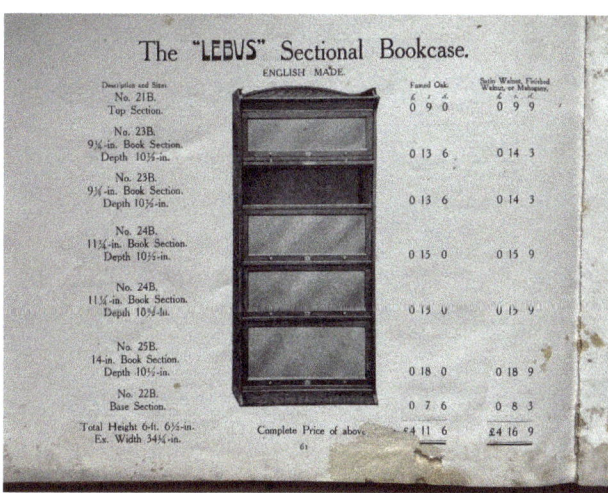

Sectional bookcase which recently came up for sale on the antiques market.
(Photographs courtesy of Mark Fudge)

Sectional bureau and corner unit.

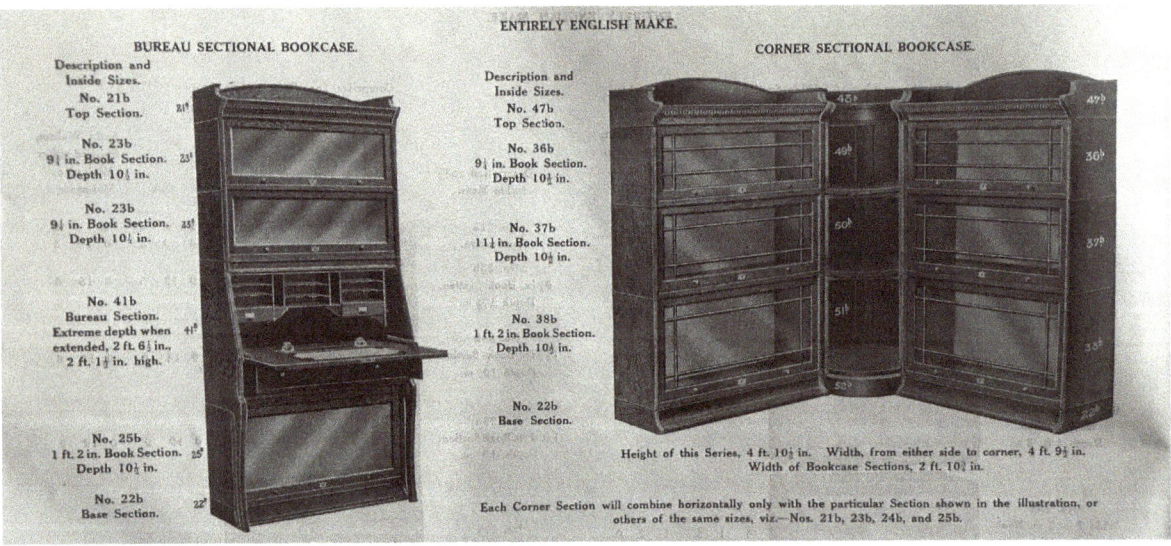

Also in the 1907 catalogue were filing cabinets with lockable shutter fronts, numbered 1 to 23. These consisted of seven different models which then came in various sizes. By 1913 there were a further four filing cabinets, identified as A to D, which are much like wooden versions of the office filing cabinets used today.

A selection of 12 revolving chairs (four with ball-bearing action) and one reading chair were listed in the 1907 catalogue. In 1913, of 40 office chairs listed the majority are revolving – one of which also tilts – three are office chairs and nine are library chairs or for reading. One other is described as a smoking chair. The 1913 catalogue includes four office stools and eight of the chairs featured were also found in the 1907 catalogue.

Selection of filing cabinets from the 1907 catalogue.

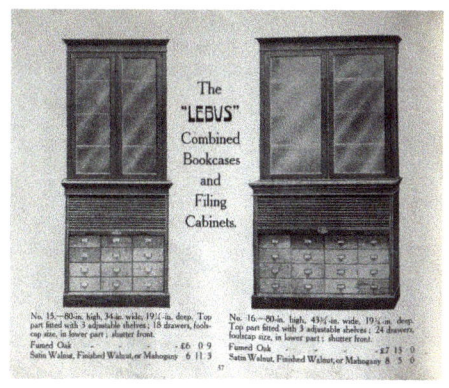

Vertical filing cabinets from the 1912 catalogue.

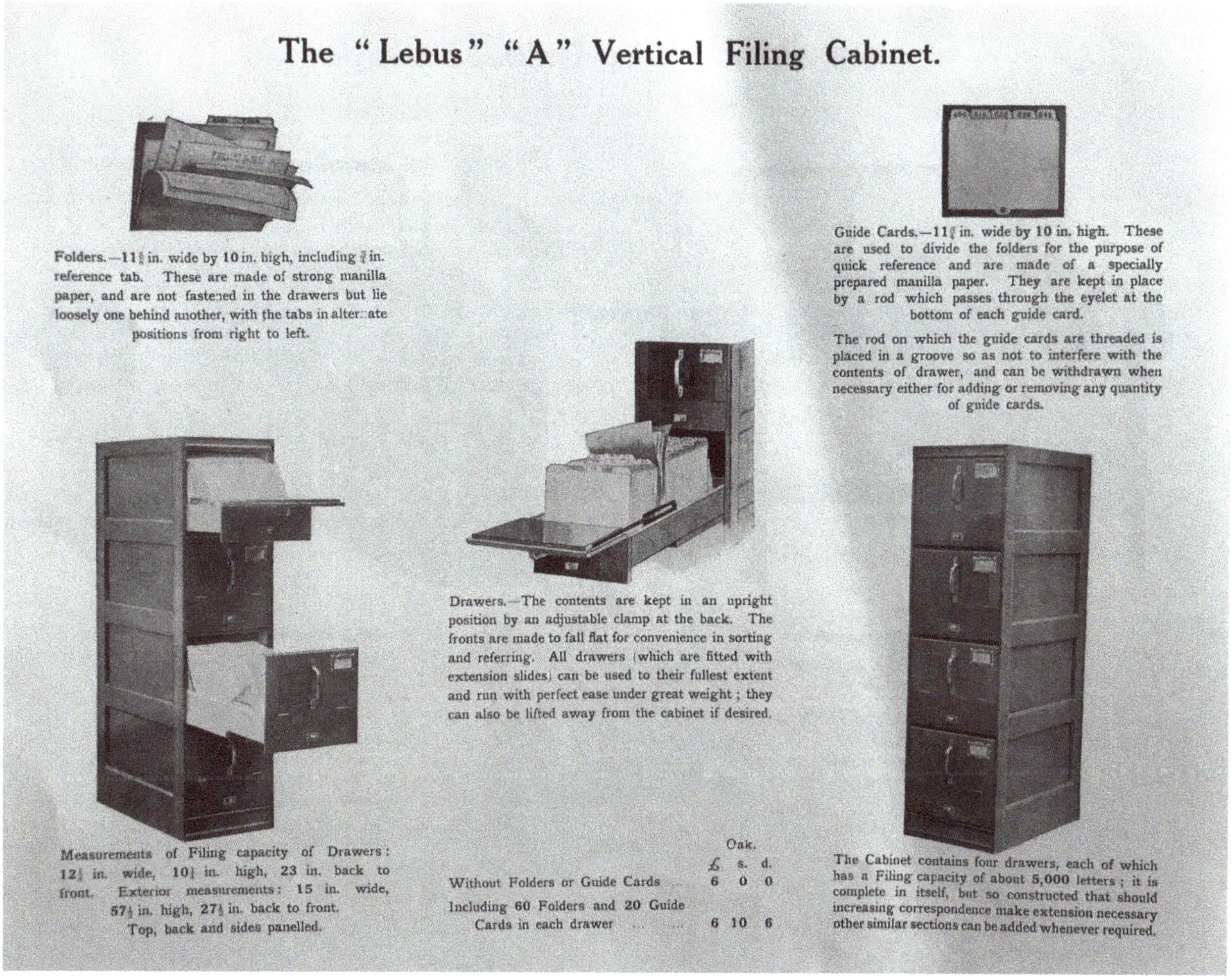

Office chairs. Six which were available in 1907 were still on sale in 1912 and 1913.

These office stools appear in the 1912 catalogue.

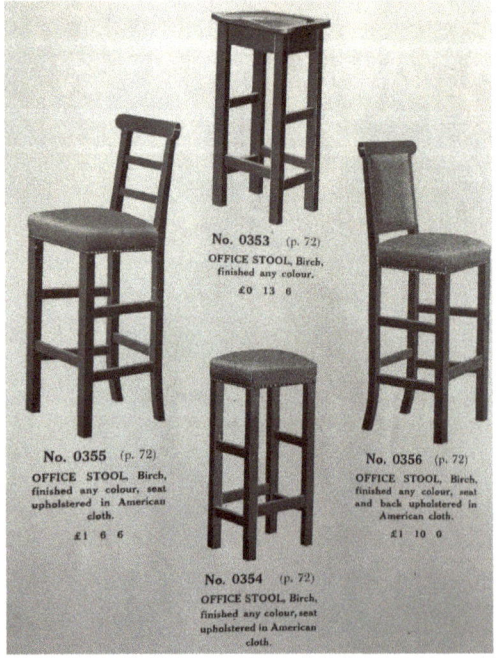

Affordable for All... Flats, Modest Terraces, Sizeable Semi-detached Houses

Art Deco/'Modern Traditional', 1919–1939

Herbert Randles Kinsley – a lieutenant in the army during World War One – was the firm's chief designer from 1919. Herbert was the son of landscape artist Albert Kinsley (1852–1945). He remained with the firm into the early years of the public company, retiring in 1951.

Art Deco design in its simplest sense was inspired by a renewed awareness of ancient Egyptian art following the discovery of Tutankhamen's tomb treasures in 1922. As for Kinsley's designs, some elements of Art Deco influence flow through Lebus pieces in the latter part of this period. There are designs that feature bold geometric shapes and ornamentation of carved wood which complimented herringbone oak parquet flooring, and accessories such as colourful Clarice Cliff crockery, Bakelite, glass and chrome. Some of the drop-centre bedroom dressing tables and dining-room sideboards could be considered as having an affinity with the style. Some Lebus designs of this period are quite eye-catching – and there are a lot of them. Some, however, retain elements of a bygone era, such as the incorporation of cabriole legs and heavily carved oak sideboards, particularly during the 1920s. Thus, a more measured description for Lebus furniture of the twenties and thirties might be 'modernist aspirations fused with traditional elements'.

This sideboard from 1926 is reminiscent of the furniture style of Lebus before World War One.

Arguably, Kinsley reached his zenith in 1939 as his design creativity seemed to soar. Kinsley produced some designs that are notable for their Art-Deco-inspired style or fusion of design influences, one example being the incomparable Admaston dining suite. This included a sideboard, GZ407, which has a fan-shaped mirror inspired by the style whilst being weighted by a sturdy oak base softened with flower and leaf motifs. The shape of some upholstered three-piece suites, such as the elegant Dolina, also draw on Art Deco style. The Bexhill bedroom suite and the Kingsland dining suite, Z5003, simply ooze class. Perhaps more than any other, the oak dining suite Z8426 epitomises Kinsley's aspirations as a designer; futuristic 'bubbles' appear to want to burst forth from their anchorage and evoke a time of space travel. This is way ahead of its time.

The Admaston dining suite and the Harbourne bedroom suite from 1937 and 1939 respectively display elements of Art Deco style. The Z5003 dining suite in natural oak with walnut cross banding from 1939 oozes class. Are these flying saucers on the Z8426 suite from 1939?

Furniture making at Lebus underwent significant change in this period but it did not come overnight: it was an evolving process. Lebus pioneered mechanised production and developed conveyor belts to facilitate movement through successive processes – developments which also enabled more sophisticated systems for unit costing and pricing.

Lebus furniture – always well constructed – became less heavy through the use of different raw materials alongside hardwood. Softwood was used for drawer panels and plywood for the backs of furniture pieces such as wardrobes, dressing tables and mirrors. Veneers were sourced worldwide and up to 30 different types were incorporated in Lebus furniture towards the latter part of this period.

During the 1920s oak furniture was offered in finishes described as 'rubbed', 'Jacobean' or 'fumed'. Some furniture was still offered enamelled. Walnut was used extensively, with some pieces decorated with gilt. Mahogany was also much used. Increasingly, French polishing was replaced by cellulose. This was produced in-house at the factory's laboratory and applied by special spray guns on moving conveyors. Lebus offered choices: oak could be finished – dark antique/Jacobean oak, bright Jacobean oak, light oak or natural oak, bright (shiny) or matt; mahogany, bright finish (a feature of several bedroom suites available in 1934, this finish disappears thereafter). Walnut veneer could be finished – brown walnut, grey walnut (bright or semi-bright) and cross-hand decoration. Burr maple and birds-eye maple were very special finishes saved for only the best bedroom suites.

Dark Jacobean oak, bright finish sample panel.

Light Jacobean oak, bright finish sample panel.

Brown walnut, bright finish sample panel.

Brown walnut, matt finish sample panel.

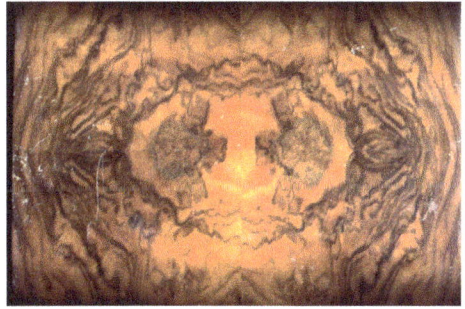

Grey walnut, matt finish sample panel.

Walnut with cross band decoration, bright finish sample panel.

These sample panels are part of the Lebus archive at Haringey Library and Archive service, Bruce Castle Museum.

As an alternative to metal, handles in various shapes and sizes were made from new materials, such as Erinoid (a patented plastic) which was used for most bedroom suites in the 1934 catalogue. A couple of the expensive bedroom suites have chromium handles in the 1937 catalogue. Polished brass and imitation ivory are used as descriptors of some handles in the 1939 catalogue, with the remainder wood, polished brass or enamelled finish.

To a furniture-manufacturing business such as Lebus, the interwar period was one of variety and opportunity. At the risk of making sweeping generalisations, there were more homes being built for people with more disposable income to spend on furnishing them.

The Addison Housing and Town Planning Act 1919 aimed to secure 'Homes for Heroes' with local authorities charged with the building of social housing with low rents. Slums were torn down and replaced. There was an emerging trend to convert larger, older houses into flats in the context of societal changes which saw family sizes becoming smaller. During the interwar period a staggering number

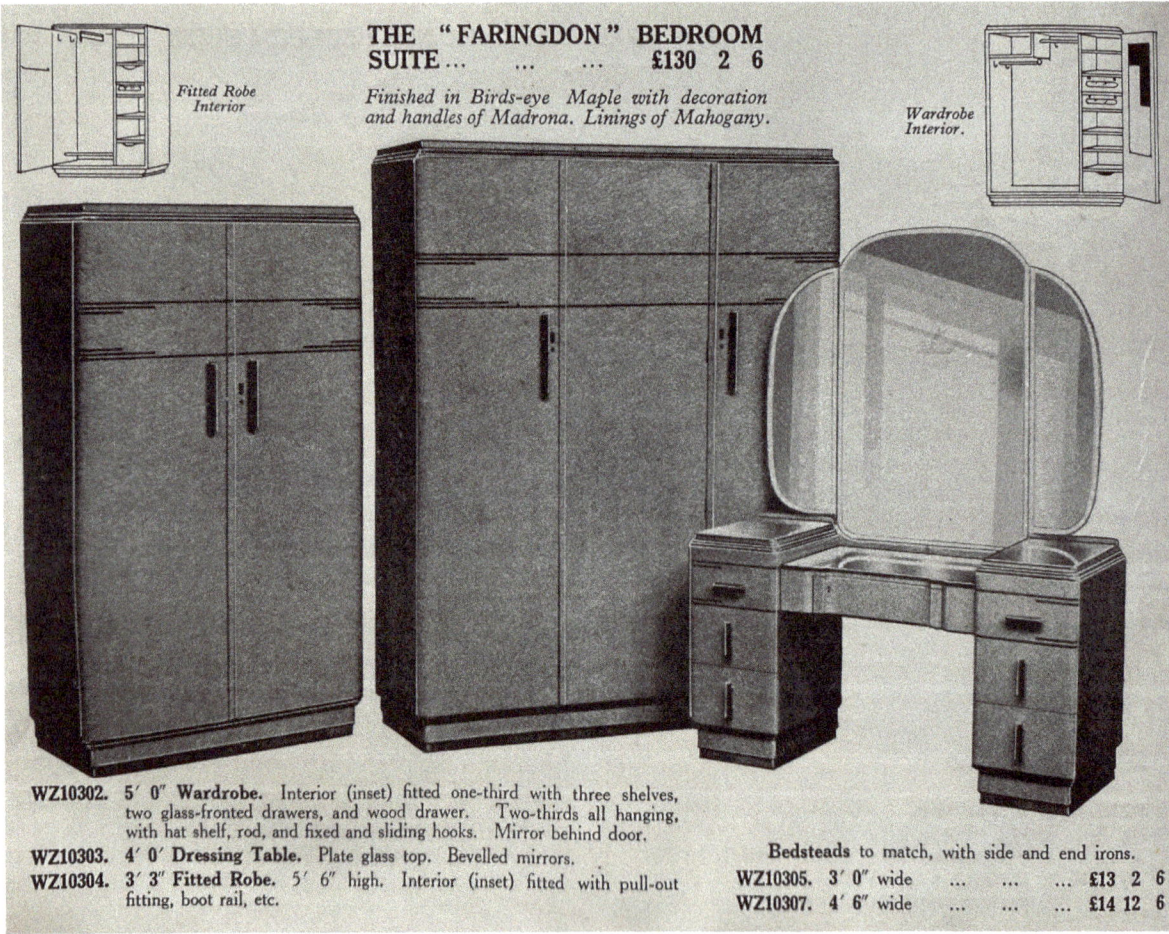

The Faringdon bedroom suite from 1939 is in birds-eye maple, an expensive finish.

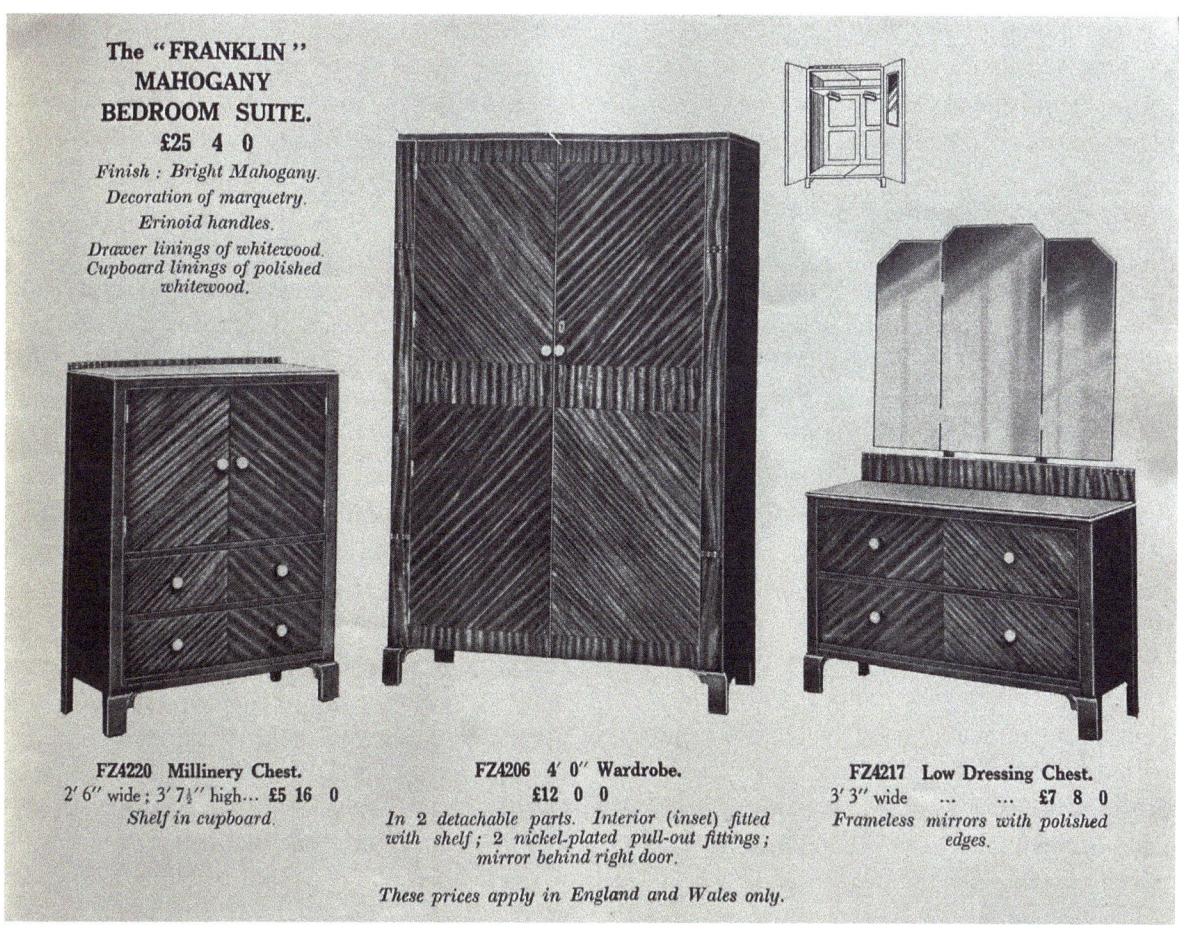

The Franklin suite from 1934 has Erinoid handles. Erinoid is a patented plastic produced from 1914 but popular during the 1920s and 1930s. It was used for most bedroom suites in the 1934 catalogue. A couple of the expensive bedroom suites in the 1937 catalogue have chromium handles. Imitation ivory is also used in some of the bedroom suites in the 1939 catalogue.

of new homes were built in and around the suburbs of towns and cities. Green-field sites were transformed by an expanse of housing and amenities such as local shops and transport networks. By 1939, a third of the population lived in new post-World War One accommodation. More people were living in accommodation with reduced, but nonetheless adequately sized, rooms.

Newly built accommodation offered variety. Many now enjoyed the luxury of owning their own homes. Whilst new 1920s houses had simply evolved from the terraced Edwardian home, most new builds of the 1930s were likely semi-detached, with a private garden and with either three or four bedrooms (the smallest of which became known as the box room). Over the front cover of the 1939 catalogue there is an advertisement for an exhibition of current Lebus furniture designs in Eastbourne and faintly written in pencil is an address in Shermanbury Road, Worthing. This was then a typical new-build semi-detached home in private ownership, likely occupied by a family of lower-middle-class status who were looking to furnish their home.

There was a surge in the supply of suitable accommodation conforming to government-set national standards designated for both social housing, with its affordable rents, and owner–occupiers. The emergence of the bungalow was prevalent too. There were purpose-built, low-rise blocks of flats with communal gardens, and flats were also built above new shops. Steel-framed Crittall windows were favoured over the traditional wooden sash.

Interwar homes featured a bathroom, inside toilet and a new-style kitchen. These tended to be small with a cooker (likely gas as this was cheaper), some storage, a table squeezed in along with facilities to wash clothes with a free-standing or wall-mounted hot-water boiler.

Open fireplaces, in varying sizes, were incorporated in bedrooms and reception rooms to provide a heat source. Most new builds had two reception rooms which may have been set up as a lounge and dining room. Alternatively, these spaces may have been a multi-purpose living room and a 'best room' – the latter, perhaps set up with a comfy three-piece suite whilst the former had a mix of comfy and dining seating, dominated by a large dining table. In many ways the use of these reception rooms was dictated by the necessity of having to light the fire and involved advanced planning, for example if family and friends were coming to visit.

The way we used various rooms in our homes had changed and this had implications for furniture manufacturers such as Lebus. Home entertaining was on the increase. Perhaps this was because people took pride in their homes, which they were happy to show off. Or because in the newly built suburbs there were fewer public houses by ratio to households. The emergence of a new furniture piece – the cocktail cabinet – is evident during this period.

Looking into 1926, 1934, 1936, 1937 and 1939

The Lebus catalogues of the 1920s appear much the same as those which preceded World War One as they are the same size, with grey hardback covers and a similar layout plus index. By the 1930s, catalogues were reduced in size to A5. Still with grey covers, they were now printed in the factory using offset printing machines at a lower cost and were updated and reissued on a regular basis (possibly as often as bi-monthly).

Whilst the representations of rooms set up for their intended use that were a feature of catalogues in the pre-World War One era are conspicuous by their absence during the 1920s, more emphasis was placed on the staging, set-up and presentation of individual furniture pieces in the 1930s catalogues. There were still the images of opened wardrobes neatly organised with clothes on hangers or folded on shelves, and accessories neatly distributed to purpose-built fittings as before World War One; but now there were linen cupboards stacked with freshly laundered, ironed towels and sheets, and living-room seating arrangements with a comfy sofa and chairs arranged around a coffee table on which sat exotic cocktails in the making. In addition, Lebus chose to compliment the catalogue with the occasional diagram revealing the inner components of upholstered items or those that demonstrated the differences between dining tabletops that were swivel or reversible, as well as those with fittings designed for detachable legs.

As for catalogues and the prices listed, some observations in the opening pages of catalogues during this period are notable. For example, the 1934 catalogue states 'these prices apply to England and Wales only'. And in 1939, a comparison between the catalogues of January and March suggests the existence of different pricing policies. In the January catalogue, a 50 percent trade discount is applied to listed prices. In the edition of March 1939 – distinguishable because of its A4-portrait-size dark-green cover along with the fact it contains a collection of only some of the complete furniture range – the trade discount is 33.3 percent. The prices quoted for exactly the same suites and furniture pieces in both the January and March catalogues are different too. For example, the Z5521 oak bedroom suite (unnamed) is £13 10s in the January catalogue and the named Bledlow suite (same catalogue number) is £10 2s 6d in March. When applying the respective trade discounts to these prices the wholesale purchase costs to the retailer are the same. This raises more questions than can be answered.

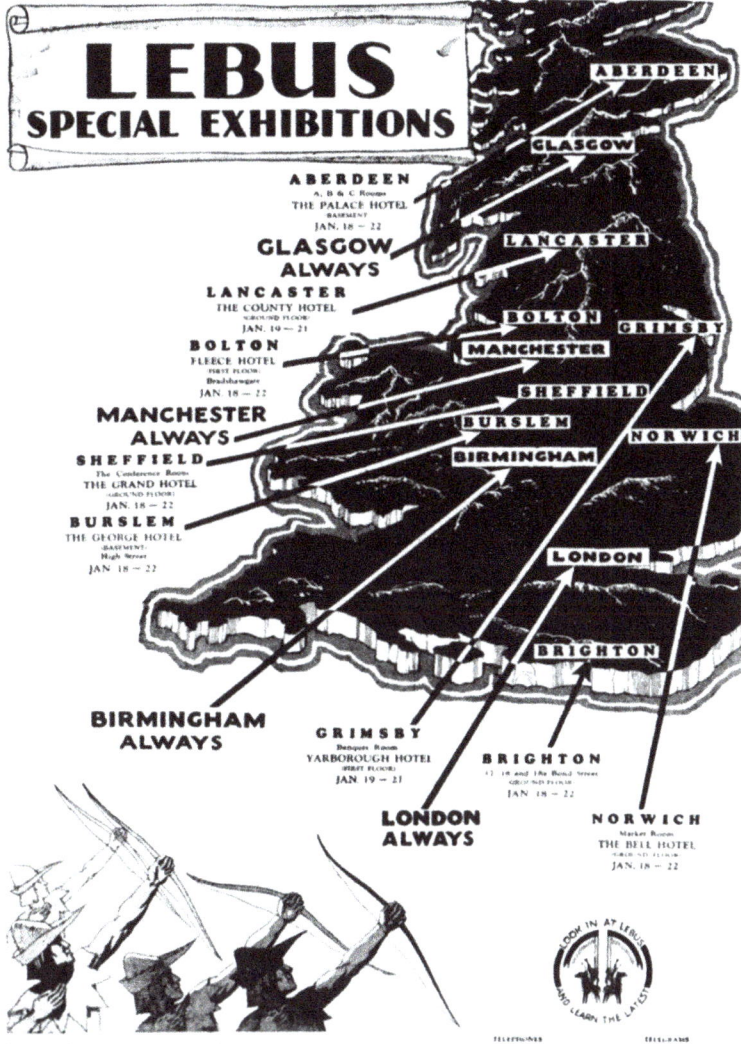

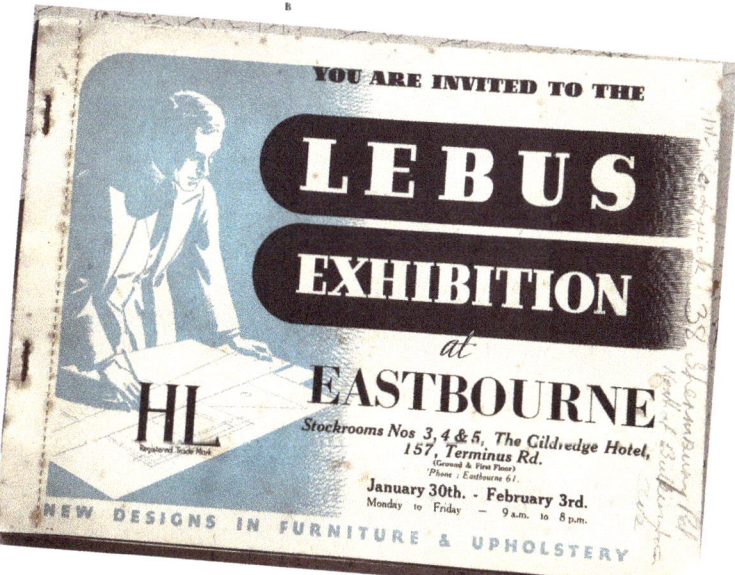

Lebus exhibited around the country often and had adverts in publications. This one is from the *Cabinet Maker and Complete House Furnisher*, 16 January 1932. The advert also shows where the Lebus showrooms are located. The advert for the exhibition in Eastbourne sits on the front of the 1939 catalogue.

Marketing furniture pieces with props and as part of a room set-up: the UZ280/1 three-piece suite from 1939 is pictured with cocktails on the coffee table.

Bedroom suite ZZ5521 (January 1939) and Bledlow (March 1939) are priced markedly differently, and yet these are the same suite. A trade discount of 50 percent applies to the January catalogue and a 33 percent discount to the March catalogue, which equates to the furniture retailer paying around the same cost price. The implication is the retail prices customers paid may have differed also between individual furniture outlets or, more likely, geographical areas.

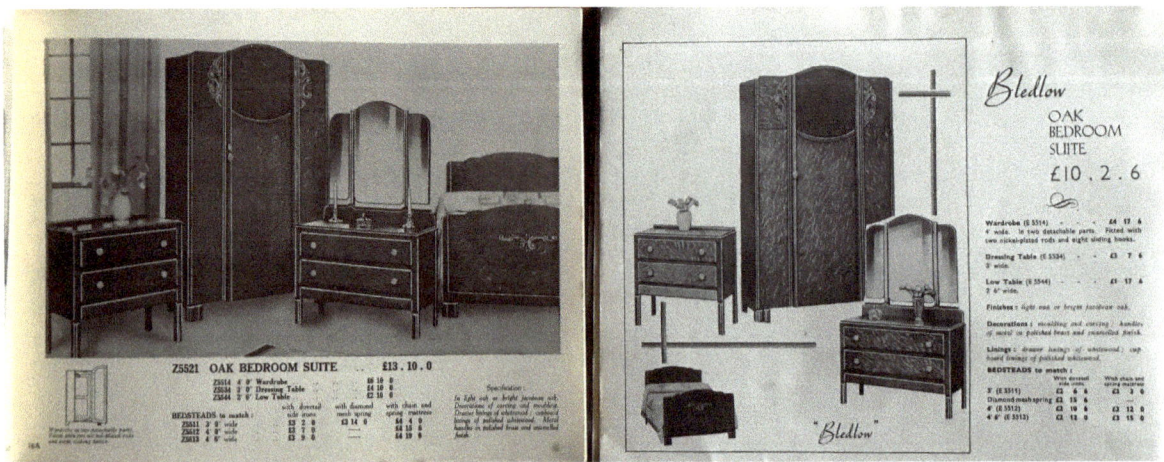

76 LOVING LEBUS

The large catalogue of May 1926 has almost 300 pages – half of which are devoted to bedroom suites. It has an index but those of the 1930s do not, making them difficult to navigate. The smaller 1937 catalogue ends on page 230 but not all numbered pages are in the correct running order, and some pages do not exist at all, so the actual number is just shy of two hundred. In some instances, where odd-numbered pages should be, they are a continuation of the previous even-numbered page with the addition of the letter 'b'.

Looking into the catalogue of 1926, it appears Lebus still made items of furniture very similar to those seen before World War One, such as revolving bookcases, shaving stands, commodes, along with a handful of oak office desks. That said, there is a considerable amount of new furniture pieces not seen before and some new descriptors: dining chairs described as 'cottage' and the use of the prefix 'lounge' with some occasional tables and coffee tables. There are space-saving furniture pieces, such as the adjustable bed chair, writing bureaus built to a smaller scale, china cabinets described as 'dwarf' and wall-mounted hat and coat racks. And for the first time we see electric standard lamps (the National Grid was being rolled out across the country at this time). The appearance of these furniture pieces sits with the notion that the size of rooms and how they were used was indeed undergoing change.

The extensive index in the 1926 catalogue.

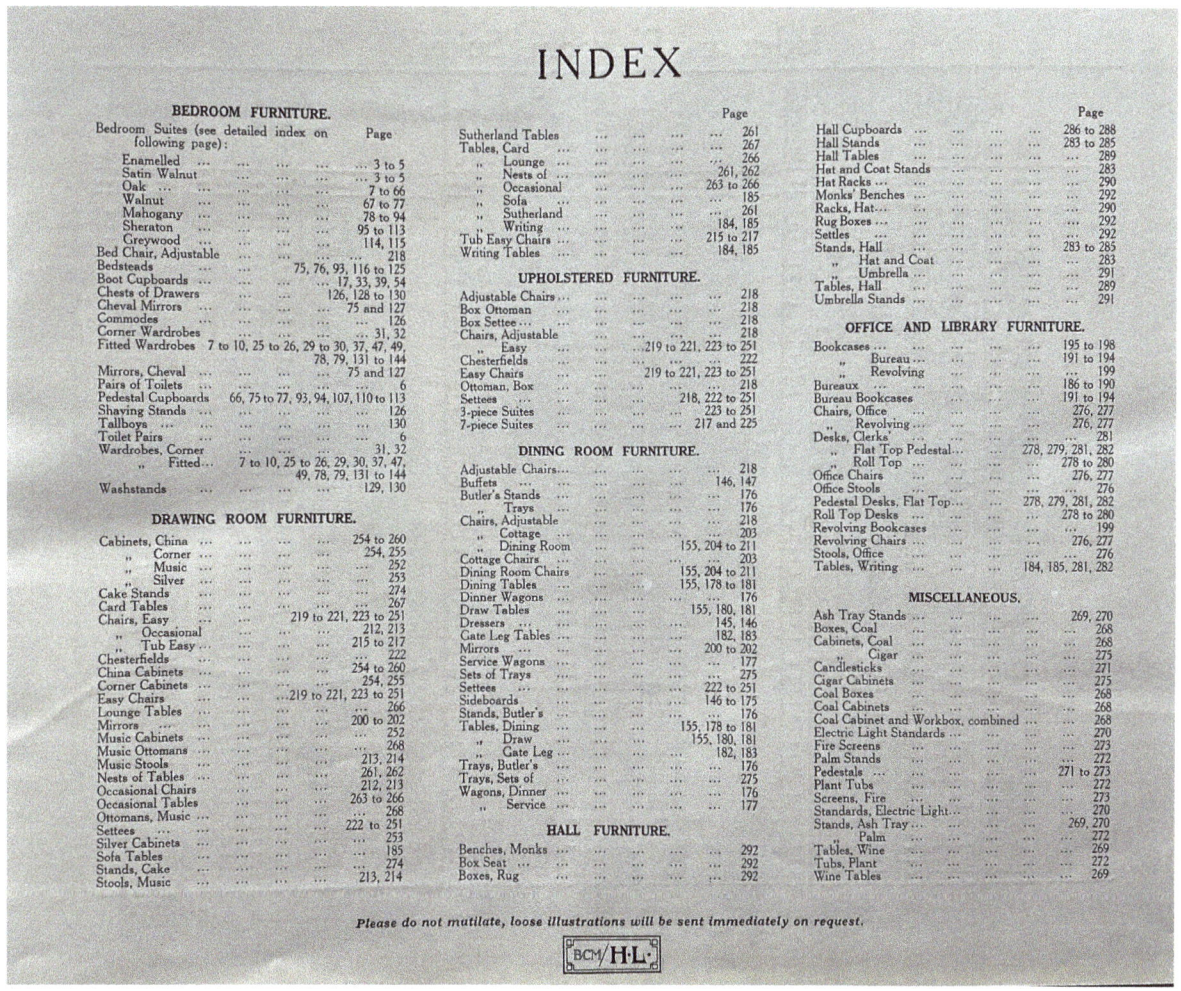

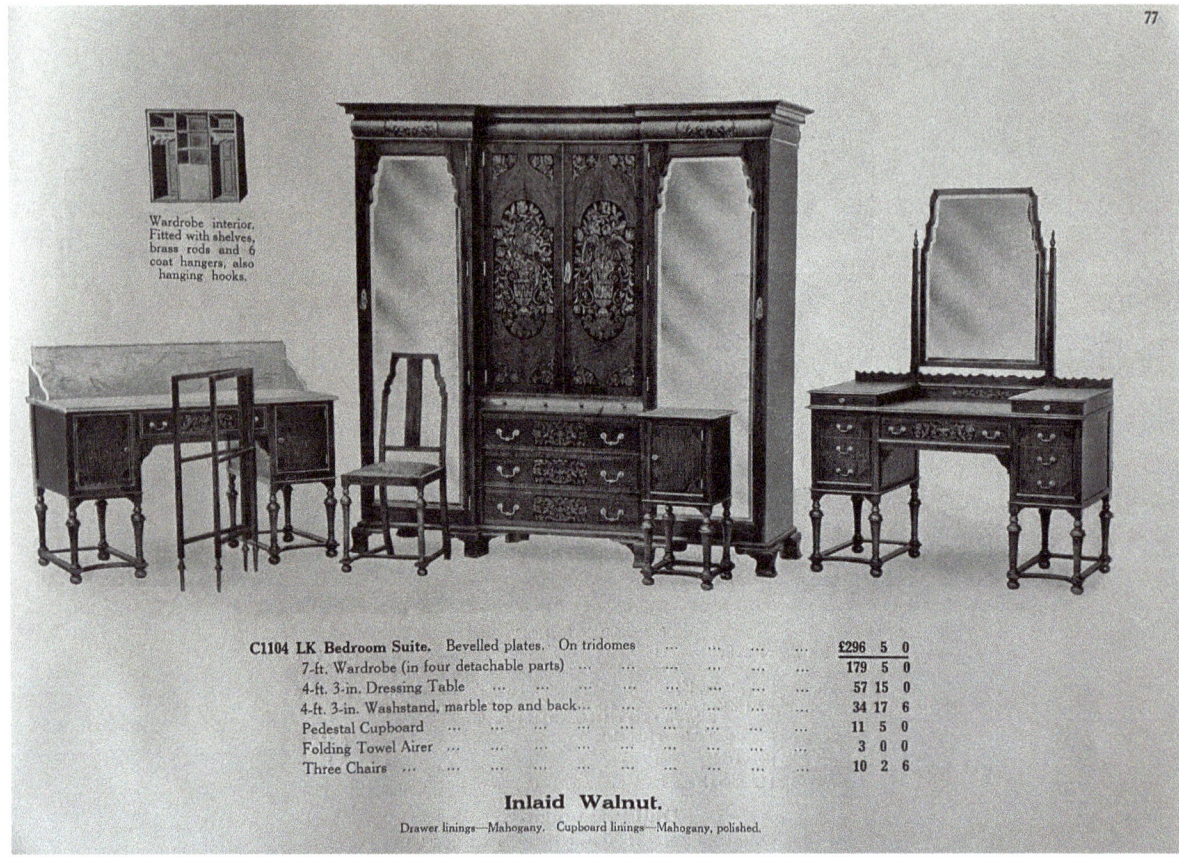

The inlaid walnut C1104 bedroom suite offered in 1926 is reminiscent of those Lebus offered before World War One.

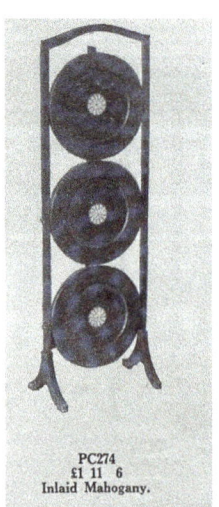

Cake stands, similar in style to those sold before World War One.

These easy chairs in Rexine (faux leather) with velveteen cushions are part of the EC15 three-piece suite offered in 1926. Their curves are much more sleek than on similar designs offered before World War One. (Image courtesy of Ian Yeates)

There are furniture items in the 1926 catalogue which reflect the customer base Lebus was now catering to: the adjustable bed chair could be an indicator that people were living in smaller homes benefitting from space-saving, dual-purpose furniture.

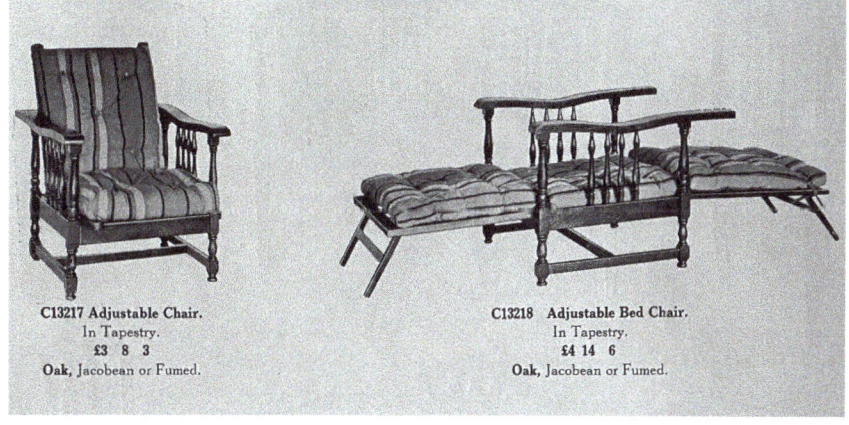

One of Kinsley's designs for draw-top tables, this TC17 has barley-twist legs. They are strong, durable and heavy solid oak pieces. This one has survived and has been refurbished by Andy of Andy Lincoln Restorations.

From the 1939 catalogue, Lebus offered tables with removable legs in a choice of three styles. Extending tabletops came in a choice of drawer leaf, reversible or swivel top. These were reintroduced after World War Two.

TC317

5-ft. × 3-ft.	… … …	£6 11 3
6-ft. × 3-ft.	… … …	£7 7 9
6-ft. × 3-ft. 6-in.	… … …	£8 5 0
7-ft. × 3-ft. 6-in.	… … …	£9 9 0

Draw Top Tables.
All quoted in full extended sizes.
Oak, Rubbed Jacobean or Fumed.

Dining Tables with detachable legs.

Finished in dark or light oak.
Tables can be supplied with various types of tops and legs as shown below

Illustration of E 5601 Table complete with legs.

Legs are held in place by strong angle-plates and large wing nuts. A few minutes to remove or replace legs!

TYPES OF TABLE TOP	Size of Top				
DRAWLEAF					
5601	4' 6" x 2' 6" open / 3' x 2' 6" closed	E 5601 £2 : 6 : 6	E 5618 £2 : 6 : 6	E 5651 £2 : 10 : 6	E 4041 £2 : 10 : 6
5602	5' x 3' open / 3' x 3' closed	E 5602 £2 : 9 : 0	E 5603 £2 : 9 : 0	E 5652 £2 : 12 : 6	E 4042 £2 : 12 : 6
5613	5' x 3' open / 3' x 3' closed	E 5613 £2 : 13 : 6	E 5614 £2 : 13 : 6	E 5657 £2 : 17 : 0	E 4051 £2 : 17 : 0
REVERSIBLE					
5604	4' 6" x 2' 6" open / 2' 6" x 2' 3" closed	E 5604 £2 : 15 : 0	E 5606 £2 : 15 : 0	E 5660 £2 : 18 : 6	
5605 Step-Top when half open	5' x 3' open / 3' x 2' 6" closed	E 5605 £2 : 19 : 6	E 5607 £2 : 19 : 6	E 5653 £3 : 3 : 0	E 4052 £3 : 3 : 0
5608 Flush-Top when half open	5' x 3' open / 3' x 2' 6" closed	E 5621 £3 : 6 : 0	E 5608 £3 : 6 : 0	E 5654 £3 : 10 : 0	E 4053 £3 : 10 : 0
SWIVEL TOP					
5610	4' x 3' open / 3' x 2' closed	E 5619 £2 : 12 : 0	E 5610 £2 : 12 : 0	E 5658 £2 : 15 : 6	E 4060 £2 : 15 : 6
5611	5' x 3' open / 3' x 2' 6" closed	E 5620 £2 : 16 : 6	E 5611 £2 : 16 : 6	E 5659 £3 : 0 : 0	E 4061 £3 : 0 : 0

Illustrations showing the action of Reversible and Swivel Tops.

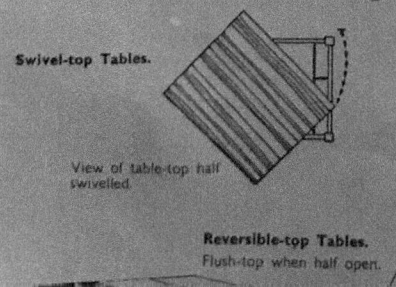

Swivel-top Tables.

View of table-top half swivelled.

View of table top completely swivelled, revealing linen and cutlery wells.

Final movement showing table-leaf being opened.

Reversible-top Tables. Flush-top when half open.

Left-hand illustration shows one leaf extended. Right-hand illustration shows leaves pulled out, revealing three compartments; Nos. 1 and 3, lined for cutlery; 2, unlined, for table linen. Patent applied for.

Reversible-top Tables. Step-top when half open.

Left-hand illustration shows table with one leaf extended. Right-hand illustration shows table with both leaves pulled out revealing well for table linen. The arrows indicate the action of the leaves.

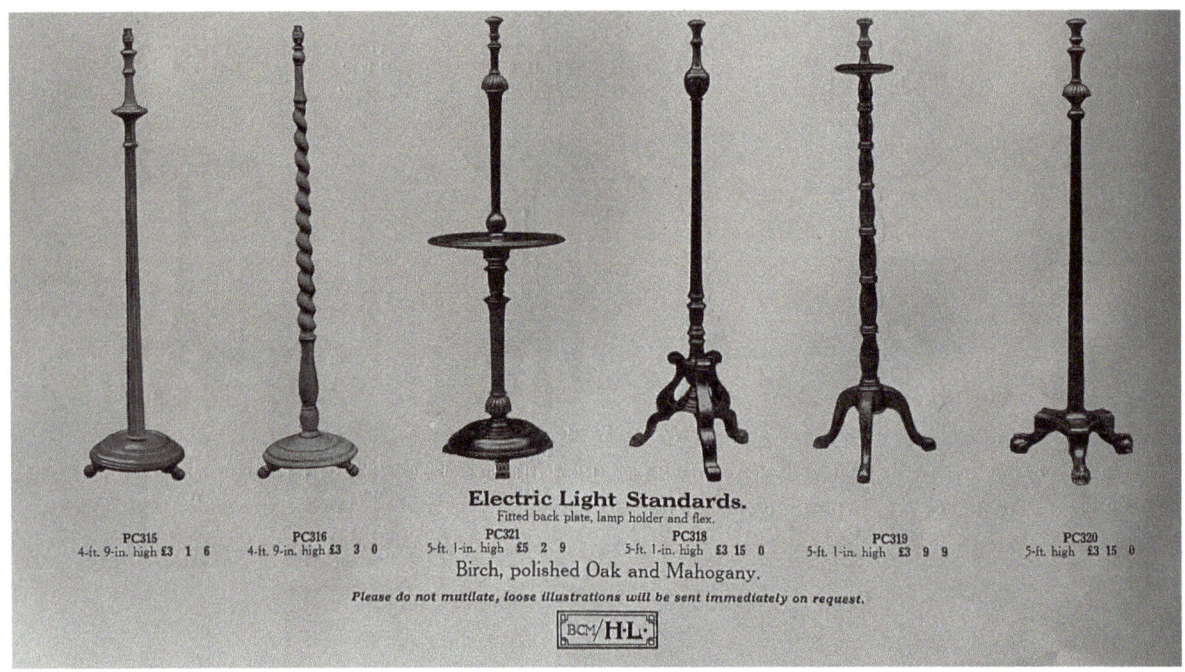

Electric standard lamps were offered in response to the fact that households were now being connected to electric power as the National Grid was rolled out. That said, Kinsley was fond of the more traditional cabriole legs with the addition of the ball claw. These design features help identify Lebus furniture to this period and this up-cycled cabinet by Lee O'Gorman, at LeeO'GormanHome (Etsy), could well be Lebus made.

In Lebus catalogues of the 1930s all suites are allocated a design name (invented or otherwise). For the most part these are listed alphabetically. Every single furniture piece is allocated an individual catalogue number, as are those in 1926. With reference to the 1926 catalogue, designs are still being registered but by the 1930s there are no longer design patent registration numbers.

Within the bedroom section of the 1930s catalogues are pages containing additional furniture pieces which could be purchased individually. There are two pages of oak and one page of walnut furniture. They include dressing-table designs which differ from the featured full suites, as well as a range of chests of drawers. Also available were furniture pieces designed to enhance storage, such as millinery cupboards (for neatly storing sheets, blankets, bedding, towels, etc.). Given these extended choices, the notion of furniture mixing is implicit; a household could mix and match any items, even oak pieces with walnut. There were no rules.

With each room, or section of the catalogue, in which suites of furniture are featured, they are listed in ascending order of price, beginning with the least expensive. Looking into Lebus furniture in the latter part of this period, walnut-veneered suites were generally priced considerably more expensively than their oak counterparts.

In offering furniture choices across a wide price band, Lebus recognised that, within its target consumer group – the upper working class and lower middle class – there were variances in disposable income. Using the choices of furniture suites and individual pieces available, it is possible to demonstrate how much it would have cost in 1937 for an assumed family with three children to furnish either: an inner-city London County Council modest terraced cottage or flat with three bedrooms (one a box room) and one reception room with small kitchen, choosing from the cheaper end of the price scale; or a suburban four-bedroom (one a box room) detached house with two reception rooms, a large kitchen and a large hall in London, choosing the furniture at the more expensive end of the price scale.

Furnishing a modest terraced cottage or flat with three bedrooms and one reception room with small kitchen, making selections from the least expensive choices in the 1937 catalogue

Bedrooms

The least expensive oak bedroom suite was the Abbotsbury, priced at £6 10s. The suite included a single wardrobe, dressing table with mirror and a low table (this was the same as the dressing table minus the mirror).

Beds with oak headboard came in a choice of five widths, with or without a combination spring and priced accordingly. (Bedsteads at two feet six inches appear first in Lebus furniture catalogues in 1937. Prior to that, the smallest was three feet.)

There were no nursery furniture pieces, such as a baby's cot, in the 1937 catalogue.

The least expensive single bedroom suite in oak was the Abbotsbury. Although a bedstead is pictured, there were various choices in oak available to buy separately. A fitted oak wardrobe – one of eight in the oak range – was available to buy separately. 'Fitted' in this context applied to the fixtures and fittings inside the wardrobe, such as hanging rail, shelves, drawers, compartments, etc. Lebus offered a range of additional bedroom furniture compatible with the oak suites which could be bought individually.

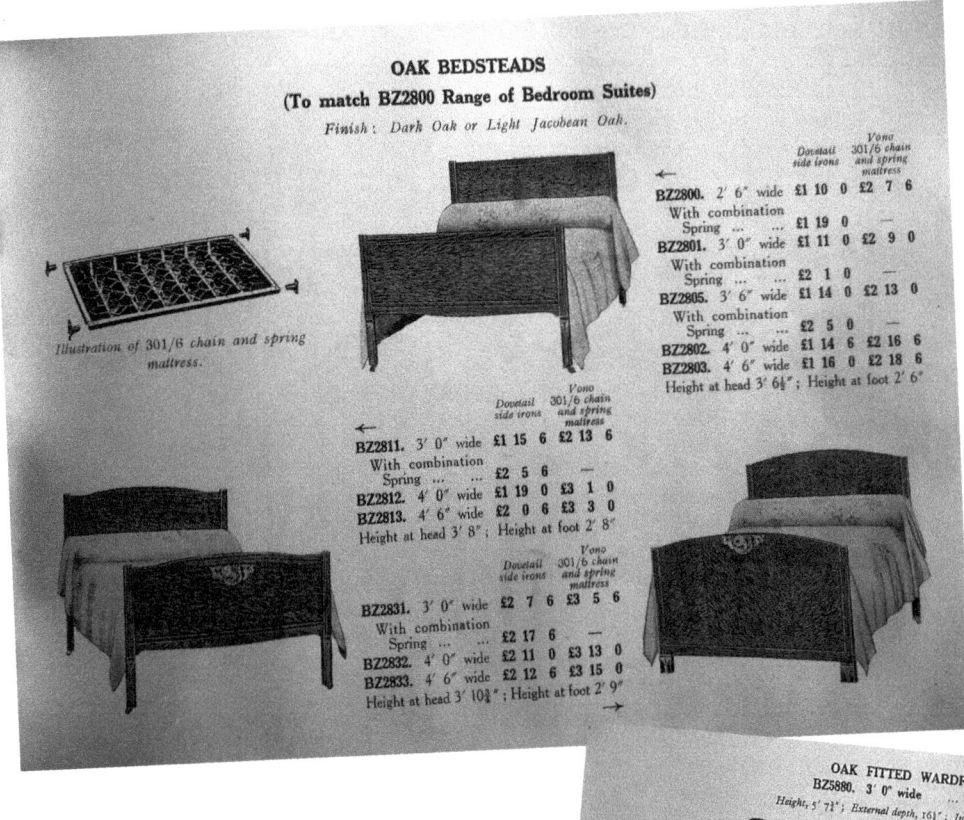

AFFORDABLE FOR ALL… FLATS, MODEST TERRACES, SIZEABLE SEMI-DETACHED HOUSES

Table: Inexpensive furniture selected and distributed across three bedrooms

Bedrooms	Catalogue number	Abbotsbury plus extra furniture items	Width	Cost
Master	BZ2802	Basic double bed	4ft	£1 14s 6d
	BZ5880	Fitted wardrobe (with shelves etc.)	3ft	£3 19s,
	BZ2844	Dressing table with mirror*	2ft	£2 3s 6d
	EZ102	Bedside cabinet	14in	£1 1s
Middle	BZ2800	Single bed (x2)	2ft 6in	£1 10s (each)
	BZ2804	Single wardrobe*	2ft	£2 14s
Small	BZ2860	Low table*	2ft	£1 12s 6d
	BZ2800	Single bed	2ft 6in	£1 10s
Total cost				Just under £18

* Furniture piece from Abbotsbury suite

Living room

The least expensive dining suite in oak was the Dansville, priced at £8 6s 6d. At least one more chair was required by our family, with another for visitors, meaning six chairs in total.

The Ealing three-piece suite was the least expensive in the catalogue. It was covered in brown Rexine (faux leather) as standard. However, the seats came upholstered in moquette (derived from the French word for carpet) using whatever was in stock at the time.

The Dansville was the least expensive oak dining-room suite.

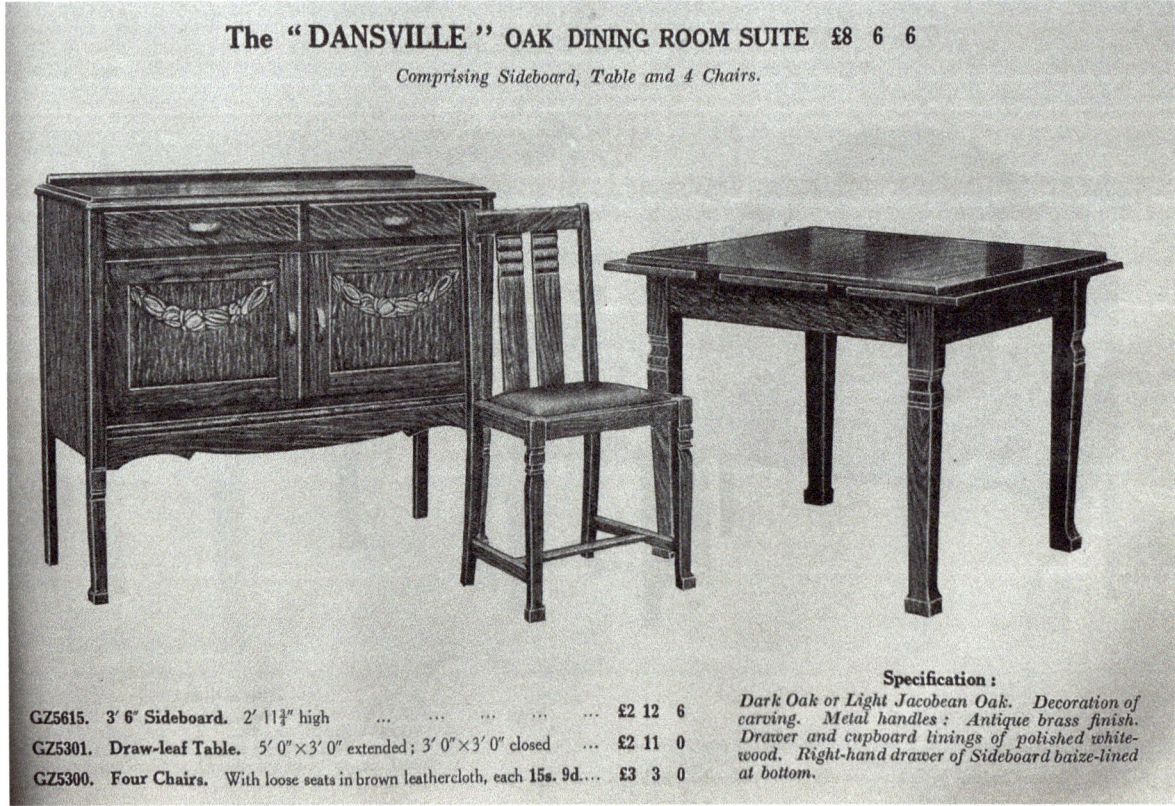

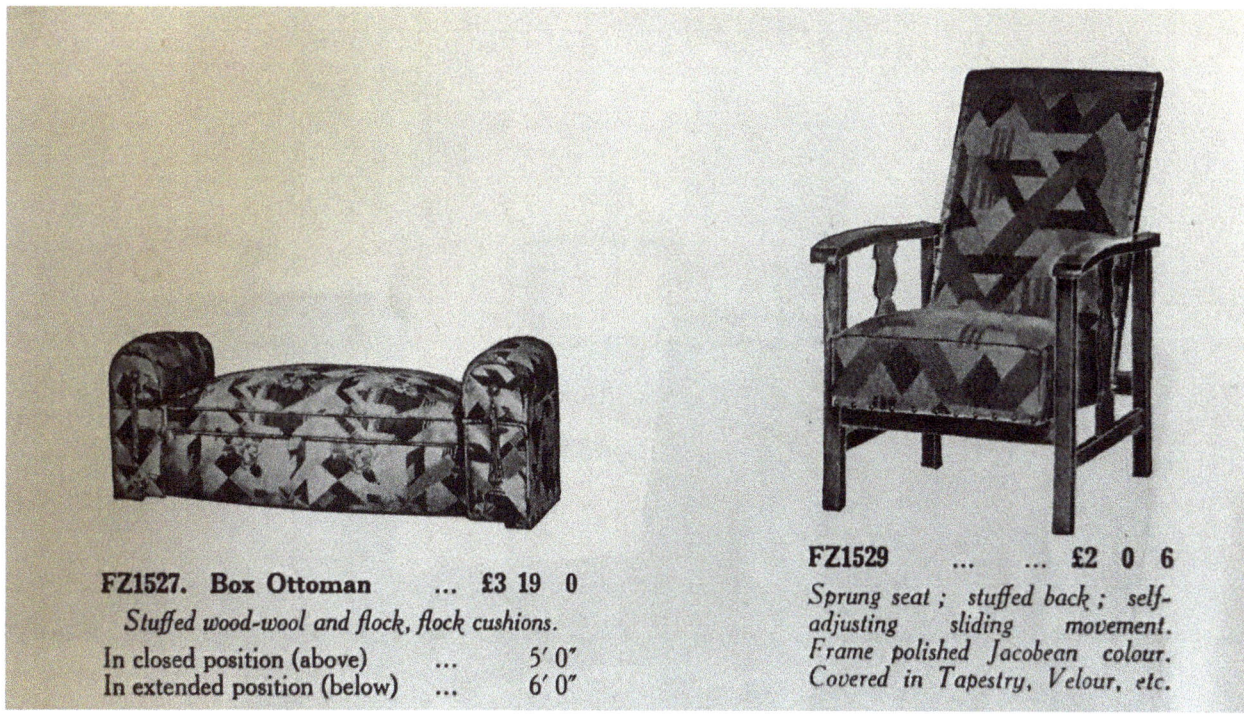

FZ1527. Box Ottoman ... £3 19 0
Stuffed wood-wool and flock, flock cushions.
In closed position (above) ... 5' 0"
In extended position (below) ... 6' 0"

FZ1529 ... ... £2 0 6
Sprung seat; stuffed back; self-adjusting sliding movement. Frame polished Jacobean colour. Covered in Tapestry, Velour, etc.

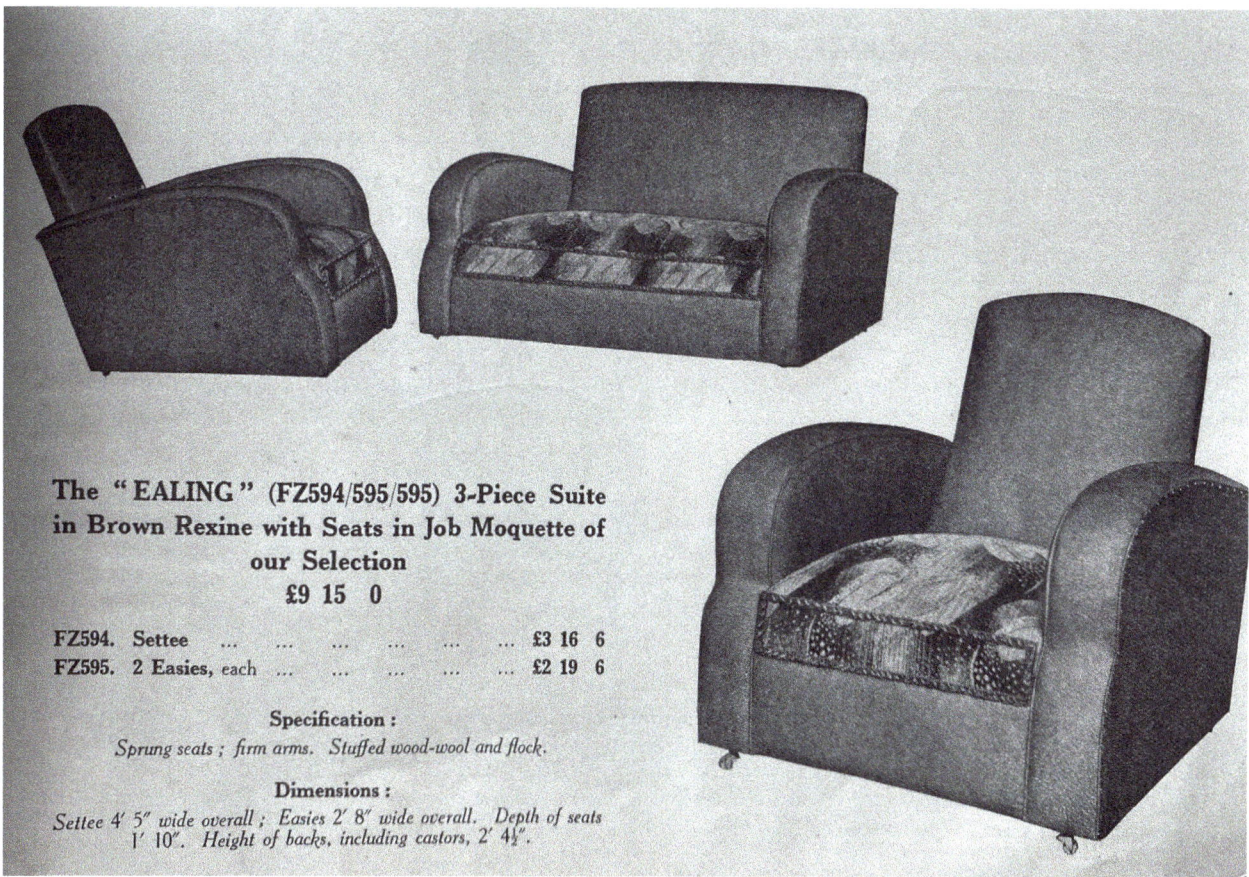

The "EALING" (FZ594/595/595) 3-Piece Suite in Brown Rexine with Seats in Job Moquette of our Selection
£9 15 0

FZ594. Settee £3 16 6
FZ595. 2 Easies, each £2 19 6

Specification:
Sprung seats; firm arms. Stuffed wood-wool and flock.

Dimensions:
Settee 4' 5" wide overall; Easies 2' 8" wide overall. Depth of seats 1' 10". Height of backs, including castors, 2' 4½".

Inexpensive comfortable seating options for the living room could be formed from a couple of fireside chairs and a box ottoman. The latter was like a two-seater sofa with the option to open out the arm rests in a seated position of up to six feet in length to accommodate three people. The FZ1527 was £3 19s. The FZ1529 was a relatively inexpensive oak framed chair with sprung seat, stuffed back with 'self-adjusting sliding movement' covered in tapestry, velour at £2 0s 6d. The two comfy chairs and ottoman together would have cost £8. Chairs in these styles would have looked just as much at home in the bedroom.

Table: Inexpensive furniture selected for the living room

Living room	Catalogue number	Dansville plus extra furniture items	Width	Cost
	GZ5615	Sideboard	3ft 6in	£2 12s 6d
	GZ5301	Draw-leaf (extendable) dining table	3ft (by 3ft) up to 5ft	£2 11s
	GZ5300	Set of four chairs – priced individually (x2)		£3 3s
				£0 15s 9d
		Ealing		
	FZ594	Two-seater settee	4ft 5in	£3 16s 6d
	FZ595	Armchairs each (x2)	2ft 8in	£2 19s 6d
Total cost				Just under £20

In reality, it was likely that a family with low income would have bought items as and when they needed, or could afford to buy, them. Alternatively, they may simply have acquired hand-me-downs.

A family could have furnished a modest terraced cottage or flat for less than £40 if choosing the least expensive choices from the Lebus furniture catalogue in the summer of 1937.

Furnishing a suburban four-bedroom (one a box room) detached house with two reception rooms, large kitchen, large hall in London, making selections from the more expensive choices in the 1937 catalogue

Bedrooms

The most expensive bedroom suite was the Salsburgh burr walnut, at £133 17s 6d. Along with the Falkirk in grey walnut and burr maple and the Faringdon in birds-eye maple at £109 and £130 respectively, these suites were likely out of the reach of many pockets.

The Fairfield in walnut at £47 5s was more realistically priced for the pocket of the consumer searching for a luxurious look. A second suite combined with items from the walnut range would have maintained a coordinated look across the bedrooms.

In some households, the box room was set up as a work room, perhaps with sewing machine or storage for other craft projects, and possibly a spare chair from a dining-room set.

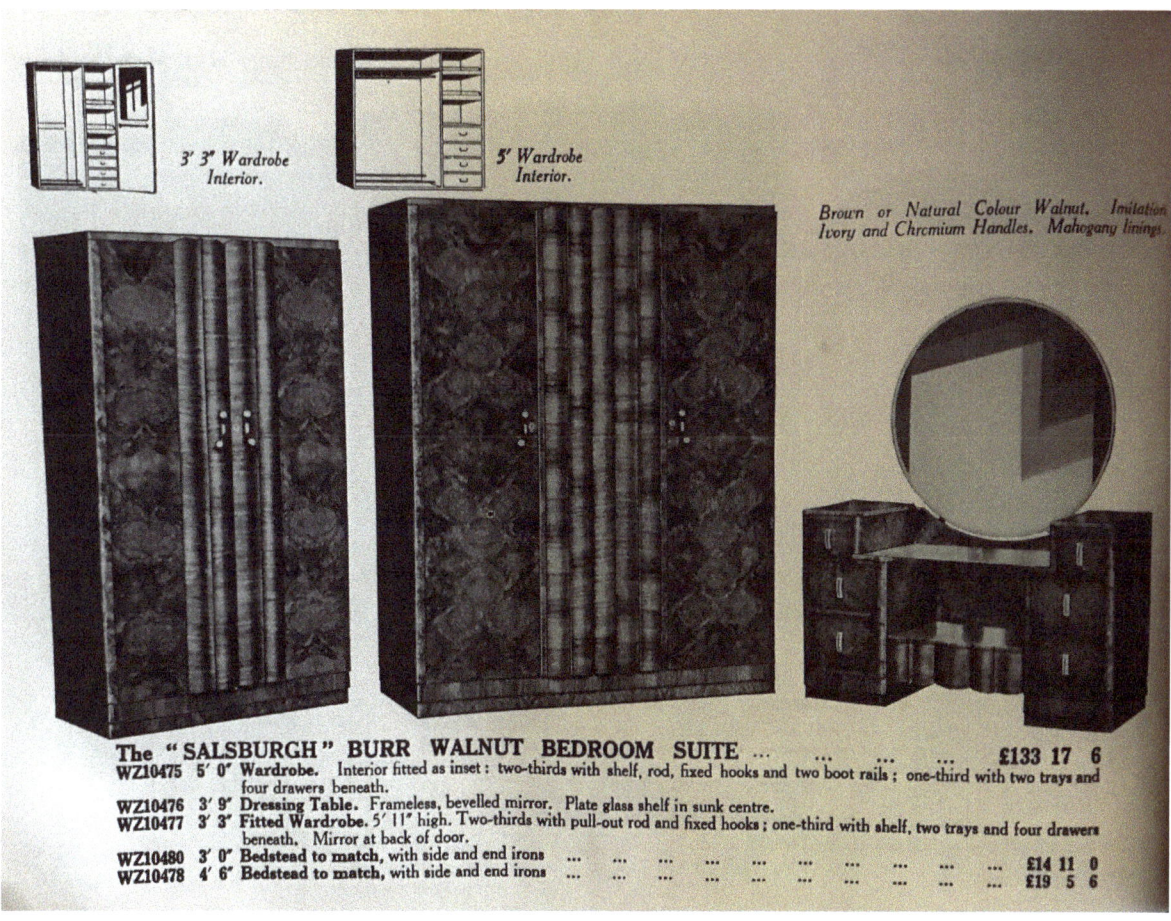

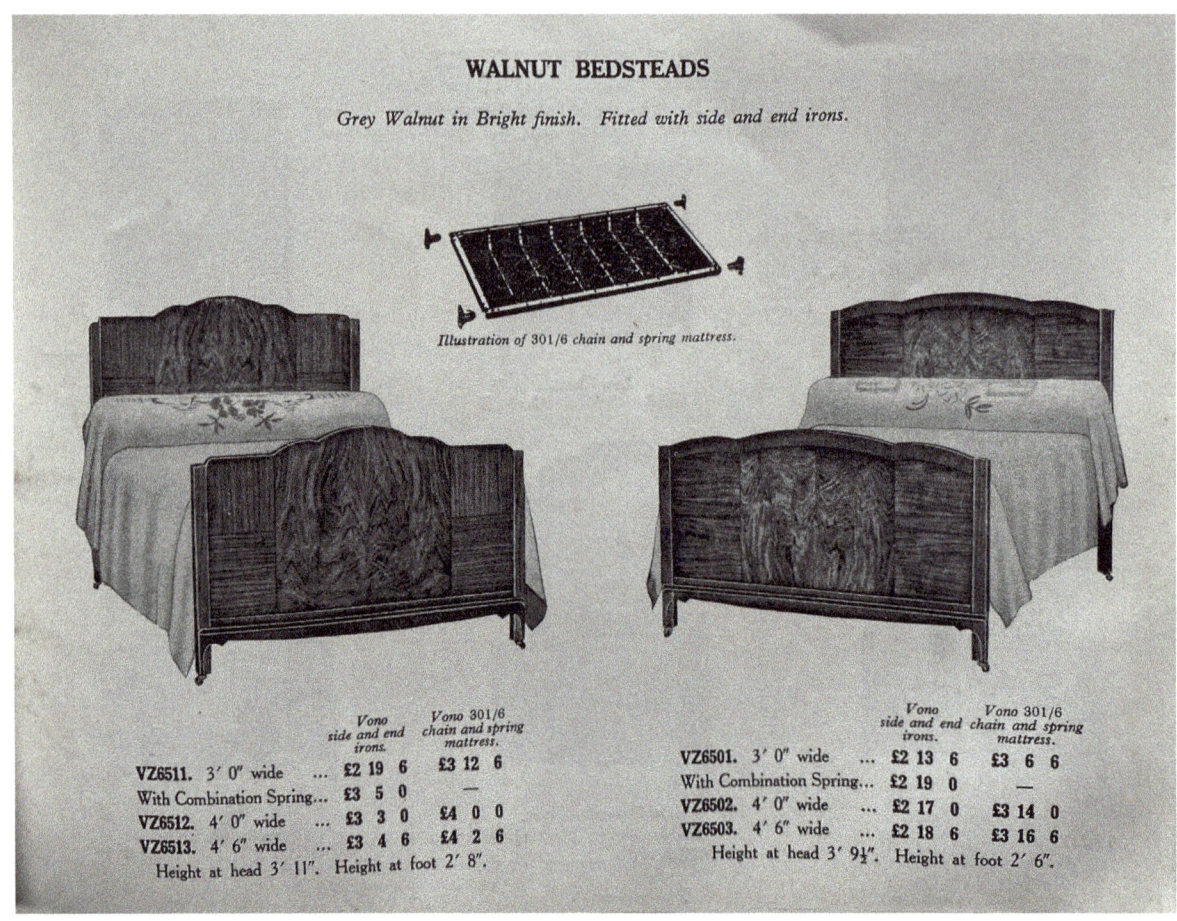

Amongst the most expensive of the bedroom suites was the Salsburgh in burr walnut. Just as with the oak suites there were bedsteads in walnut to match, along with a choice of fitted wardrobe. There were also additional walnut bedroom furniture pieces which could be added to blend, including dressing tables, chests of drawers and a millinery chest.

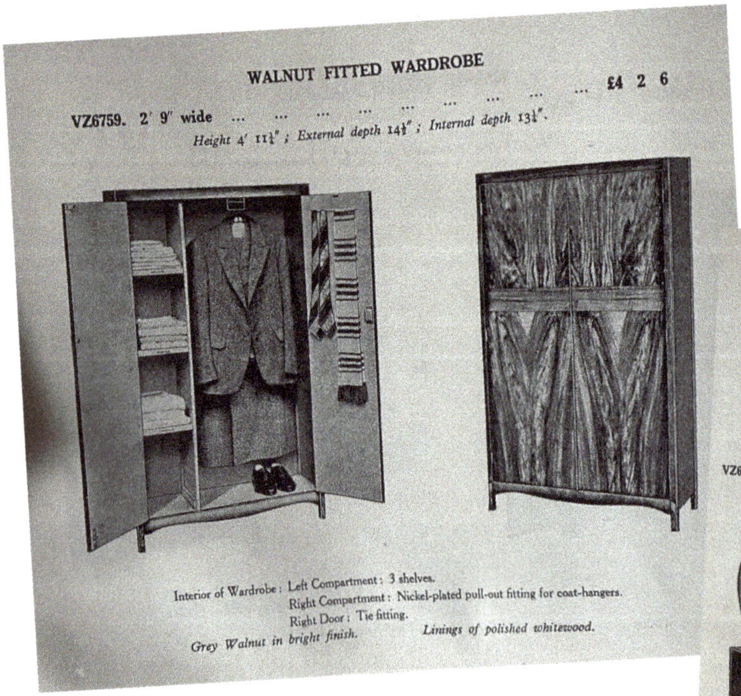

Table: Expensive furniture selected and distributed across three bedrooms

Bedrooms	Catalogue number	Fairfield (x2) plus extra furniture items	Width	Cost
Master	WZ10557	Wardrobe*	4ft	
	WZ10559	Wardrobe*	2ft 9in	
	WZ10558	Dressing table with frameless mirror*	3ft 6in	£47 5s (for suite)
	WZ10562	Double bedstead	4ft 6in	£12 7s 6d
	Z6121	Beside cabinets (x2)		£2
Middle	WZ10562	Double bedstead	4ft 6in	£12 7s 6d
	WZ10480	Single bedstead	3ft	£9 16 6d
	WZ10557	Wardrobe*	4ft	
	Z6121	Beside cabinet		£2
Small	WZ10480	Single bedstead	3ft	£14 11s
	WZ10559	Wardrobe*	2ft 9in	
	WZ10558	Dressing table with frameless mirror*	3ft 6in	
Box room	VZ6519	Millinery chest	2ft 6in	£3 3s
	VZ6518	Chest of drawers	2ft 6in	£2 9s 6d
Total cost				£165

* Furniture piece from Fairfield suite

Dining room

The most expensive dining suite in oak was the Broughton at £127 2s 6d. It came with two carvers and a standard set of four dining chairs plus two extra, making eight chairs in total.

A desirable and handy piece to add to the dining room was the 'tea wagon', as it was described in the catalogue – or drinks trolley, as we would probably say today.

Alongside bookcases, bureaux and bureau-bookcases was the secretaire, a furniture piece which combined a china cabinet with a bureau.

A mirror above the fireplace or sideboard would have completed the look.

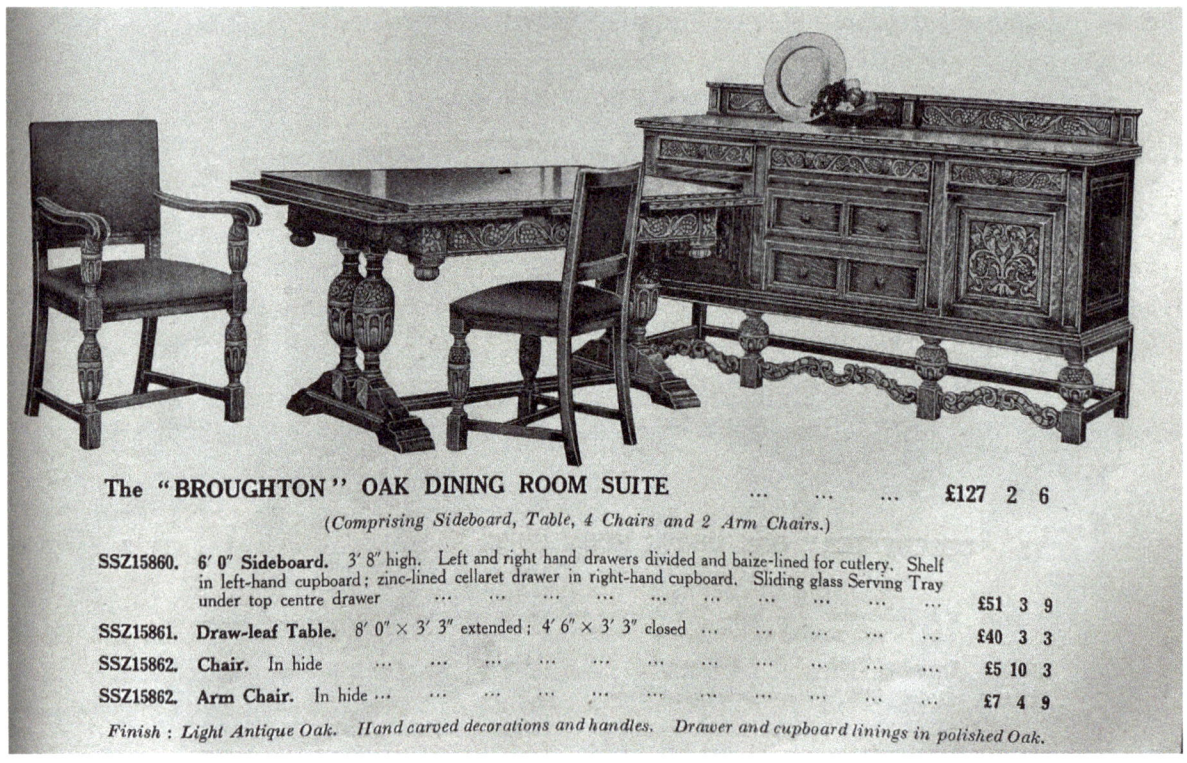

The carved, ornate and detailed Broughton was the most expensive dining-room suite. A secretaire was a popular furniture piece of the period as it was versatile; with glass-fronted doors it could be used as a china cabinet or bookcase, as well as being a disguised bureau work-desk. A tea trolley was a classic furniture item of the period; the TZ11047 was a handy, space-saving piece as it was collapsible when not in use.

Table: Expensive furniture selected for the dining room

Dining room	Catalogue number	Broughton plus extra furniture items	Width	Cost
	SS715860	Sideboard	6ft	£51 3s 9d
	SS715861	Draw-leaf (extendable) dining table	3ft 3in (by 4ft 6in) up to 8ft	£40 3s 6d
	SS715861	Six chairs – priced individually		£5 10s 3d
	SS715862	Carver – priced individually (x2)		£7 4s 66
	TZ11047	Tea trolley		£2 5s
	RZ11618	Secretaire		£12 8s 6d
	PZ11161	Mirror		£2 12s
Total cost				Just under £155

RZ11618. Secretaire ... £12 8 6
4' wide. Lined fall. Polished interiors and pigeon-hole fitment. Adjustable shelves. Shelf in centre cupboard. Oak, Walnut or Mahogany.

RZ11704. Bookcase ... £3 18 0
3' wide. 4' high. Lead-light doors. 2 fixed shelves. Brown Oak.

RZ11676. Secretaire ... £8 9 6
4' wide. Light Antique or Brown Oak. Fitted with adjustable shelves.

Sitting room

A choice of 13 three-piece suites was on offer. Price differentials largely came down to the size of the individual pieces because of the amount of material required and choice of stuffing.

There was a wide choice of additional furniture items which could be purchased for the sitting room.

Three-piece suite choices for the sitting room included the Thurgarton. With around half of the three-piece suites on offer in 1937, the customer could opt for individuality and provide their own suitable, hardwearing fabric at an advised amount with prices quoted for completed job. In the case of the Thurgarton, the suite required 22 yards (just over 20 metres).

China cabinets were popular. Once a furniture item that could only be afforded by the upper classes, they were now affordable to those of working and middle class. There were 20 different designs.

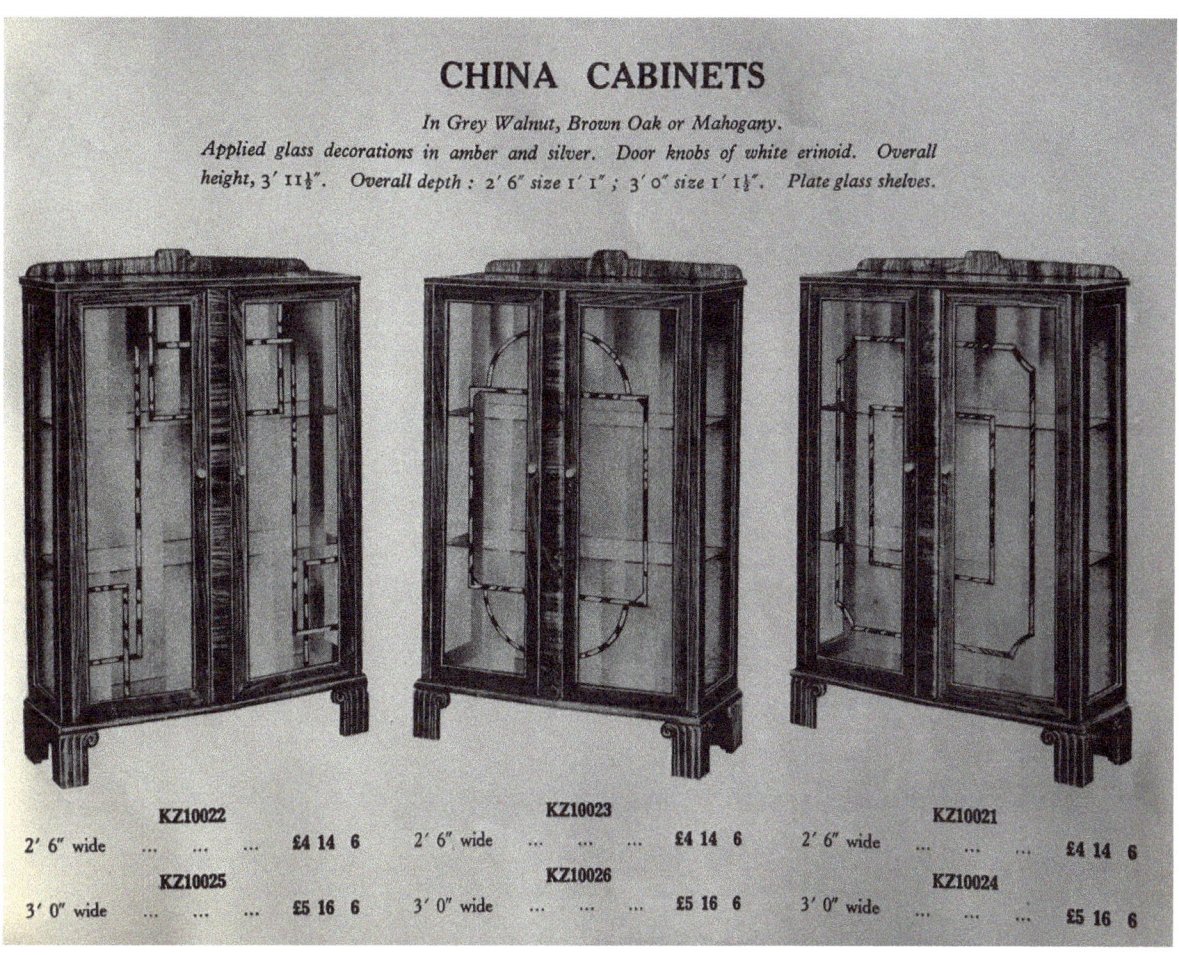

The Dinard was a stylish side table. Chosen from an array of china cabinets, any one of them would have looked stunning in any period sitting room. A cocktail cabinet, complete with silver-plated accessories, brought Hollywood glamour.

A relatively new item of furniture for the period was the cocktail cabinet. The choice came down to one, since a second design had 'withdrawn' across it in red capital lettering (printed not stamped manually).

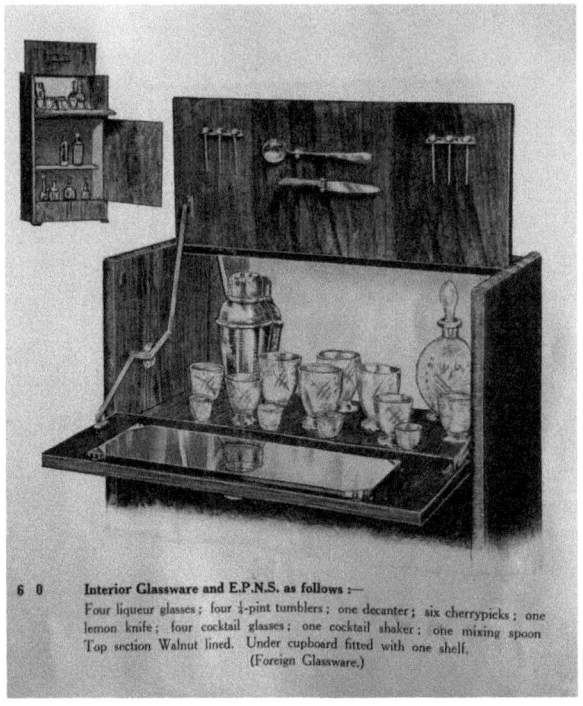

Interior Glassware and E.P.N.S. as follows:—
Four liqueur glasses; four ½-pint tumblers; one decanter; six cherrypicks; one lemon knife; four cocktail glasses; one cocktail shaker; one mixing spoon. Top section Walnut lined. Under cupboard fitted with one shelf.
(Foreign Glassware.)

Table: Table of furniture selected for the sitting room

Sitting room	Catalogue number	Thurgarton		
	UZ1001	Three-seater settee	6ft	£26
	UZ1001	Armchairs each (x2)	2ft 8in	£7 11s 6d
	KZ10080	China cabinet		£8 6s
	KZ10015	Cocktail cabinet	2ft 6in	£8 6s
	TZ11099	Revolving bookcase		£2 19s
	TZ11082	Gossip table		£3 11s 6d
	TZ11030	Nest of tables		£1 9s 6d
	TZ11031	Occasional table		£1 1s
	PZ11160	Mirror		£1 8s
Total cost				Around £60

Hall

Many detached or semi-detached suburban houses built during the interwar period had large hallways to welcome guests and hang coats. The most expensive options here were the ZZ11505 hall cupboard at £7 14s and the BZ5858 hallstand at £3 2s 6d.

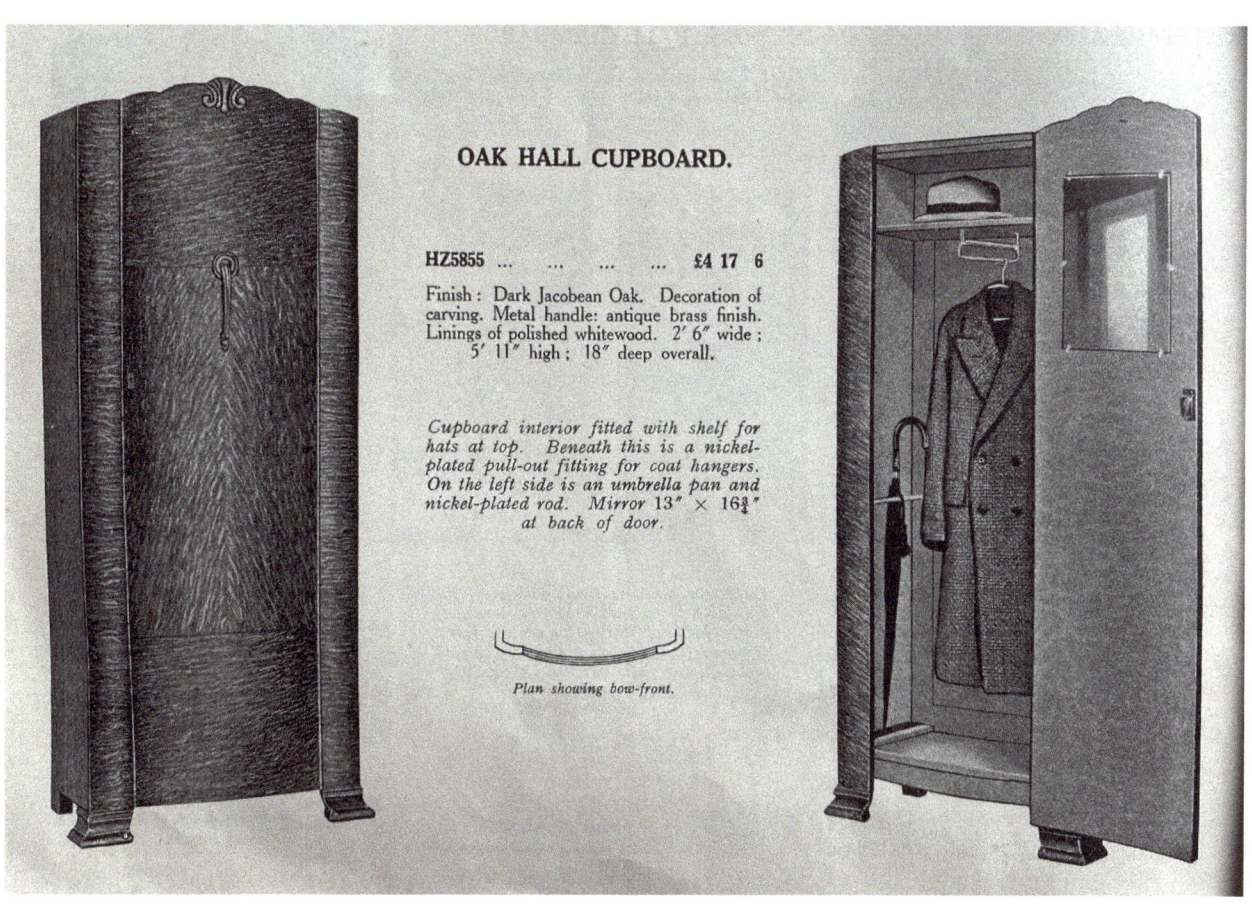

A family in their four-bedroom detached or semi-detached suburban house could have spent around £300 if choosing the most expensive choices from the Lebus furniture catalogue in the summer of 1937.

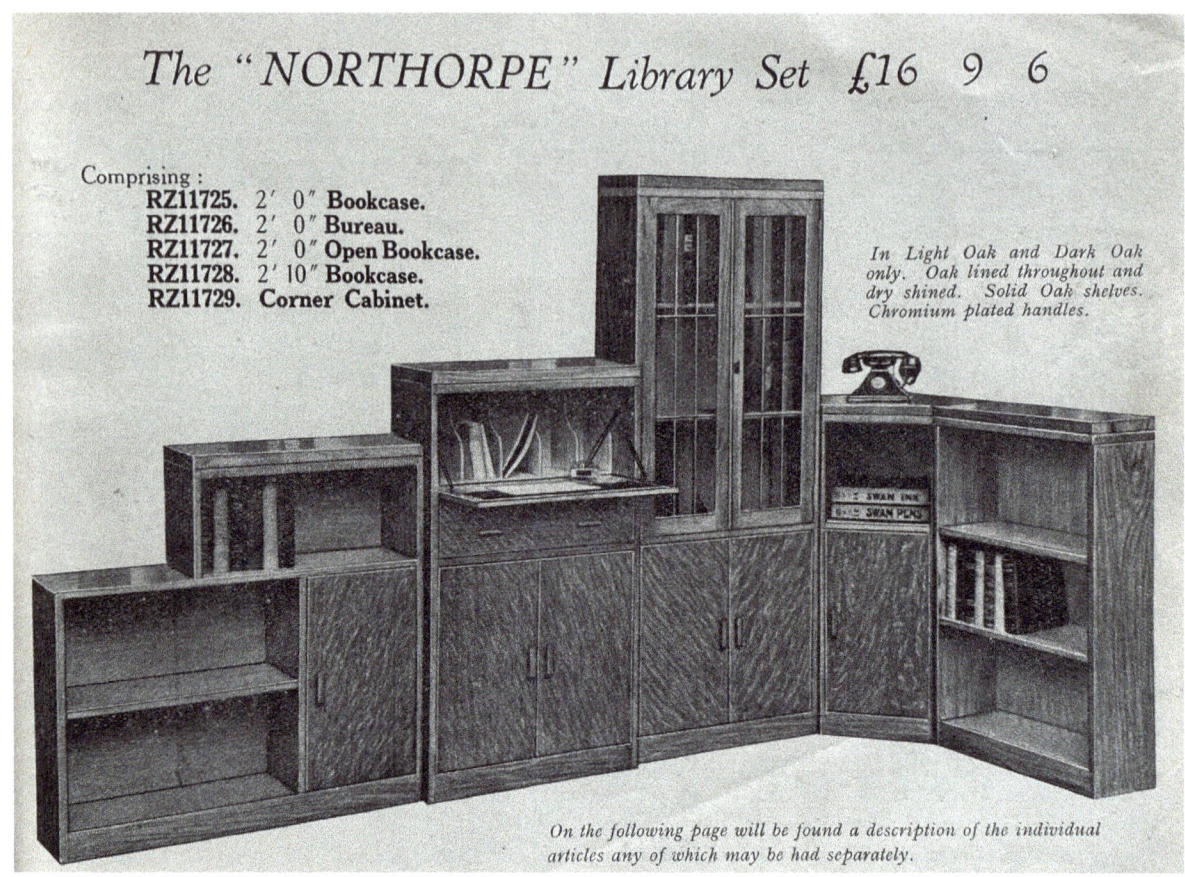

This modular home library system in the 1937 catalogue is quite special. There were five individual pieces of furniture, which collectively gave a home office all it needed. Of course, these could be bought separately, or it was possible to buy more than one of any of them, such as the bookcases.

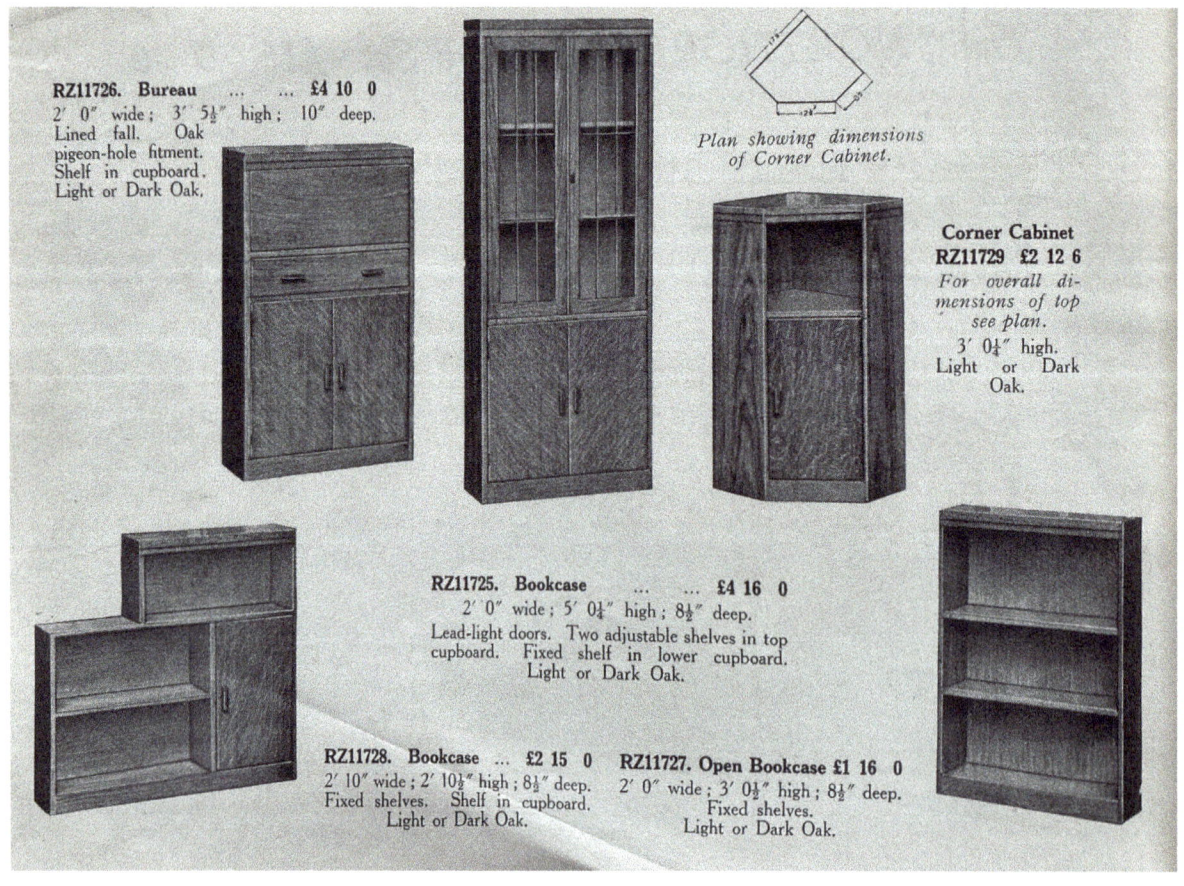

Candy-floss Colours Morphed into Neon Bold

Utility Furniture and Mid-century Modern, 1943–1970

Herbert Randles Kinsley straddled the periods either side of Lebus's conversion into a public company in 1947, and remained chief designer throughout the Utility furniture era.

Cyril Rostgaard, of Danish origin, succeeded Kinsley in the post of chief designer of cabinet furniture in 1951. Furniture ran in the family – his father, Theodore, was a furniture manufacturer in Denmark. Harry Whittaker was the chief designer of upholstery.

Furniture production at Lebus recommenced soon after World War Two; cabinet making remained at the Tottenham Hale plant while upholstery moved to Woodley, Reading in 1950.

At this time, British furniture manufacturers were bound by strict government controls. As a member of the government's Furniture Working Party (and its one-time chair), Sir Herman Lebus was in a prime position to influence national policy. The volume of furniture that each individual firm could make and sell was dictated by the amount of wood they were allocated according to a formula set by this committee.

As its name suggests, Utility furniture was basic and practical, with more emphasis placed on its function and less on how it looked. Despite the fact that Lebus offered a choice of stained mahogany alongside oak, there was little to distinguish furniture made by one manufacturer from another, save for one small thing: each furniture piece had to be stamped to identify it as Utility furniture, and each manufacturer had its own unique identity number. The number allocated to Lebus was 304.

These markings on the back of a Lebus piece give much information: '304' is the licence number allocated to Lebus to produce Utility furniture; on the ticket, 'B1956' is actually the design number (not the year) and 'JOB' stands for Jacobean oak bright finish.

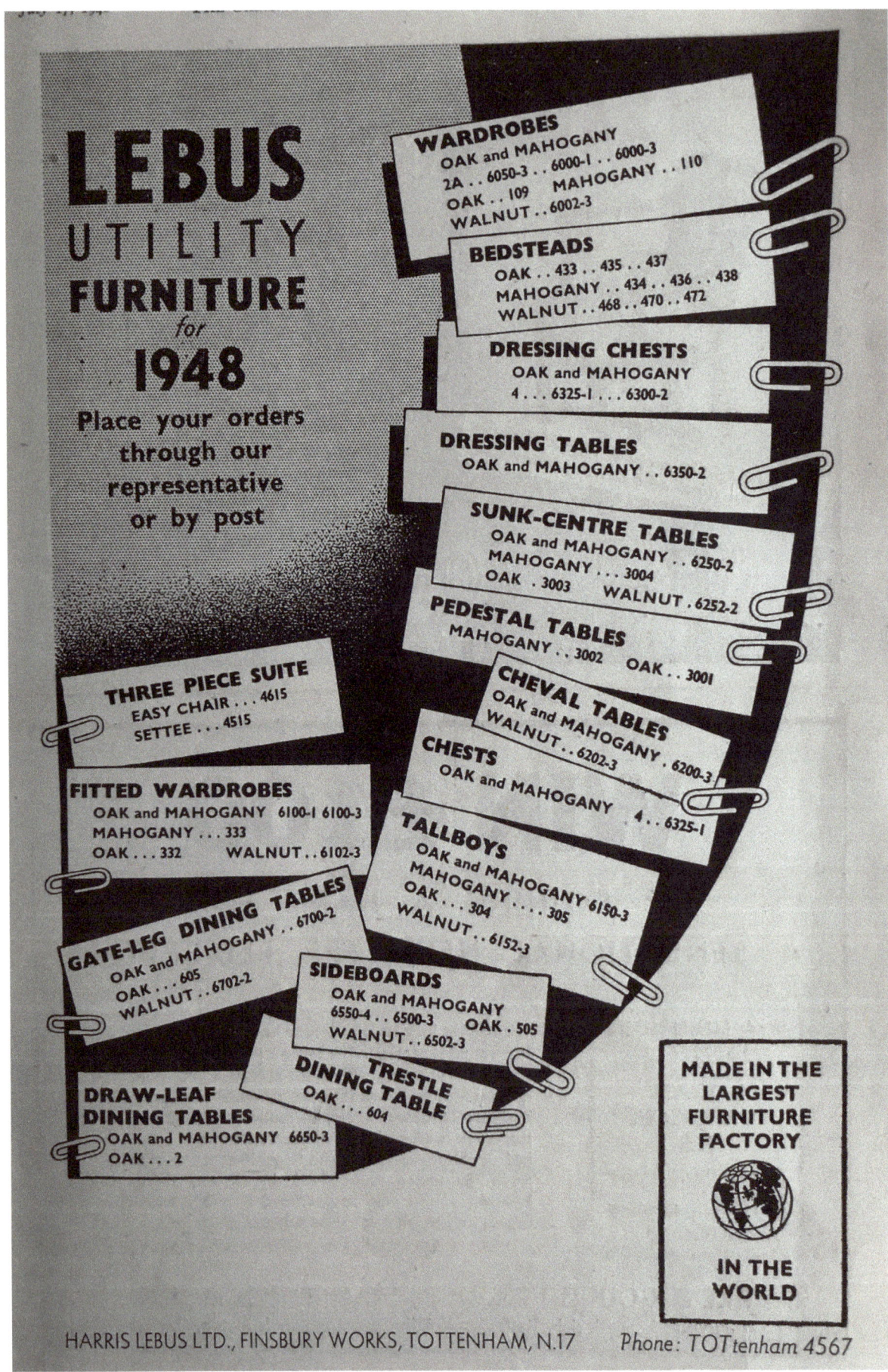

Advertisement for Lebus Utility furniture appearing in the 17 July 1948 edition of the *Cabinet Maker and Complete House Furnisher*. Not only does this show the broad range of furniture that Lebus was producing, but also their respective catalogue numbers.

Lebus celebrated the lifting of design restrictions with this full-page advertisement in the *Cabinet Maker and Complete House Furnisher*, 18 December 1948.

When rumours around the impending relaxation of price and design controls began to circulate early in 1948 there was renewed optimism amongst both manufacturers and consumers. And although controls on hardwoods remained in place until April 1949 (and the sourcing of plywood and veneer was not without its difficulties beyond this), designers were at last free to unleash their creativity.

Lebus celebrated freedom of design with advertisements in furniture magazines. However, in practice the firm took a cautious approach because the sales team felt that the independent retailers they worked closely with would not stock furniture that was different from what the majority of the furniture-buying public were used to.

An article titled 'Our products' which appeared in the in-house magazine provides a valuable insight into the company's thinking around its furniture designs and relevance to the consumer (*Lebus Log*, No. 1, June 1954). 'We felt whereas there existed a potential market for contemporary furniture, hitherto it had had two main limitations… it was too expensive and… the designs had been too extreme for the majority of people.'

Lebus continued to manufacture furniture targeted at consumers at the lower end of the market, but design would prove to play an increasingly crucial role in the choices the consumer made. The Festival of Britain, which opened on 3 May 1951 on London's South Bank, was visited by thousands. A latent desire for colour and pattern was awakened. Following the Queen's Coronation in 1953, the television set became a must-have for households up and down the land, and the emergence of ITV in 1955 brought advertisements directly into the home. New magazines which leaned towards interior design – for both men and women – carried advertisements and the concept of 'do it yourself' (DIY) grew. People enjoyed trips to the cinema and came to the realisation that the glossy, ideal interiors and Hollywood glamour could now be within everyone's reach. There were textiles in colourful, patterned fabrics for curtains, soft furnishings and upholstery, along with ceramics in colour and pattern for bright, bold dinner, tea and coffee sets. The home setting in which furniture would be placed was changing with a wide choice of emulsion paints in varied colours alongside an array of wallpaper designs. Candy-floss colours morphed into neon bold.

Central heating became both desirable and affordable, and by keeping rooms of the house or flat at a consistent, ambient temperature, households were free to use space differently. New-build accommodation tended to be plain and box-like. Where rooms were small, space-saving combination furniture helped households make more of their home – bed settees, fold-down dining tables – and the oh-so-useful tea trolley. Open-plan interiors began to trend, with zones for dining and relaxed sitting and entertaining created using open-shelved, free-standing, moveable room dividers.

As the decade wore on, Lebus embraced change, experimenting with new raw materials. Although working predominately with timber, hardboards and veneers, particle-boards and laminated plastics were increasingly used in kitchen furniture, where they were often teamed with aluminium. With the recommendation of the Furniture Development Council that manufacturers brand their furniture, Lebus introduced a small-coin-sized metal button with 'HL' in the middle and 'Lebus furniture' around the edge which was embedded inconspicuously, usually on the interior of a door or drawer. (As the decade wore on this was replaced with small plastic stickers.)

Looking into 1953 and 1954

Catalogues with black-and-white photographs were produced three times a year and printed in-house. With reference to the catalogue of spring 1954, there is a certain familiarity with both the content and the format. The majority of the furniture is for the bedroom, followed by the dining room, with oak and walnut finishes. There is much in common with Lebus pre-World War Two designs – dark wood stain and bright (shiny) finishes and echoes of Art Deco style. There is a proliferation of the use of the acorn and some pleasant surprises design-wise.

Bedrooms

Of 87 pages of bedroom furniture in 1954, 15 were walnut suites along with the remainder in oak.

This single wardrobe and small chest of drawers were amongst some of the earliest furniture produced after the Utility scheme finished.

Chislehurst oak bedroom suite from the 1954 catalogue and two pieces – chest of drawers and dressing chest – from the suite up-cycled by Haleh Kaveh of HalehDesigns (Etsy).

This wooden-handled dressing table has been rejuvenated into a stylish, sophisticated piece for the contemporary bedroom by Deborah Weston. Originally it formed part of the Prestwick oak bedroom suite found in the 1953 catalogue.

A few suites on offer have been brought over from 1953; one of them is the Chislehurst from the Z6 oak range.

The interchangeable oak bedroom range formed a major part of the bedroom choices in both the 1953 and 1954 catalogues. The concept of interchangeable furniture afforded the opportunity for the consumer to add pieces to a suite, there and then, or at a later date when funds permitted. Designs changed, but these were often subtle – the shape of a carving perhaps – but crucially the intent was that newer designs would blend with previous purchases a customer may have made. Of course, there was always the choice for contrasting through 'mix and match', such as combining walnut pieces with oak.

Some of the varied handles found on 1950s furniture.

CANDY-FLOSS COLOURS MORPHED INTO NEON BOLD   105

Variation on a theme: a selection of furniture items from the interchangeable oak bedroom range made to supplement suites. The concept of the oak interchangeable bedroom range afforded the opportunity for the consumer to add pieces – which, crucially, matched perfectly – to a suite either at the point of purchase or later, when funds permitted. Of course, mix and match had always been an option for the consumer, for example with Lebus bedroom furniture before World War Two; however, the encouragement to do this was now explicit. Not only could you mix and match furniture pieces made the same year, but those made in different years. You could even mix oak and walnut furniture.

Z2918 fitted wardrobe from the oak interchangeable choices in 1954.

![Southport Walnut Bedroom Suite catalogue page]

THE "SOUTHPORT" WALNUT BEDROOM SUITE £55 13 6

Model No. Z8174	4' 0" Wardrobe	£22 0 6
Model No. Z8175	3' 6" Sunk-centre Dressing Table	£17 18 6
Model No. Z8176	2' 6" Tallboy	£15 14 6

Extra for Wardrobe mirror 19/3.

Bedsteads to match with brackets :

Model No. Z8172	4' 0" wide	£9 5 6
Model No. Z8173	4' 6" wide	£9 9 0

SPECIFICATION: Brown or Grey Walnut: bright finish. Decoration of carving and moulding. Metal handles. Lacquer finished cupboard linings.

Wardrobe in two detachable parts. Interior fitted with two rods and revolving hook for hanging, 24" × 12" mirorr if required. Tallboy fitted with rod for hanging, four side shelves and tie-spring on inside of door.

The Southport in walnut is one of several bedroom suites appearing in both the catalogues of spring 1953 and spring 1954, indicating that it was popular. Note the carving and contour features of the design.

This small millinery cupboard, which has carving and contour features similar to those of the Southport suite, has been up-cycled by Alison of FloatingBlackDog (Etsy).

CANDY-FLOSS COLOURS MORPHED INTO NEON BOLD

BEDSTEADS

SPECIFICATION: Exterior veneer Walnut on face side of panels polished to match all Walnut colour Bedroom Suites.

Model No. Z4061	3' 0" wide	£5 5 0
Model No. Z4060	3' 6" wide	£5 17 9
Model No. Z4062	4' 0" wide	£6 9 6
Model No. Z4063	4' 6" wide	£6 16 6

Fitted with brackets.

Just as for the oak bedroom suites, Lebus offered a range of additional furniture pieces to match walnut suites, including this bedstead from the Z4 range.

The beauty of this single-sheet veneer on the front of the bottom set of drawers on this high chest has been restored and enhanced through the creativity of Robyn at Onward Interiors.

Dominika Winska's artistic treatment of this 1950s millinery cupboard appears to recreate a burr walnut effect.(Scraped and Brushed, Etsy)

In 1954, four new bedroom suites stood out: the Z7 range had a polished natural oak finish that was light and unfussy, with sleek lines. The Cheltenham was one such suite. There was also a selection of additional pieces to match this range just as there were with the oak and walnut suites.

Lebus offered some oak suites, such as the Cheltenham, in a new, lighter finish described as 'natural'. Note the modern fabrics of the window dressing used to stage the suite. The dressing table with roll-top jewellery or make-up storage feature has been up-cycled by Jenni.

CANDY-FLOSS COLOURS MORPHED INTO NEON BOLD

SPECIFICATION:

Exterior veneer Oak polished natural colour, wax finish. Cupboard and drawer interiors lacquered and polished.

WARDROBE: *In two detachable parts. Interior fitted with two rods for hanging and three corner shelves. 24" × 12" mirror if required.*

DRESSING TABLE: *Fitted with roll-front trinket compartment divided into three sections.*

Illustrated with metal handles. If required with wood handles, please specify.

THE "CHELTENHAM" BEDROOM SUITE — £43 14

Model No.	Description	Price
Z7104	3' 6" Wardrobe	£19 2
Z7105	3' 3" Sunk-centre Dressing Table	£15 2
Z7116	2' 6" Low Chest	£9 9

Extra for Wardrobe mirror 19/3d.

Bedsteads to match with brackets:

Model No.	Width	Price
Z7101	3' 0" wide	£5 11
Z7102	4' 0" wide	£6 13
Z7103	4' 6" wide	£6 19

SPECIFICATION:
Exterior veneer Oak polished natural colour, wax finish. Cupboard and drawer interiors lacquered and polished.
SIDEBOARD: *Interior fitted with full-width, full-length shelf. Right-hand drawer divided and bottom sprayed with green Rayon for cutlery.*
DRAW-LEAF TABLE: *Fitted with detachable legs.*
DINING CHAIRS: *Fitted with loose, sprung seats in green or red leathercloth.*

THE "SANDOWN" DINING ROOM SUITE	£42 0 3
Model No. Z6117 4' 0" Sideboard	£19 11 6
Model No. Z6104 Draw-leaf Table	£10 1 9
2' 6" × 3' 0" closed : 2' 6" × 5' 0" extended.	
Model No. Z6100 Dining Chair, each	£3 1 9
Extra for Chairs covered in Tapestry 4/3d. each.	

A handful of dining-room suites in polished natural oak were also a new feature in the 1954 catalogue. The Sandown suite has a slick, modern style.

Dining furniture

There were 30 pages of dining suites in 1954, with a flexible choice of individual dining tables. On offer were draw-leaf, swivel or reversible tabletops, each available in a choice of three different leg designs. In addition was a range of five space-saving gate-leg (fold-down) dining tables – two with cupboards and one with a cutlery/napkin drawer.

The Glasgow oak dining suite is from 1953 and has a modern edge to its design.

Dining suites in alternative styles and finishes from 1954: the Worthing suite in walnut had a modern look, while the Gainsborough in mahogany has elements of Queen Anne style seen in suites before World War One.

This 1950s sideboard has been up-cycled into a cocktail cabinet by Gosia at GM Up-cycling Studio. She has really brought out the qualities of the walnut veneer.

CANDY-FLOSS COLOURS MORPHED INTO NEON BOLD 113

Sideboard with ball feet up-cycled by Fran and Carl, TaylorThompson (Etsy).

SPECIFICATION:
Exterior veneer Oak polished Golden or Jacobean colour, bright or matt finish. Drawer and cupboard interiors lacquered and polished.
SIDEBOARD: Interior fitted with full-width shelf in each cupboard. Top drawer divided and bottom sprayed with green Rayon for cutlery.
DINING CHAIRS: Fitted with loose, sprung seats in brown or green leathercloth.

THE "ARUNDEL" DINING ROOM SUITE	£52 2 9
Model No. Z2561 4′ 6″ Sideboard	£24 1 3
Model No. Z2563 Refectory Table 2′ 6″ × 3′ 6″ closed : 2′ 6″ × 5′ 6″ extended.	£13 14 6
Model No. Z2560 Dining Chair, each	£3 11 9

The sideboard with the Arundel suite is one of two with these spectacular decorative ball feet with curved supports. These were new in 1954. A similar design has been up-cycled by Leo, Leoquentfurniture.

Of 21 dining suites in the 1954 catalogue, 14 were in traditional oak, with two in walnut veneer and another in mahogany. The others were four new stand-out dining suites in the Z6 range with their natural oak finish and modern look.

In recognition that homes had smaller spaces, the gate-leg table was available in both 1953 and 1954. The Z3022 is pictured in the darker Jacobean oak.

Three-piece suites

Twenty-one pages of three-piece suites and upholstered seating were on offer in 1954. There is one bed settee and six designs for open-arm easy chairs, along with two new wing-back easy chairs.

116 LOVING LEBUS

Upholstered seating in different styles. The Hertford suite, with its traditional style, had a bed settee (the other suite with a bed settee was the Beverley). The most modern-looking was the Windsor suite, which came with or without wing backs. The Eastbourne (one of the few suites pictured with a three-seat settee) has a style of arm reminiscent of some of the Art Deco suites before World War Two.

THE "WINDSOR" THREE-PIECE SUITE
Comprising Model No. Z5856 Settee and two Model No. Z5857 Easy Chairs. Covered in Tapestry or Uncut Moquette. Self welted only.
From £42 12 9 to £54 15 3 covered in H.L. range of Uncut Moquettes.
THE "CONWAY" THREE-PIECE SUITE (As above but without wings)
Comprising Model No. Z5850 Settee and two Model No. Z5851 Easy Chairs.
From £39 4 9 to £49 17 6 covered in H.L. range of Uncut Moquettes.
SPECIFICATION: *Cable sprung seats and sprung backs. Latex foam seat cushions. Upholstered with woven fibre and felt.*

THE "EASTBOURNE" THREE-PIECE SUITE
Comprising Model No. Z5862 and two Model No. Z5861 Easy Chairs. Covered in Uncut Moquette or Non-crush Velvet. Self welted.
From £50 17 0 to £71 16 9 covered in H.L. range of Uncut Moquettes.
Specification: *Sprung seats, backs and arms. Spring filled seat cushions. Upholstered with woven fibre and felt.*

Looking back on this period in 1975, Ken Bennett, who was managing director in the latter years of Lebus Upholstery, recalled: 'We produced… designs of three-piece suites which we called our "Z" range. These were cheaper than most other manufacturers and very good value for money. These ranges immediately became very popular and we were suddenly inundated with orders for three-piece suites, our open-arm easy chairs and bed settees.'

Kitchen free-standing units

Shortly after the launch of furniture for the kitchen, the stand-alone tall (larder) cabinet Z1101 featured in the Spring 1953 catalogue. It had fixtures and fittings with the carcase finished in a cream enamel paint, doors finished in a choice of pale shades of green, red or blue hammered enamel paint with a polished black plinth. It was also offered in a darker shade of green in 1954 as model Z1106 as well as in oak veneer as model Z1102.

'They were also one of the only manufactured larders with curves on the cabinet corners and top shelf', wrote Russ of Resto-Worx Furniture shop, Redruth Cornwall in an online chat with the author. Russ mentioned another difference which distinguishes Lebus kitchen larder cabinets when it comes to the work surfaces: 'They were famous for their armour-glass-work surfaces. It was foil backed, like a mirror, and coloured, with the word *Armourplate* (a registered trademark of Pilkington Brothers Ltd) embossed on the glass'. In effect, it was safety toughened glass, scratchproof and bullet

The free-standing kitchen (larder) cabinet Z1102 which first appeared in the 1954 catalogue is the second model of this furniture piece and is finished in the more traditional dark Jacobean oak. This would indicate a demand for such finishes. Features unique to the Lebus range are the curved outer edges, the curved upper shelf and the Armourplate work surface.

proof! Lebus did, after all, have experience with bullet-proof glass, having made complete aircraft during both World War One and World War Two. Russ added: 'Lebus were the only manufacturer, to my knowledge, to use this' – the majority of other manufacturers opted for enamel or Formica (a newer material at the time).

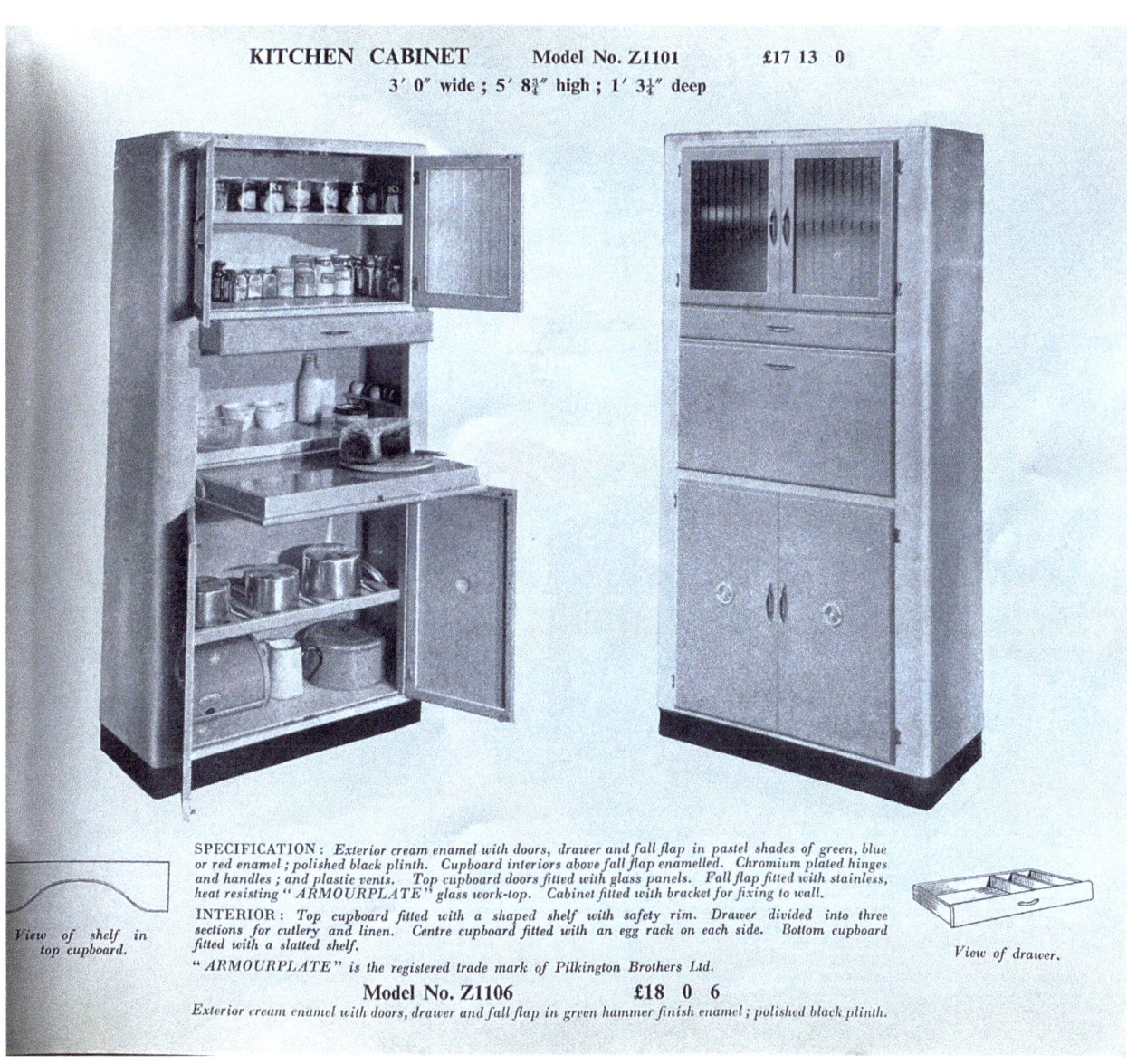

The Z1101 had different glass-fronted doors at the top of the cabinet.

Russ at Resto-Worx, Cornwall, kindly supplied this image of his own restoration of one of these pieces, which he has painted in vivid red.

KITCHEN CABINETS

3′ 0″ wide : 2′ 11⅝″ high : 1′ 4⅛″ deep.

Model No. Z1108   £10 10 0

SPECIFICATION : *Exterior cream enamel or exterior cream enamel with drawer and doors in pastel shades of blue, green or red enamel ; polished black plinth. Plastic vents and chromium plated hinges and handles.*

Model No. Z1109   £10 13 6

SPECIFICATION : *Exterior cream enamel with drawer and doors in green hammer finish enamel ; polished black plinth. Plastic vents and chromium plated hinges and handles.*

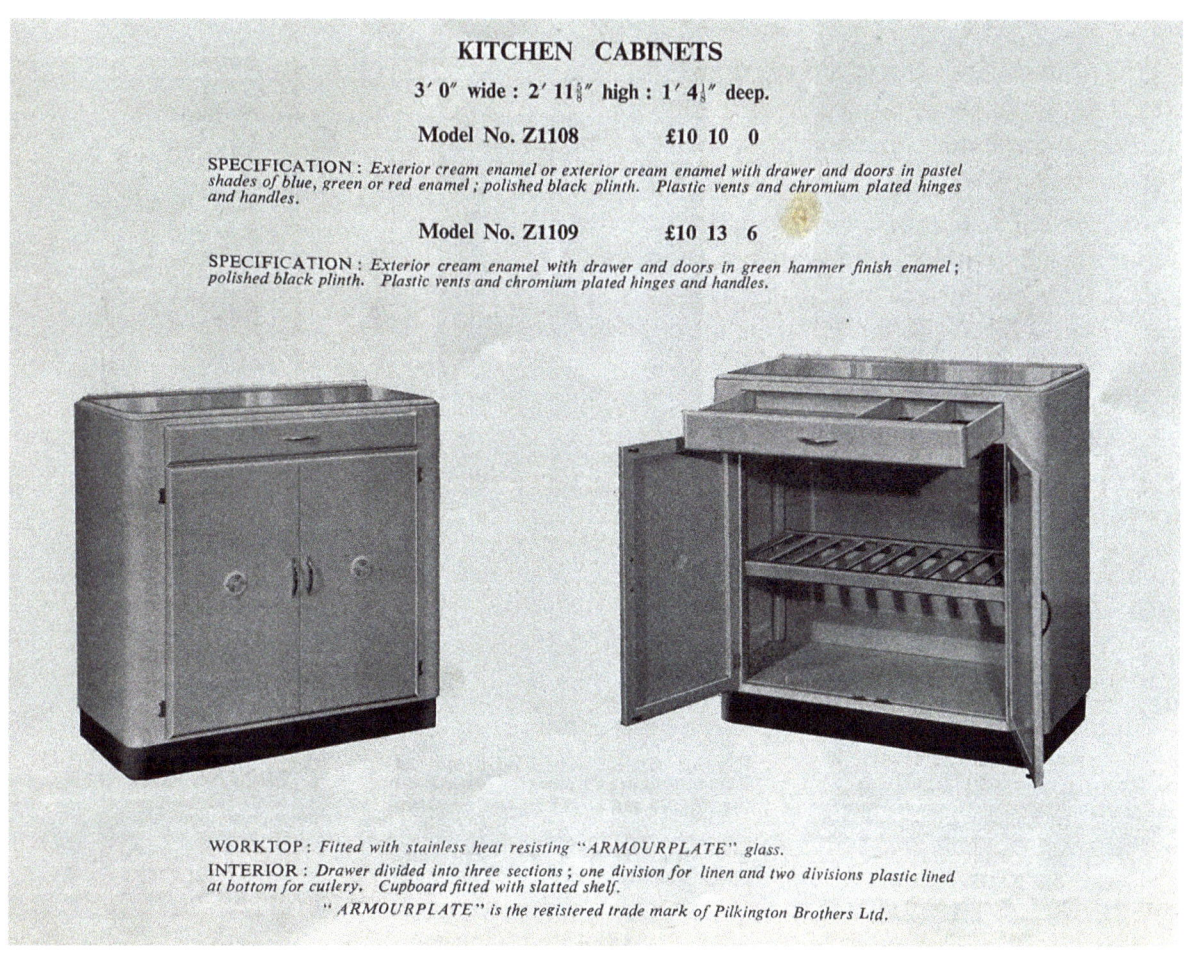

WORKTOP : *Fitted with stainless heat resisting "ARMOURPLATE" glass.*
INTERIOR : *Drawer divided into three sections ; one division for linen and two divisions plastic lined at bottom for cutlery. Cupboard fitted with slatted shelf.*
"ARMOURPLATE" is the registered trade mark of Pilkington Brothers Ltd.

KITCHEN CABINETS

BROOM CUPBOARD
Model No. Z1110   £8 11 6
SPECIFICATION : *Exterior cream enamel or exterior cream enamel with door in pastel shades of blue, green or red enamel ; polished black plinth.*
Model No. Z1111   £8 15 0
SPECIFICATION : *Exterior cream enamel with door in green hammer finish enamel ; polished black plinth.*
INTERIOR : *Fitted with adjustable shelf ; two hooks and a broom clip each side.*

Exterior view of Model Nos. Z1110 and Z1111 Broom Cupboards and Model Nos. Z1112 and Z1113 Store Cupboards.

2′ 0″ wide : 5′ 9½″ high : 1′ 4⅛″ deep. Fitted with chromium plated hinges and handles.

STORE CUPBOARD
Model No. Z1112   £9 12 6
SPECIFICATION : *Exterior cream enamel or exterior cream enamel with door in pastel shades of blue, green or red enamel ; polished black plinth.*
Model No. Z1113   £9 15 6
SPECIFICATION : *Exterior cream enamel with door in green hammer finish enamel ; polished black plinth.*
INTERIOR : *Fitted with five adjustable shelves ; three hooks each side.*

A collection of free-standing kitchen units which complimented the Z1101 were brand new in 1954. These included a waist-height cupboard with Armourplate work surface, Z1108, and two tall cupboards – one of which made an ideal broom cupboard (Z1110) and the other ideal for storing food and kitchen utensils (Z1112).

In effect, it was possible to build up a complete free-standing kitchen in a colour scheme of either pale green, blue or red.

This entire range was also available in the familiar fifties shade of darker hammered green.

Three additional pieces to match were also available: a waist-height cabinet with work surface, and two tall, slim cupboards – one for brooms and one with shelves for storage. The three were offered in the same choice of finish as the original stand-alone, tall kitchen (larder) cabinet: carcase finished in a cream enamel paint, with a polished black plinth and the doors in the same choice of pale green, red or blue hammered enamel.

Hall

For the hall were various hallstands. One, Z4085, was on offer in 1954 at a cheaper price than the previous year – £9 2s 9d as compared to £10 8s.

Model No. Z4085 £10 8 0
2'3" wide, 5'11" high, 12" deep.
*Fitted with seat and rug box.
17" x 11" mirror.*

Lebus continued to offer hall furniture, including this hallstand – one of two on offer in both 1953 and 1954.

Miscellaneous furniture

Finally, there were several pages of miscellaneous furniture in the 1950s catalogues, including china cabinets, occasional tables for the lounge, some bookcases, bureaux, bureau-bookcases, a secretaire and some hallstands. A handful of furniture suites and individual pieces are repeated from 1953, such as a bureau-bookcase, some occasional tables and a stool.

Secretaire.
Model No. Z3029.   £22 5 3
3′ 6″ wide ; 3′ 7½″ high ; 1′ 0½″ deep.
Light Tan or Jacobean Oak ; bright finish. Decoration of carving and moulding. Wood handles. Lacquer finished drawer and cupboard linings. Lead-light doors.
Fitted with Mahogany pigeon-hole fitment, polished fall and three adjustable wood shelves in each bookcase compartment.

George Lilly at Ex Amino has rejuvenated this Lebus secretaire from 1953 and reinvented it as a cocktail cabinet for the contemporary home.

Looking into 1956 – Link

A new range launched at the end of 1956 emphasising 'Link' as the brand name – a bright blue plastic diamond elongated horizontally was affixed to every furniture piece and stated: 'Lebus Link furniture'.

Link was made with solid oak exteriors and oak veneer, with drawer and cupboard linings of mahogany and mahogany veneer, and with metal handles finished in satin brass. Afromosia wood – with the same colour palette and feel of teak – was used in the making of some Link pieces.

Link proved extremely popular and the range ran for several years. In 1960 a brand-new set of Link designs featured in an exhibition in America to showcase a broad range of British businesses at the Coliseum, beside New York's Central Park. In 17 days there were 300,000 visitors to the exhibition and it generated significant orders, not only in New York, but also in Vancouver and Winnipeg, Canada.

A striking change of tack was evident with the launch of the Link range, not just the fact that Lebus initiated a robust marketing campaign, but that advertisements were created with the end consumer in mind. And for the first time, Lebus upholstery and cabinet furniture pieces were pictured in glorious colour.

Advertising was characterised by numerous catchy marketing strap-lines with different marketing media used. 'Thinking of Linking' was the common theme of five one-minute Link films made at Elstree Studios for cinema advertising. Magnificent sets were built for each film including streets, shops, houses and gardens. Pearl and Dean, who were famous for cinema advertising, were the producers. In the spring of 1958, the films appeared in 450 cinemas up and down the country.

It was evident in the marketing for Link that Lebus was aiming both to attract new customers and to please its loyal base. Phrases such as 'original modern furniture for modern homes, but with all the grace and charm of a bygone age' affirm this.

Just look at 'Link' – at the pleasing curves, at the strong but slender legs. Classic in its simplicity, contemporary in its compactness and adaptability, 'Link' furniture represents a new approach to modern design.

From the range of 'Link' pieces in these pages, you will find plenty to choose for every room for every home. Each piece can be bought separately, and you can devise innumerably lovely room arrangements – all with astonishing variety-in-harmony. Furnish a complete house with 'Link' or start with a few essential pieces and build up gradually – either way you'll be delighted with the elegance and versatility of this new furnishing idea.

Lebus built upon the tried and tested notion of interchangeability with Link:

> A special point about 'Link' is the way it will blend with other furniture you already have. Few people can afford to set up a home that is completely new throughout, and the modern fashion is, of course, for blending good traditional with good modern furniture. That's one of the charms of 'Link' – it looks so well with older furniture… To achieve the variety-in-harmony which is characteristic of 'Link', all the pieces are completely interchangeable.

Lebus was all too aware that its customer base experienced variations in disposable income. The firm set out with the expressed intent in its Link marketing to reach out to embrace those who could afford more alongside those who could afford less. Link furniture was placed in three price bands.

A fold-out leaflet, 'The new beauty of "Link"', shows the complete range of furniture pieces in their respective price bands: there was one set of designs with a choice of two finishes in the lowest of the price bands; another range with a choice of two finishes in a higher price band; and a further selection available in one finish only that were more expensive again.

A living-room set-up with a modern setting appeared in a magazine advertisement dated 22 September 1956 showing designs in the harvest oak and sable oak range. The advertisement began with the question: What's the first thing a woman looks for in a dressing table? A subsequent question asks: And what does a man expect from an armchair? The advertisement does go on to answer these questions (fifties sexism is best left in the past!).

CANDY-FLOSS COLOURS MORPHED INTO NEON BOLD

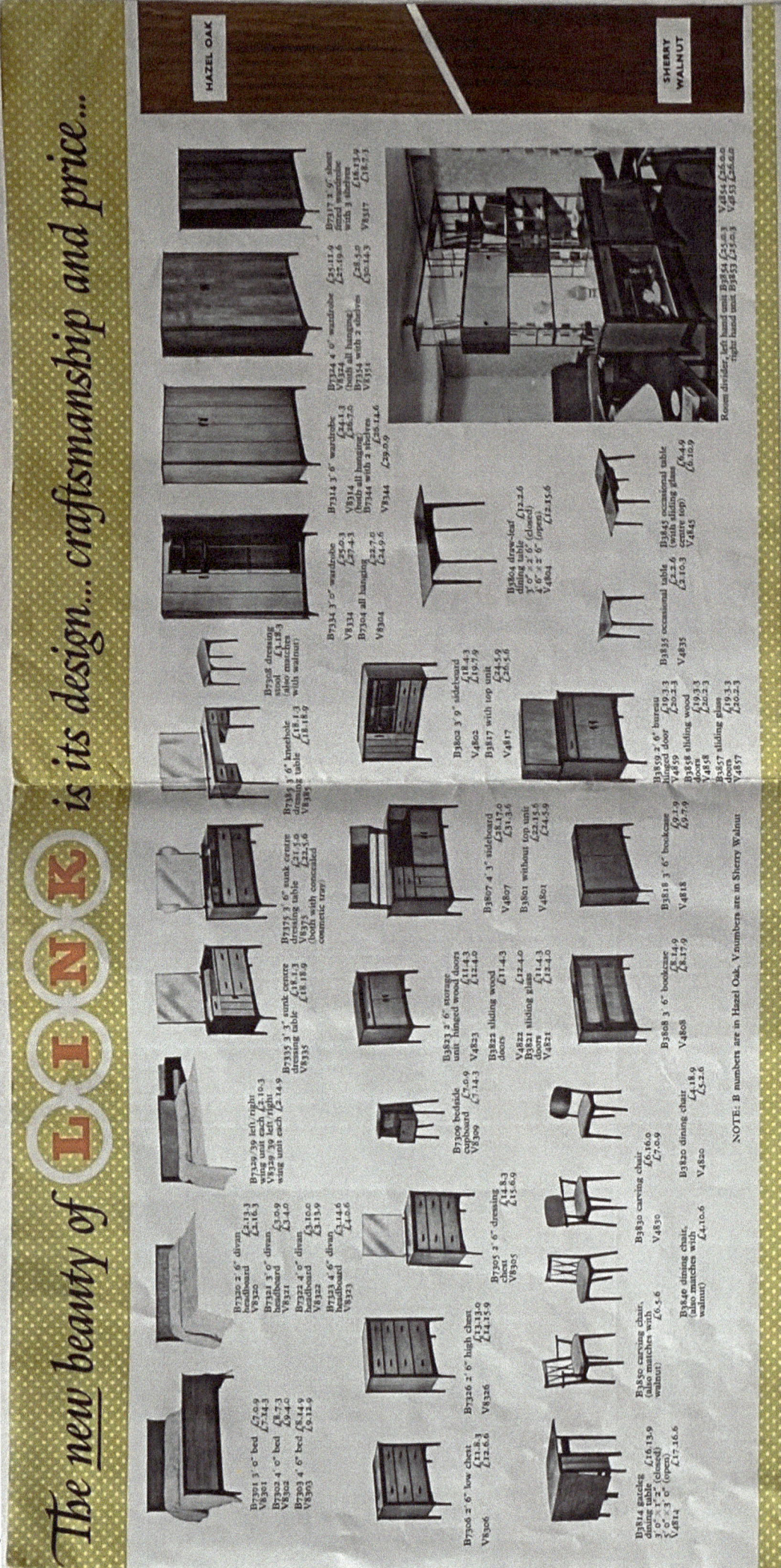

The complete Link range.

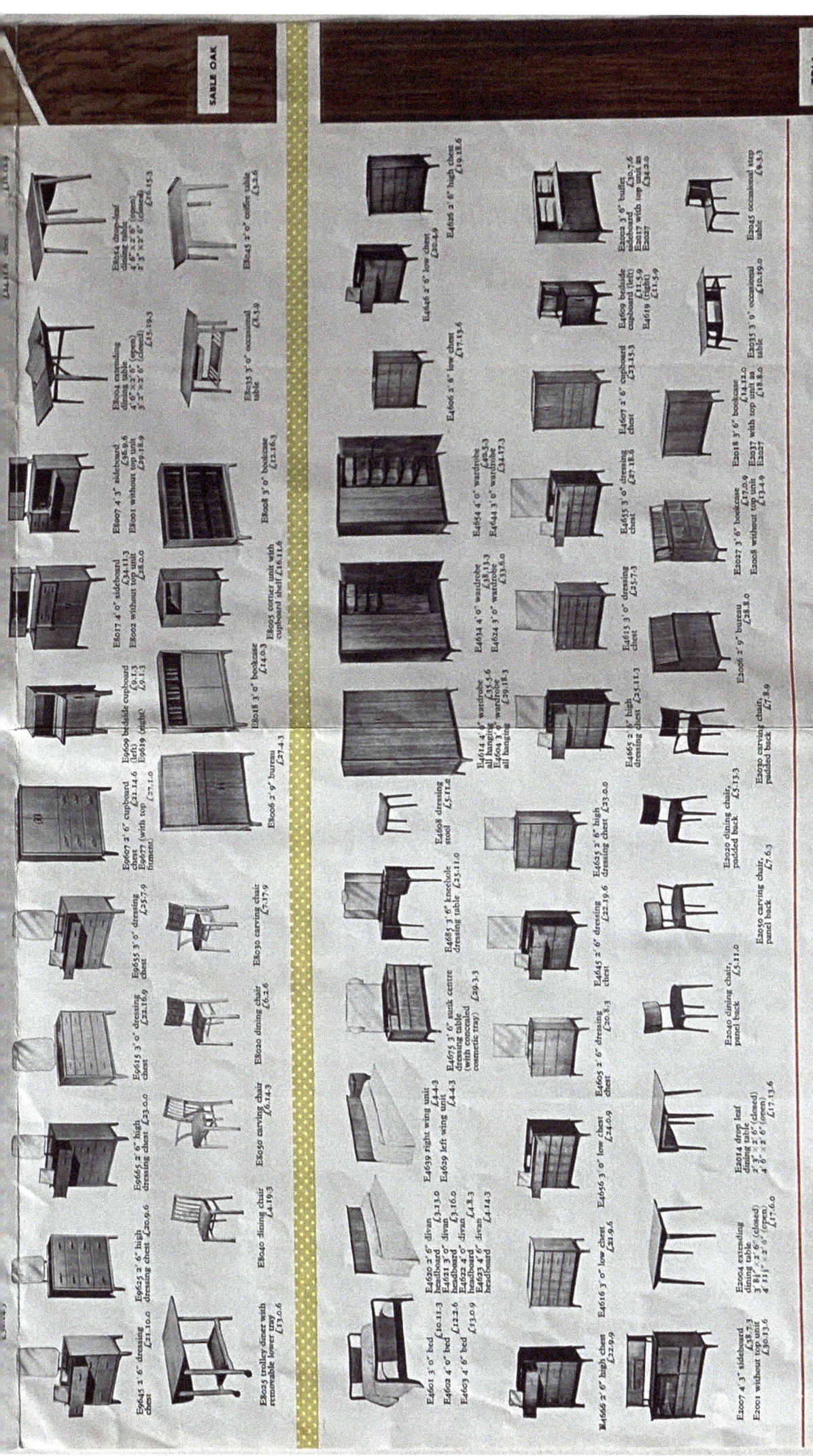

'...for the smaller home and costing a little less...'

The set of designs available in the darker shades of hazel oak and sherry walnut were intended for the smaller home and were the least expensive. Catalogue references for these pieces were prefixed with either the letter 'B' or 'V' respectively.

'...for the larger home and costing a little more...'

The set of different designs in the lighter shades of harvest oak and sable oak were intended for the larger home and were more expensive. Catalogue references for these pieces were prefixed with the letter 'E'.

The most expensive of the three designs came in a tola finish, with catalogue references prefixed also with the letter 'E' (followed by a '4' or a '2').

Front of 'The new beauty of "Link"' leaflet.

Furniture from the hazel oak and sherry walnut range: a sideboard in sherry walnut with top, V4807, along with dining chairs in hazel oak with cross wood back and seat pads in green vinyl, B3840.

Full-page magazine advertisement, 20 October 1956, showing designs in the harvest oak and sable oak range for a double bedroom. The advertisement posed the question: 'A home full of furniture or a little at a time?'

Pictured in the advertisement are: four-foot double bed E9602, four-foot wardrobe E9614, dressing table E9675 and stool E9608, bedside cabinet (right side) E9619, tallboy E9607 and occasional table E8035.

Alongside the E9675 were two further choices of dressing table in the harvest oak and sable oak range: E9635 and E9685 (pictured with stool E9608). All the dressing tables had small drawers with the blue plastic trays for holding small items, such as jewellery or make-up.
(Image of E9675 dressing table courtesy of Nigel T. Wybrow)

IDEAL HOME MARCH 1958

Must top quality furniture always have top prices?

Here's a lovely piece of furniture—simple, elegant, unmistakably contemporary, yet with the grace of tradition behind it. This sideboard would blend in with fine furniture of any period— or, with other Link pieces. With its softly gleaming wood, and beautiful finish, it looks ruinously expensive. But in fact, Link is the *least expensive* of all good, modern furniture.

4'0" sideboard with top unit (above) £34.12.0

4'3" sideboard £30.19.9

Dining table £19.7.9

Dining chair £6.8.6

Carving chair £8.3.6

Occasional table £8.11.0

Bookcase £15.3.6

Armchair from £20.9.3

3-seater settee from £42.4.0

Also available 2-seater settee from £31.11.9

Prices for Northern Ireland and the North of Scotland on application.

Learn more about Link. This is some of the furniture from the Harvest Oak range. But go to your shop and see its golden colour and the details of craftsmanship in its construction. Compare it with the slightly more expensive range in light bronze, gleaming Tola wood, and take the opportunity of looking at the less expensive range in Sherry Walnut and Hazel Oak. Link pieces can be bought separately or as suites and they will blend with the furniture you already have.

New Link Kitchen Furniture. Link now offer you colourful contemporary kitchen furniture—and it isn't expensive either! There are many exciting, practical units for you to choose from. Hard-wearing plastic surfaces, different colours to suit your taste, all the "extras" that usually cost so much— Link gives you these and much more.

Look at Link. We can send you a catalogue showing all the Link pieces, their sizes and prices. Write to: LEBUS, Dept. IH11, 17 Maddox St. London, W.1.

Link is made in the world's largest furniture factory by LEBUS, *famous for over 100 years.*

costs less

than any other good contemporary furniture. Look in the shops and see for yourself.

77

Lebus prided itself on producing low-cost, quality furniture as this magazine advert for Link from *Ideal Home*, March 1958, emphasises. The advertisement began with the question: 'Must top quality furniture always have top prices?' Some of the Link pieces pictured include: sideboard without top unit E8007, bookcase with glass doors E8008 and occasional table E8035. Extending dining table and carver chairs (as before) and dining chairs E8020. The upholstered seating shown is the easy chair U81 and three-seat settee U80, in two tone – white/oatmeal seats, backs, inside arms and chocolate/black sides and base.

CANDY-FLOSS COLOURS MORPHED INTO NEON BOLD

This image of sideboard with top E8001 is courtesy of Matt and Stuart, Hadham Vintage.

Alongside the firm's assumptions that its broad customer base lived in accommodation of various sizes and that there was a direct correlation between this size and income, Lebus demonstrated an understanding that the way homes were configured and the way space was used had been, and was, changing. Individual rooms had become just that bit smaller. Rooms with dual functions, such as the kitchen–breakfast room and the lounge–diner were becoming the norm in new houses and flats. The concepts of open-plan living and zoned spaces were emerging in new builds.

In recognition of these changing patterns, Lebus introduced a brand-new concept in furniture – the Link room divider. This is featured in 'The new beauty of "Link"' fold-out leaflet and was realistically set up to create

Extending dining table E8004 and carver chair E8030 from the harvest oak and sable oak range. (Image courtesy of Nigel T. Wybrow)

An up-cycled carver dining chair E8050 by Leanda and Donna at Fab Vintage Interiors (Etsy).

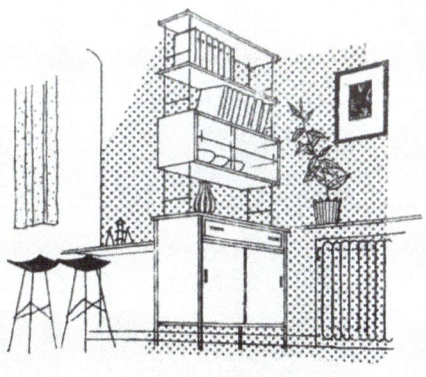
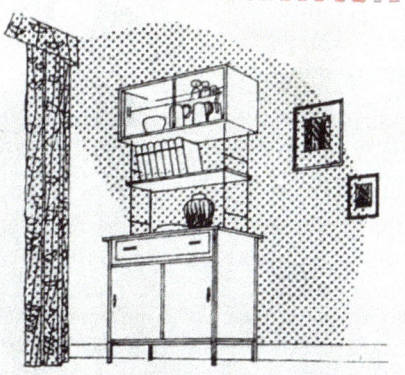
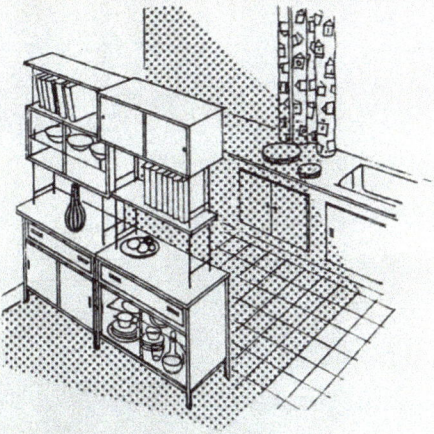

LINK'S VERSATILE ROOM DIVIDER

TALL OR SHORT – WIDE OR NARROW, this remarkable Link piece can be adapted to any number of new furniture ideas. Use one, two or even three units as a room divider; place it, single or double, flat against a wall as a cupboard unit. If you look closely at the photograph you will see that we show two complete units, each made up from six detachable sections. As the drawings illustrate, you just choose the combination that perfectly matches your space. With fittings too – adaptability is the theme. There is a choice of hinged wood, sliding wood or sliding glass doors for the base section and of sliding wood or sliding glass doors for the top section. Then as a further concession to personal taste you have a choice of wood finishes. In Hazel Oak or Sherry Walnut, Link's lovely room divider can bring exciting flexibility to your furniture planning.

MADE BY LEBUS IN THE WORLD'S LARGEST FURNITURE FACTORY

living zones – a living-room space and a dining space. The Lebus Link room divider came with a choice of two units. Each unit had six detachable sections which could be set up in various combinations to suit. As well as the open shelving there were display and storage cupboards with doors. There was a choice of hinged wood, sliding wood or sliding glass doors for the base section, and of sliding wood or sliding glass doors for the top section. Each of these units was available in two finishes: hazel oak (B3854 and B3853) or sherry walnut (V4854 and V4853).

To compliment 'The new beauty of "Link"' leaflet came a second (also fold-out) leaflet,[8] 'Now plan the perfect "Link" furniture scheme for your own home'. This was a very special leaflet – it was innovative and may have been the first of its kind. This leaflet folded out to

---

[8] The two leaflets survive in their original envelope, postmarked 12 March 1957. The address is in Holders Hill Drive, Hendon, a five-bedroomed semi-detached 1930s build.

The leaflet 'Now plan the perfect Link furniture scheme for your own home' was innovative since it included a scaled grid-plan of a room onto which a potential customer could draw their own room, which could then be 'furnished' with cut-out scaled-down shapes of the Link furniture pieces on offer.

HAZEL OAK / SHERRY WALNUT						HARVEST OAK / SABLE OAK				TOLA			
B7301	11	V8314	8	V4817	2	E9601	11	E9616	26	E4601	11	E4607	5
V8301	11	B7344	8	B3804	3	E9602	12	E9656	26	E4602	12	E4609	14
B7302	12	V8344	8	V4804	3	E9603	13	E9686	26	E4603	13	E4619	14
V8302	12	B7324	9	B3814	4	E9611	11	E9605	5	E4620	20	E2002	17
B7303	13	V8324	9	V4814	4	E9612	12	E9645	5	E4621	21	E2007	1
V8303	13	B7354	9	B3850	25	E9613	13	E9625	5	E4622	22	E2001	1
B7320	20	V8354	9	B3840	24	E9643	31	E9665	5	E4623	23	E2004	28
V8320	20	B7317	10	B3830	25	E9653	31	E9615	26	E4639	19	E2014	27
B7321	21	V8317	10	V4830	25	E9620	20	E9655	26	E4629	19	E2040	24
V8321	21	B7306	5	B3820	24	E9621	21	E9607	5	E4675	6	E2050	25
B7322	22	V8306	5	V4820	24	E9622	22	E9609	14	E4685	6	E2020	24
V8322	22	B7326	5	B3808	15	E9623	23	E9619	14	E4608	18	E2030	25
B7323	23	V8326	5	V4808	15	E9639	19	E8017	1	E4614	9	E2006	10
V8323	23	B7305	5	B3818	15	E9629	19	E8002	1	E4604	7	E2027	15
B7329	19	V8305	5	V4818	15	E9685	6	E8007	1	E4634	9	E2008	15
V8329	19	B7309	14	B3859	5	E9675	6	E8001	1	E4624	7	E2018	15
B7339	19	V8309	14	V4859	5	E9635	6	E8004	32	E4654	9	E2037	15
V8339	19	B3823	5	B3858	5	E9608	18	E8014	27	E4644	7	E2035	29
B7335	6	V4823	5	V4858	5	E9614	9	E8025	34	E4606	5	E2045	30
V8335	6	B3822	5	B3857	5	E9604	7	E8040	24	E4646	5		
B7375	6	V4822	5	V4857	5	E9634	9	E8050	25	E4626	5		
V8375	6	B3821	5	B3835	16	E9624	7	E8020	24	E4666	5		
B7385	6	V4821	5	V4835	16	E9654	9	E8030	25	E4616	26		
V8385	6	B3807	1	B3845	17	E9644	7	E8006	17	E4656	26		
B7308	18	V4807	1	V4845	17	E9606	5	E8018	33	E4605	5		
B7334	7	B3801	1	Room divider	5	E9646	5	E8005	35	E4645	5		
V8334	7	V4801	1			E9676	5	E8008	33	E4625	5		
B7304	7	B3802	2			E9626	5	E8035	36	E4665	5		
V8304	7	V4802	2			E9696	5	E8045	30	E4615	26		
B7314	8	B3817	2			E9666	5			E4655	26		

The numbers in the right hand column in red indicate the cut-out silhouettes on opposite page.

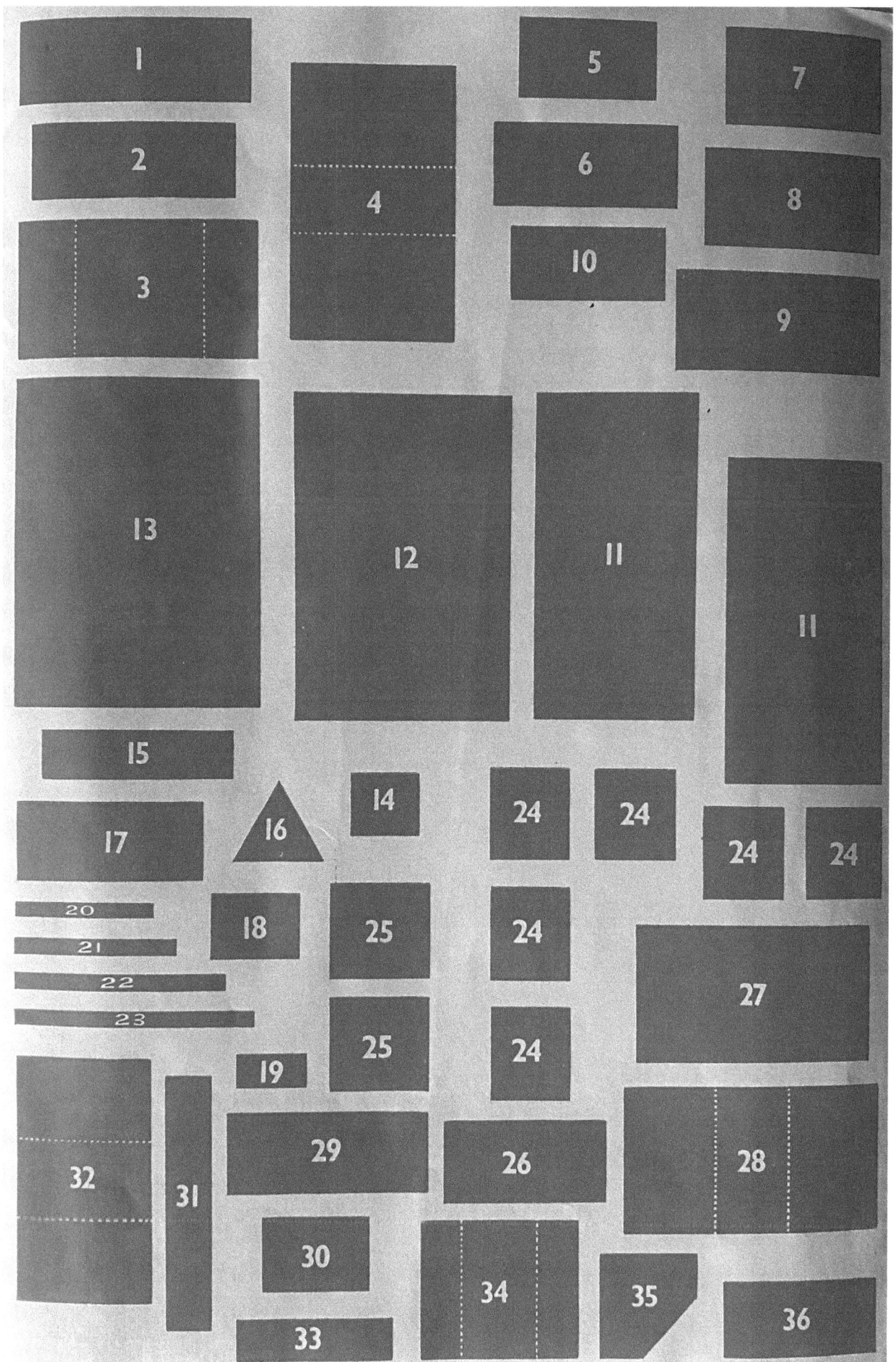

CANDY-FLOSS COLOURS MORPHED INTO NEON BOLD

reveal several pages of graph-paper squares for customers to draw in a scale version of a room in their home which they were thinking of furnishing with Link pieces. (The correlation of this scale to feet and inches is not specified.)

Printed in the leaflet were shapes, to scale, which were representative of the floor space required for various Link furniture pieces. These shapes could be cut out and placed in a mock-up room accordingly. For example, the V4807 sideboard corresponded (amongst several other pieces of furniture) to shape number one. Of course, if planning to add Link pieces to an existing furniture scheme, a prospective customer could size-up, draw and cut out shapes corresponding to their existing furniture.

'The new beauty of "Link"' leaflet included an image of every single piece of Link furniture, complete with its dimensions, unique catalogue number and price. Link furniture offered a wide variety of choice. In all, there were four variations of sideboard and six different dressing tables. Chests of drawers were designed in such a way that they need not be confined to the bedroom – they sat just as comfortably in living rooms, lounges, dining rooms, halls or bed-sits/studios. Link offered a choice of dining chairs, three different upholstered suites, along with armchairs and a settee.

The Link range had been loved by the buying public and was a great success for the firm. However, although important to Lebus, the Link range was amongst hundreds of other products. As the Link brand faded away during the early 1960s, Lebus focussed on its many other designs.

The choice of Link upholstered pieces which appeared in the leaflet 'The new beauty of "Link"'.

A bedroom design set-up dated September 1958 which also appeared in *Ideal Home*. It was different: Link 'six' was finished in an off-white called chinchilla.

It appears there were further additions to the Link range over time.
(Image of Link integrated headboard and bedside tables courtesy of Annabelle, lille_vinge_fly)

A new Link sideboard appeared as a later piece.

Looking into 1965

Furnishing bedrooms still constituted the major area of the business and Lebus continued to offer an extensive choice of furniture in its interchangeable oak bedroom range. The firm acquired another business in the field, which it brought under its wing – Eventide Bedding[9] – and with coming of the 'baby boom' generation, Lebus offered a range of nursery furniture. A significant amount of development had also taken place in the design and manufacture of kitchen furniture.

Alongside hardwoods and plywood, Lebus was using aluminium, melamine and laminated plastics in some of its furniture. As the introductory notes to the Lebus catalogue of 1965 state: 'observe the many styles and designs… in various colours and finishes including the latest treatments of wood-grain plastics… the latter being resistant to heat, scratches, stains, etc.'

With reference to the 1965 catalogue, aside from the cover (in a shade of polished copper), the contents are exclusively black and white, and in a new world of colour and vibrancy they appear comparably dreary. This mattered because sales representatives relied on catalogues to convince independent retailers to sell Lebus ranges and they, in turn, relied on these images to persuade customers to choose the company's furniture. The sales team, however, had additional marketing material to work with in the shape of full-colour leaflets that accompanied and showcased new Lebus ranges. With their vibrant graphics and catchy strap-lines, these came into their own during the 1960s.

---

9 Eventide (Bedding) Limited Shoreditch, based in Leonard Street, Shoreditch, was originally established by Thomas Nicholson just before World War One, then taken over by his son Walter, who successfully made the transition to a public company in 1954 and was ready to retire. With ongoing contracts with the Admiralty and a strong export market, Eventide Bedding was well known to consumers in the south of England.

In colour: an undated 1960s brochure listing five bedroom suites was a refreshing addition to the black-and-white images of a Lebus catalogue. Three suites were mahogany veneered – Cameron, Solent and Harlington – with the remaining two suites oak veneered – Wendover and Lamorna. The latter with its light shade was described as polished in the 'fashionable chinchilla colour'. A section of the leaflet which launched the Consul bedroom range in 1960 described this as 'unit furniture with that elegant difference'.

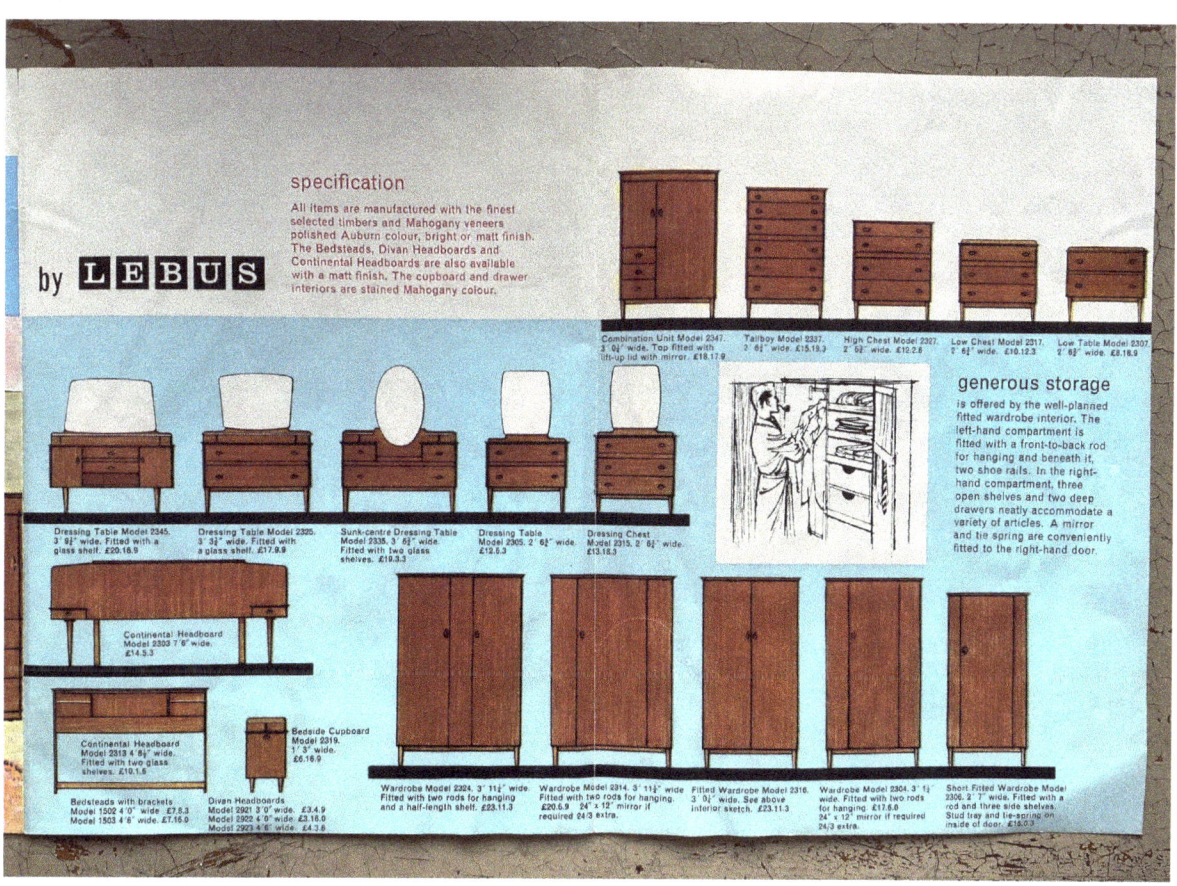

Children's bunk beds from 1965. The nursery furniture was painted white with a choice of colour for the door and drawer fronts of either pink or blue.

Kerstin Parsonage at Forget Me Knot Designs has been inspired by a baby's nursery with her reinvention and redecoration of a Lebus tallboy/linen cupboard. There is a story behind this furniture piece: Kerstin acquired it from a lady whose grandmother had bought it brand new in the late fifties. During World War Two, in New Milton, New Forest, the grandmother helped deliver babies in her own home for expectant mothers who were unable to pay (in the days before the NHS).

BUNK BEDS

1391	£14 13 0	
	With mesh springs.	
1393	£32 4 6	
	With mesh springs and spring interior mattresses.	
1062	£25 7 0	
	With reversible Polyether foam mattress.	

LADDER

1394	£1 9 6	
	Beech polished natural colour. Overall dimensions: 6' 6¾" long: 2' 6" wide: 4' 8¾" high. Single bed size 6' 6¾" long: 2' 6" wide: 2' 4¾" high. Beds secured with four catches.	

Bedroom suites

Whilst the interchangeable oak bedroom range looked sleek and unfussy, its dark, shiny 'autumn' colour left it looking somewhat dated. The range consisted of these pieces:

- Five different regular height wardrobes
- One of a shorter height
- A fitted wardrobe (with mirror on the inside of one door, a tie rack and five compartments)
- Nine different dressing tables (though one is withdrawn)
- Five chests of drawers (one with a mirror mounted above)
- Two designs of divan headboards (each available in two sizes, with only one of these designs available as a single-bed option)
- A combination wardrobe with chest of drawers
- A choice of two tallboys
- A millinery cupboard
- One bedside cabinet.

Alongside the interchangeable oak bedroom range, Lebus offered a choice of 42 other bedroom suites. The majority came with natural wood veneer with a handful of suites finished in man-made materials. Of the natural wood veneers, eight were oak, 13 mahogany, four teak, two ash and one tola. Fourteen suites were of a man-made finish.

Eventide mattresses, divan bases and headboards could be purchased either separately or as a package. There were four designs: Scintilla, Starmist, Stellar and Zodiac. Each was offered in five sizes: two feet six inches, three feet, three feet six inches, four feet, four feet six inches.

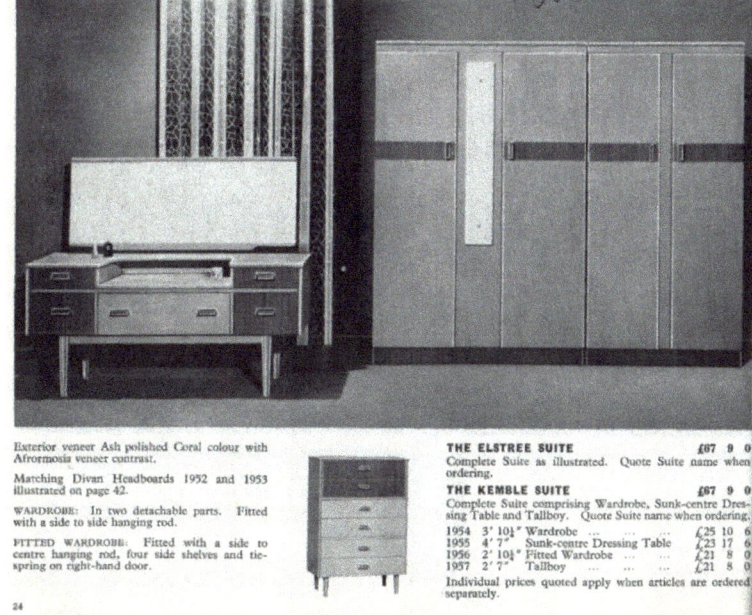

Ash veneered, the Elstree and Kemble suite was polished coral colour, which can be seen with this fitted wardrobe.

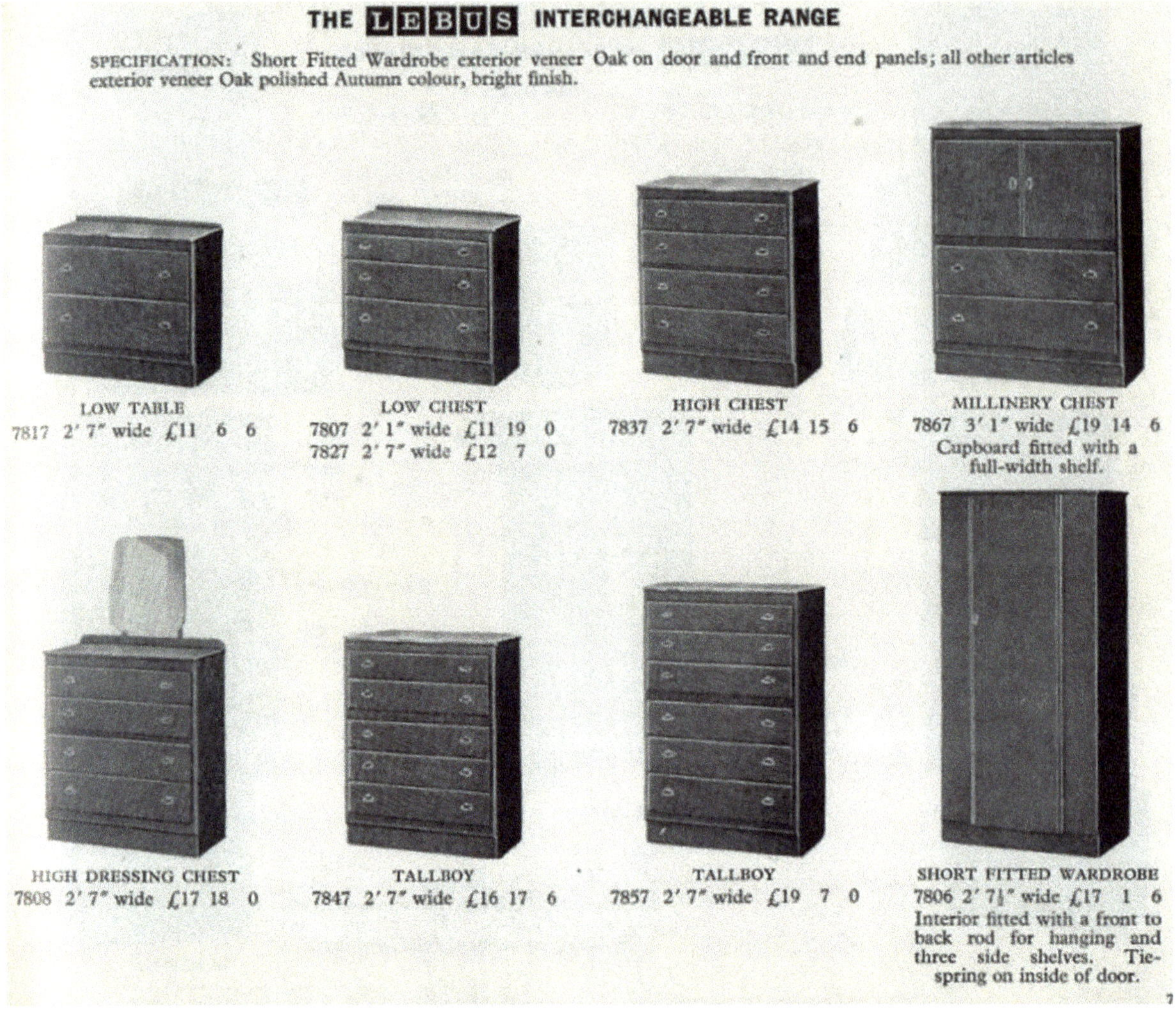

THE LEBUS INTERCHANGEABLE RANGE

SPECIFICATION: Short Fitted Wardrobe exterior veneer Oak on door and front and end panels; all other articles exterior veneer Oak polished Autumn colour, bright finish.

LOW TABLE	LOW CHEST	HIGH CHEST	MILLINERY CHEST
7817 2' 7" wide £11 6 6	7807 2' 1" wide £11 19 0	7837 2' 7" wide £14 15 6	7867 3' 1" wide £19 14 6
	7827 2' 7" wide £12 7 0		Cupboard fitted with a full-width shelf.

HIGH DRESSING CHEST	TALLBOY	TALLBOY	SHORT FITTED WARDROBE
7808 2' 7" wide £17 18 0	7847 2' 7" wide £16 17 6	7857 2' 7" wide £19 7 0	7806 2' 7½" wide £17 1 6
			Interior fitted with a front to back rod for hanging and three side shelves. Tie-spring on inside of door.

The interchangeable oak bedroom range in 1965: despite a sleek look, its veneered, dark, shiny finish stood out against the lighter suites. An oak tallboy looks amazing after being rejuvenated by Annick T. Lynn.

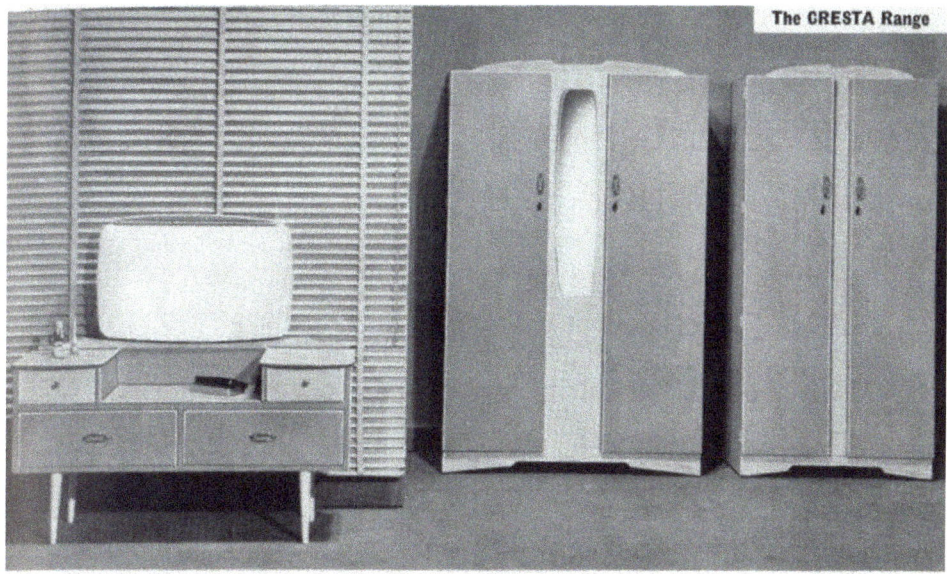

The Cresta suite was described as 'fine grain effect polished oyster grey and sea foam colour with light stone colour Melamine'. A Cresta double wardrobe which matches the suite demonstrates this.

The CAPITOL Range

Exterior veneer Oak with Mahogany veneer contrast polished Honey colour, matt finish or Autumn colour, matt finish.

Divan and Continental Headboards and other matching articles illustrated on pages 16, 17, 18 and 19.

WARDROBE: In two detachable parts. Fitted with a side to side hanging rod.

FITTED WARDROBE: Fitted with a side to centre hanging rod, four side shelves and 18" × 12" mirror and tie-spring on right-hand door.

		£	s	d
SUITE as illustrated		83	19	6
4804	3' 10¼" Wardrobe	26	7	0
4845	5' 4" Sunk-centre Dressing Table	31	5	6
4806	2' 10¼" Fitted Wardrobe	26	7	0

The Capitol range had been launched in 1962 and was still going strong three years on.

The Cameron bedroom suite in mahogany with wardrobe and dressing table is one of five suites featured in the colourful leaflet of bedroom suites. This dressing table in the same design is finished a lighter shade.
(Image courtesy of Micksmitzy)

CANDY-FLOSS COLOURS MORPHED INTO NEON BOLD   145

The Wendover in darker oak with its dressing table.

A collection of up-cycled bedroom furniture. Below and opposite top: a bedside cabinet stylishly updated by Paul at Vintagioustyle and a dressing table which has been given a sophisticated, luxury look with paint and designer wallpaper by Julie Cooper at Amélie Bespoke Furniture. Opposite bottom row, left to right: a combination unit and tallboy with Mark at Justbeauvintage, and a chest of drawers by Keren at Vintage Furniture Revival, Facebook.

CANDY-FLOSS COLOURS MORPHED INTO NEON BOLD

Sideboards and dining furniture

A dining suite continued to be a requisite in the sixties home. A mix of modern as well as traditional designs was on offer. A couple of oak suites, dark stained with glossy finish, are throwbacks almost certainly to the designs pre-eminent in the immediate post-World War Two period and, to an extent, to those of even earlier. Of 28 individual dining-room suites on offer, 26 had natural wood veneers and two had man-made.

Since each furniture piece making up a suite had its own catalogue number, it seems likely that these were available to purchase separately.

In addition to the suites there was a choice of seven sideboards available to purchase individually. Most were six feet one inch in length (except 7731, at five feet four inches, and 7651, at four feet seven inches). Four sideboards were finished in wood veneers and three in man-made. Suggestions were made in the catalogue as to which dining tables – extendable or space-saving drop leaf – would best match a sideboard, along with dining chairs. In effect, these were the same as those which had been listed as part of a suite.

From the considerable variety available in the catalogue's dining-room section the eventual consumer had, effectively, a completely free choice over buying matching furniture or a mixture of styles and finishes to create their own look.

Lebus had a stained ('Autumn' shade), shiny-finished oak offering in a traditional style, just as it had for a good number of years. Alongside the sideboard and dining chairs came a choice of dining tables. The gate-leg table along with the sideboard and dining chairs collectively made up the Bexhill suite. With an alternative choice of draw-leaf table, along with the sideboard and chairs, this collectively made up the Culworth suite. It was the choice of dining table which effectively determined the name of the suite. To add further variety, the seats of the dining chairs in 'leathercloth' (faux leather) were available either in one of the shades described as 'Rose' or in (dark) green.

An alternate, fresher, modern offering in oak but with a light shade ('honey' colour) came in the form of either the Hounslow suite with its draw-leaf table 7684 (pictured) or the Brierley suite with its gate-leg table 7673. (The matching sideboard 7682 with drawers of teak veneer contrast was the same for both suites.) Further choices came in the form of the vinyl seat pad for the chairs 7680, which could be black, green, red or off-white.

SIDEBOARD: Fitted with a full-width shelf in each cupboard. Top drawer divided and bottom covered with blue plastic material for cutlery.
DINING CHAIRS: Fitted with loose seats in brown or green leathercloth.
110

THE BEXHILL SUITE			£63 6 0
Exterior veneer Oak polished Autumn colour, bright finish.			
2211	4′ 7½″ Sideboard	... ...	£26 19 0
9034	Gate-leg Table		£19 7 0
	3′ 0″ × 1′ 2″ closed: 3′ 0″ × 4′ 11″ extended.		
3450	Dining Chairs, each	... ...	£4 5 0
THE CULWORTH SUITE			**£57 15 6**
With 4074 Draw-leaf Table inset	... ...		£13 16 6
	2′ 6″ × 3′ 0″ closed: 2′ 6″ × 4′ 6″ extended.		

CANDY-FLOSS COLOURS MORPHED INTO NEON BOLD 149

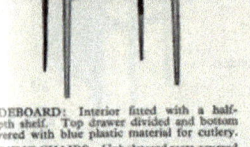

Teak was a popular choice in the 1960s and several suites were built around teak-veneered sideboards on offer in 1965. The Crawley and Keswick suites were built around the four-foot-one-inch teak-veneered sideboard 7622 along with dining chairs 4280. The gate-leg table 4283 made up the Crawley suite and the draw-leaf table 7624 made up the Keswick suite.

The adjacent page of the catalogue made suggestions of dining chairs which would harmonise: the 7600 with seat pad upholstered in moquette of tan, green, red, grey or black vinyl, and the 7640 with full back rest and seat pad covered in vinyl – black, green, red or off-white. By combining the sideboard with one of the two tables and choice of one set of dining chairs from the two listed, it was possible to build up *four* different suites. (The sideboard 7601 is a given in each of them.)

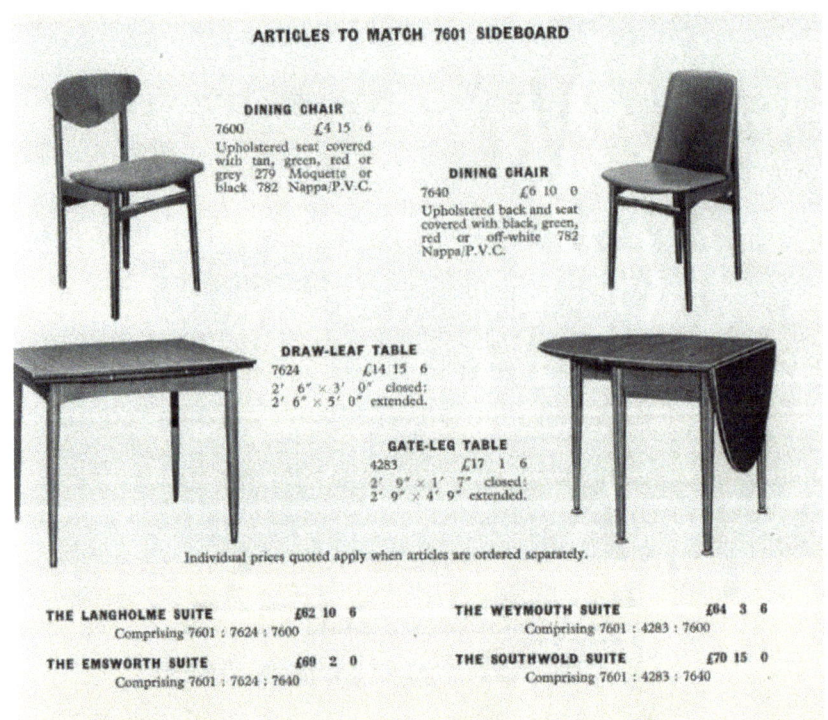

With the choice of gate-leg table 4283, the Weymouth suite uses the 7600 chairs and the Southwold the 7640. Similarly, draw-leaf table 7624 combines with the 7600 chairs to form the Langholme suite, and with the 7640 chairs to form the Emsworth.

Altogether there were six colours for the upholstery for the various chairs on offer.

One sideboard on offer was a mix of mahogany wood veneer, and walnut and burr walnut Melamine veneers. The legs were ebonised with brass ferrules and glides. This dining table and chairs found in Barney McGrew's vintage furniture shop are a close match. A further set of chairs have been given this fabulous makeover.

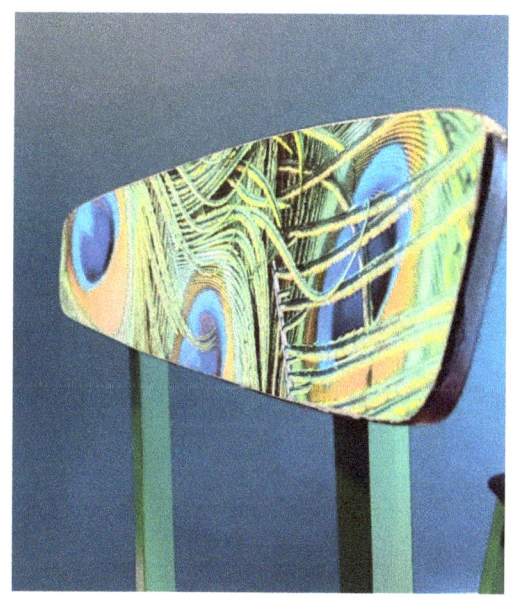

CANDY-FLOSS COLOURS MORPHED INTO NEON BOLD 151

This gate-leg table is a close match for the 7733, which was a suggested pairing with a maple Formica sideboard.

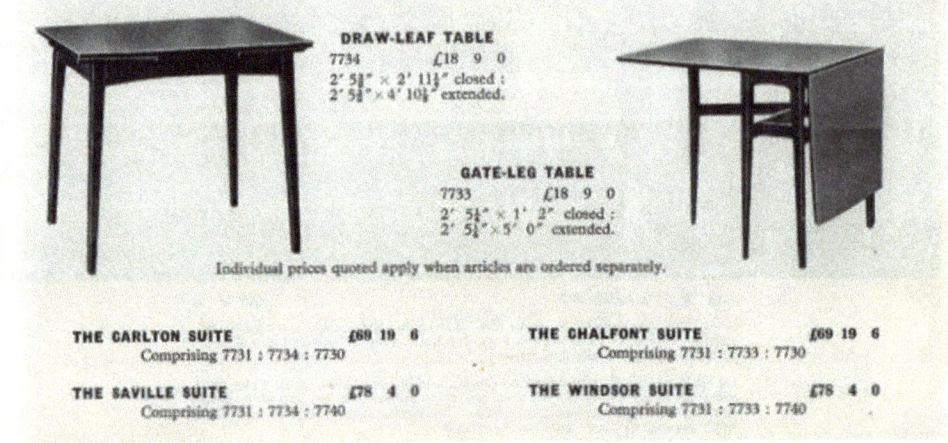

Showcasing some of the Lebus sideboards from the mid-sixties. Above: Siobhan has opted for a simple yet sophisticated paint treatment of this mid-1960s sideboard. This sideboard was commissioned by Heal's department store, London.

CANDY-FLOSS COLOURS MORPHED INTO NEON BOLD   153

Lounge

There were 30 individual three-piece suite designs on offer. The majority of these came with the option of a sofa to sit three people, except for nine suites which offered a two-seat sofa. There were eight easy-/armchair designs which could be bought individually.

The catalogue entry in 1965 for the low–mid-priced Silverdale three-piece suite at a cost of just over £70, consisting of a three-seater sofa 5696 and two chairs 5695. This was the only suite in which colour choices were specified. Options available were described thus: 'Classic presentation is in olive green, walnut, red or smoke colour, 787 Astrakhan Nappa (high-performance faux leather that is soft and supple) with contrasting 780R off white Nappa on sides of backs and insides of arms. Alternatively, the contrasts can be omitted and Astrakhan Nappa used all over. If required 780 can be used with, or without 780R contrasts. Gold colour welts and buttons.' These colours harmonise with the dining-chair seat fabrics. A number of suites came with a choice of four different cover materials (and in some cases six) which, in effect, ramped up the choices. It is assumed sales representatives carried upholstery fabric samples with them.

154 LOVING LEBUS

The least expensive of the suites were the Cambrian, with two chairs 0671 and three-seater sofa 0672, and the Cannock, with the alternative two-seater sofa 0670. Added to the mix was a choice of four different coloured fabrics for both suites, which in ascending price order were E, L, D and C. The Cambrian prices ranged from a little over £51 to a little over £61 and the Cannock from a little over £44 to a little over £53.

The most expensive of the suites were the Caversham, with two chairs 5181 and three-seater sofa 5182, and the Thames, with the alternative three-seater sofa 5856. The difference between the two suites was that the Thames suite came in one upholstery option – hide effect superlon 781 – with matching seat covers for only £143 14s 3d. The Caversham suite was offered in a choice of four different coloured fabrics, which in ascending price order were C, H, M and U, from a little over £121 to £143 14s 3d.

The Melrose three-piece suite with three-seater studio couch (sofa-bed). Modern in appearance, it was covered in a mid-brown fabric with a linen/cotton appearance with seat pads in a matching material with off-white squares. The hand ends of the arm rests were finished with an Afrormosia wood protection panel. (Images courtesy of Max)

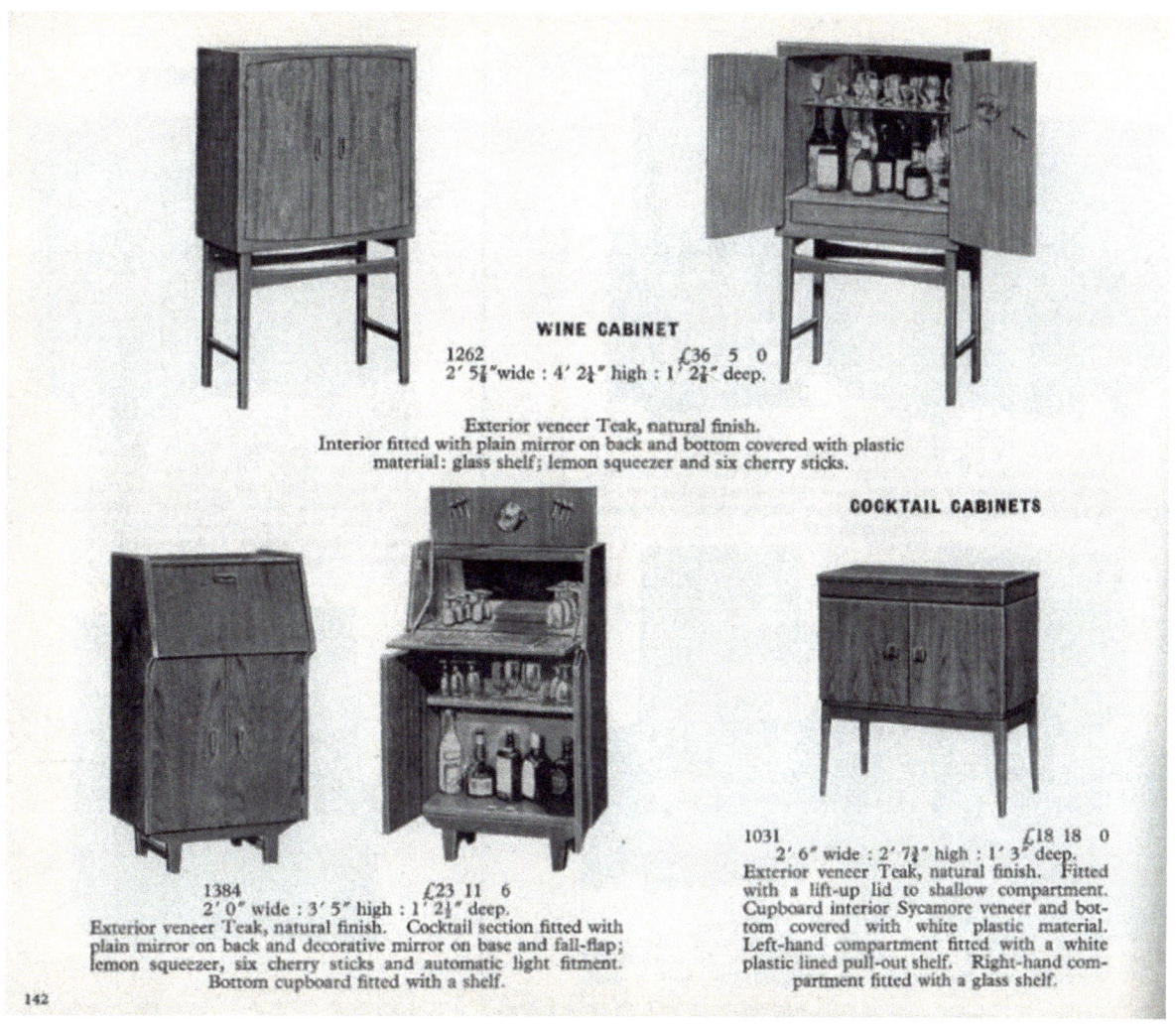

Home entertaining – cocktail cabinets.

The mix of traditional and modern in the 1965 catalogue is exemplified in the miscellaneous mix of furniture to complete the home. There were coffee tables, bureaux, bookcases, sleek modern cocktail cabinets and china cabinets – some reminiscent of pre-war designs with their cabriole legs.

A furniture piece which stood out was the fold-away home office with its stylish design and finish. The unit is pictured with a typewriter – perhaps a reflection of the fact that some professional typists worked at home either for child-care reasons or because of freelance work. The cabinet is available in three veneered finishes: walnut matt finish, mahogany polished amber colour matt finish, and teak in natural finish. When opened, there was a knee space, and the inside of the door when opened at a 90-degree angle offered a further work surface.

Having introduced the room divider in the fifties, Lebus offered a choice of two room divider units. Clearly, these were popular in the modern home to delineate space.

Alongside the room dividers were a selection of modular, flexible wall units. These were a stylish addition to the modern lounge since they allowed for display and storage of books, ornaments (coloured ceramics and glassware), television, vinyl records and record players.

2504 £16 7 0
3' 6" wide : 3' 8" high : 1' 0¼" deep.
Exterior veneer Walnut. Fitted with two glass shelves and lined back.

A china cabinet from the 1965 catalogue, model number 2504, has been the inspiration for Percy and Albert of Percy and Albert interiors. They have found two of these and lovingly updated, decorated and repurposed both into gin cabinets using different paint and designer wallpapers.

HOME OFFICE
3' 9" wide : 2' 5¾" high : 1' 7" deep.
1165   £32 8 6
    Exterior veneer Walnut, matt finish.
2096   £30 5 0
    Exterior veneer Mahogany polished Amber colour, matt finish.
6550   £36 4 6
    Exterior veneer Teak, natural finish.

Home office. Quite an amazing piece of furniture which, when closed, looks like a modest cabinet and yet opens up to create a small office area at home.

A choice of room dividers, a furniture concept which Lebus first introduced as part of its Link range almost a decade earlier.

6518   £30 17 6
3' 11¾" wide : 5' 8¾" high : 1' 0" deep.
Exterior veneer Teak, natural finish. Cupboard divided into two compartments; right-hand compartment fitted with a shelf.

1009   £29 1 0
3' 0" wide : 5' 8¼" high : 11¾" deep.
Exterior veneer Mahogany polished Amber colour. Bottom cupboard divided into two compartments; right-hand compartment fitted with a shelf.

Flexible, modular wall units were a popular choice in the 1960s home. Note how the television unit dominates. The unit was a useful display and storage space for a radio, record player and records, glassware, best china, books, magazines, ornaments and so forth.

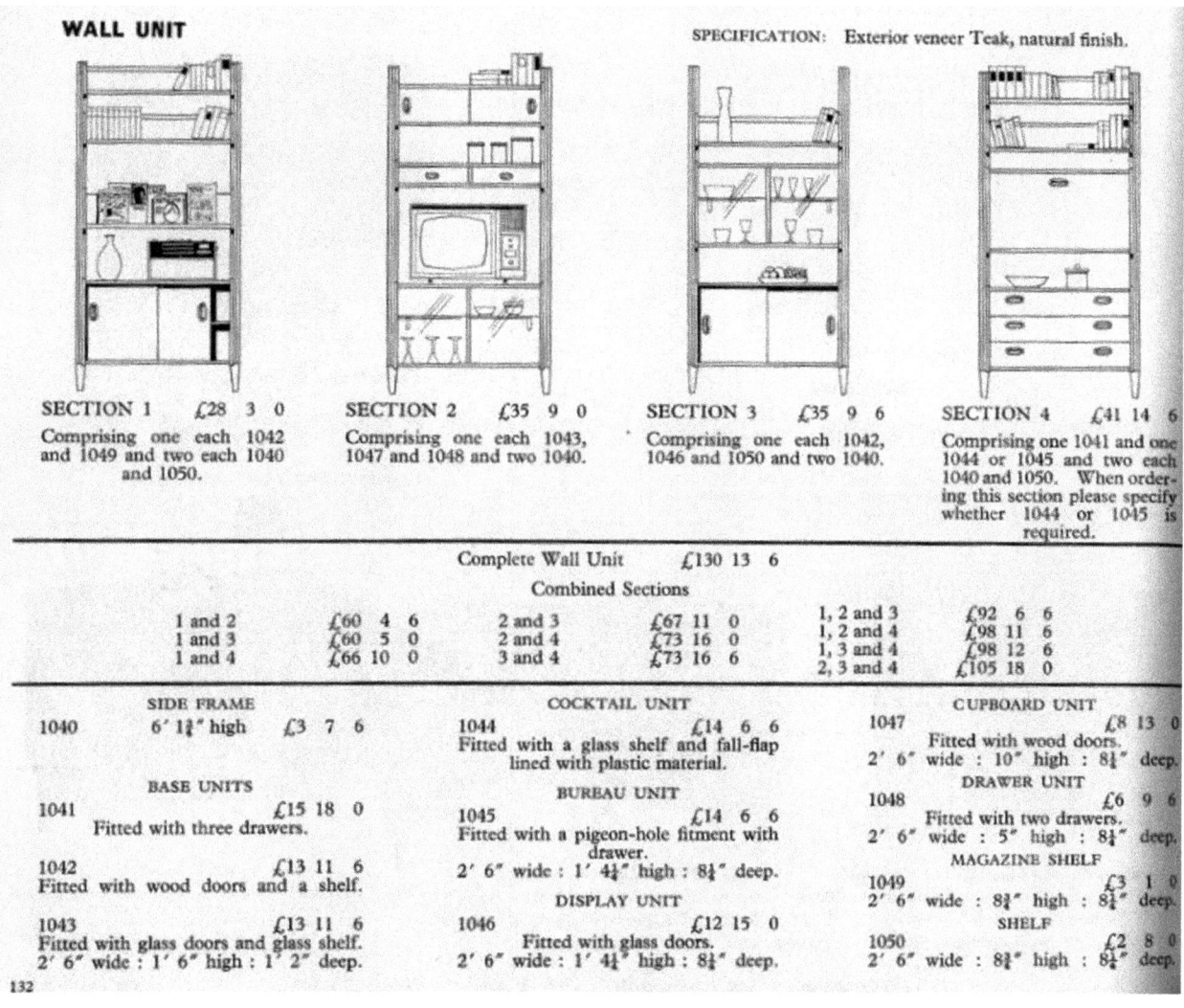

WALL UNIT SPECIFICATION: Exterior veneer Teak, natural finish.

SECTION 1 £28 3 0
Comprising one each 1042 and 1049 and two each 1040 and 1050.

SECTION 2 £35 9 0
Comprising one each 1043, 1047 and 1048 and two 1040.

SECTION 3 £35 9 6
Comprising one each 1042, 1046 and 1050 and two 1040.

SECTION 4 £41 14 6
Comprising one 1041 and one 1044 or 1045 and two each 1040 and 1050. When ordering this section please specify whether 1044 or 1045 is required.

Complete Wall Unit £130 13 6
Combined Sections

1 and 2	£60 4 6	2 and 3	£67 11 0	1, 2 and 3	£92 6 6
1 and 3	£60 5 0	2 and 4	£73 16 0	1, 2 and 4	£98 11 6
1 and 4	£66 10 0	3 and 4	£73 16 6	1, 3 and 4	£98 12 6
				2, 3 and 4	£105 18 0

SIDE FRAME
1040   6' 1¾" high   £3 7 6

BASE UNITS
1041   £15 18 0
Fitted with three drawers.

1042   £13 11 6
Fitted with wood doors and a shelf.

1043   £13 11 6
Fitted with glass doors and glass shelf.
2' 6" wide : 1' 6" high : 1' 2" deep.

COCKTAIL UNIT
1044   £14 6 6
Fitted with a glass shelf and fall-flap lined with plastic material.

BUREAU UNIT
1045   £14 6 6
Fitted with a pigeon-hole fitment with drawer.
2' 6" wide : 1' 4¼" high : 8¼" deep.

DISPLAY UNIT
1046   £12 15 0
Fitted with glass doors.
2' 6" wide : 1' 4¼" high : 8¼" deep.

CUPBOARD UNIT
1047   £8 13 0
Fitted with wood doors.
2' 6" wide : 10" high : 8¼" deep.

DRAWER UNIT
1048   £6 9 6
Fitted with two drawers.
2' 6" wide : 5" high : 8¼" deep.

MAGAZINE SHELF
1049   £3 1 0
2' 6" wide : 8¾" high : 8¼" deep.

SHELF
1050   £2 8 0
2' 6" wide : 8¾" high : 8¼" deep.

Kitchens

Lebus offered a range of modern kitchen furniture that was bright and colourful as well as offering flexible and practical solutions for sixties living. There were modular free-standing units (much like the larders from the fifties but sleeker and with a modern edginess). There were free-standing base cabinets which could be fitted around cookers and the sink and draining-board areas.

There were also matching cabinets that could be affixed to the wall above the free-standing units to create the feel of a fitted kitchen.

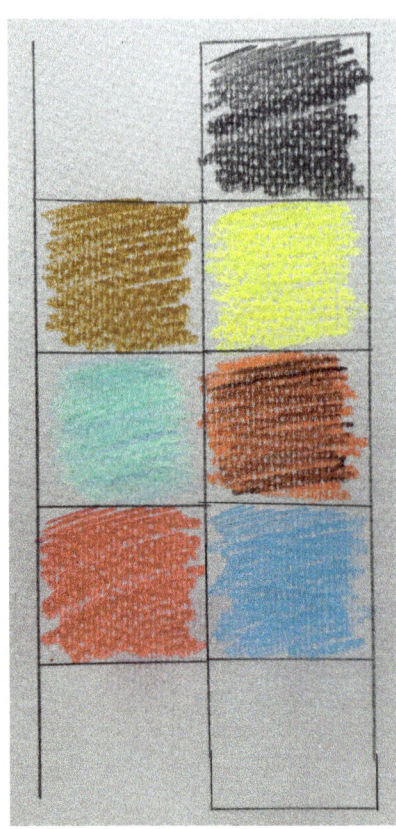

The Lebus free-standing flexible units were ideal for the modern kitchen, especially if the kitchen space was small. Whilst fitted kitchens were available, not everyone could afford to have them, in part because of the fitting process. These were a useful alternative. They could also be taken with you when moving house.

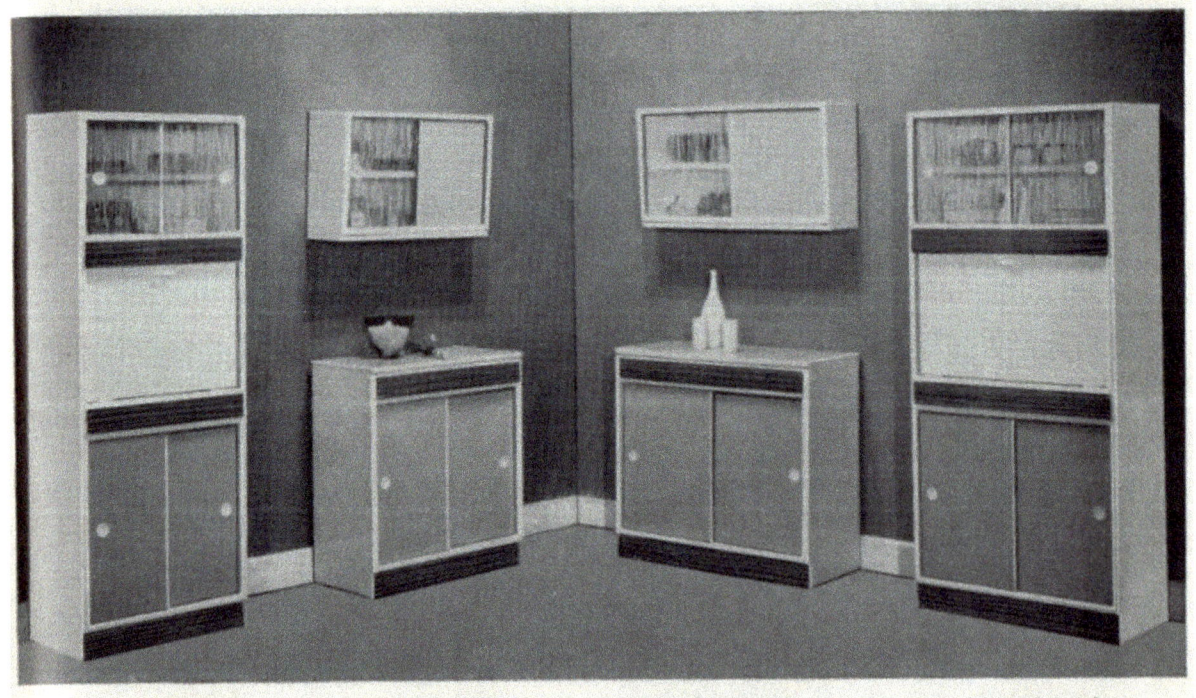

KITCHEN CABINET	WALL UNIT	WALL UNIT	KITCHEN CABINET
2651 £14 15 6	2655 £6 5 0	2653 £7 8 0	2650 £16 8 6
2' 0" wide : 5' 8½" high : 1' 4¼" deep.	2' 6" wide : 1' 7" high : 10" deep. Fitted with a full-length shelf.	3' 0" wide : 1' 7" high : 10" deep. Fitted with a full-length shelf.	2' 6" wide : 5' 8½" high : 1' 4¼" deep.
		2656 £8 13 0	
		4' 0" wide : 1' 7" high : 10" deep. Fitted with a full-length shelf.	
	BASE UNIT	BASE UNIT	KITCHEN CABINETS: Top cupboard fitted with a shelf 7" wide. Drawer divided and bottom covered with blue plastic material. Bottom cupboard fitted with a shelf 7" wide.
	2652 £9 17 0	2654 £11 9 6	
	2' 6" wide : 2' 9" high : 1' 4¼" deep.	3' 0" wide : 2' 9" high : 1' 4¼" deep.	BASE UNITS: Fitted with a drawer divided and bottom covered with blue plastic material. Cupboard fitted with a shelf 7" wide.

SPECIFICATION: Exterior white enamel. Drawer fronts, plinths and Kitchen Cabinet front panels Walnut grained Melamine. Sliding doors mushroom, lemon, copper, turquoise, blue, red or yellow colour enamel. Kitchen Cabinet fall-flap inside and Base Unit tops covered with beige marble patterned Melamine.

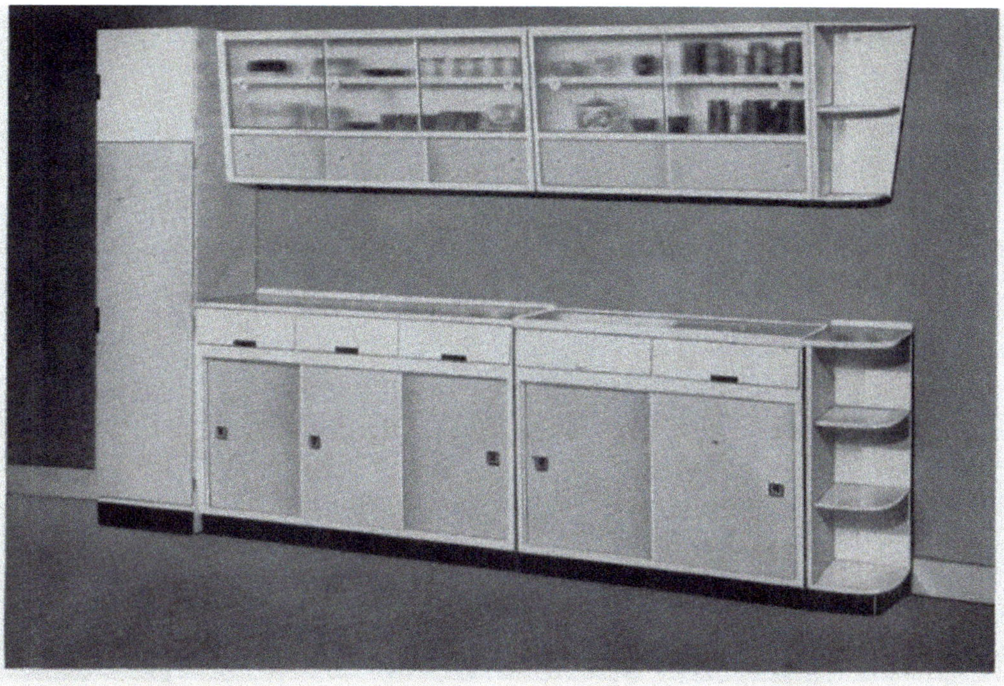

Top row– left to right: 6542 4′ 6″ and 6541 3′ 6″ Wall Units, 6539 Wall End Unit.
Bottom row– left to right: 6544 1′ 6″ Storage Cupboard, 6533 4′ 5¼″ Base Unit, 6536 3′ 6″ Sink Unit, 6546 Base End Unit.

THE NAPOLI KITCHEN RANGE

SPECIFICATION: Exterior white enamel with black plinths. Work-tops covered with charcoal Capri pattern Formica. Blue, red or yellow enamel doors. Wall Units: white enamel interiors. Sink Units: white vitreous enamel with chain, plug and waste fitting; taps are not included.

STORAGE CUPBOARD

6544		£16 7 6

1′ 6″ wide : 6′ 5¼″ high : 1′ 7″ deep.
Top compartment fitted with a shelf and white enamel door. Bottom compartment fitted with three shelves.

WALL UNITS

	Width		
6538	2′0″	(*Not illustrated*)	£6 5 0
6540	3′0″	(*Illustrated on page 123*)	£7 15 6
6541	3′6″		£8 12 0
6542	4′6″		£10 5 0

1′11¼″ high : 11¼″ deep.
Top cupboards fitted with a shelf. 6540-1-2: Two compartments in bottom cupboards.

WALL END UNITS

6539		£3 6 0

11¼″ wide : 1′ 11¼″ high : 11¼″ deep.
Reversible for left or right-hand.

BASE UNITS

	Width		
6534	1′9″	(*Illustrated on page 123*)	£11 0 0
6531	2′11¼″	(*Not illustrated*)	£15 8 6
6532	3′5¼″	(*Illustrated on page 123*)	£17 5 0
6533	4′5¼″		£21 6 6

3′1″ high : 1′6¼″ deep.
6531-2-3: Left-hand drawers divided and bottom lined for cutlery, shelf in cupboards.

BASE END UNITS

6545	(*Illustrated on page 123*)	£7 4 0
6546		£7 4 0

11¼″ wide : 3′1″ high : 1′6¼″ deep.

122

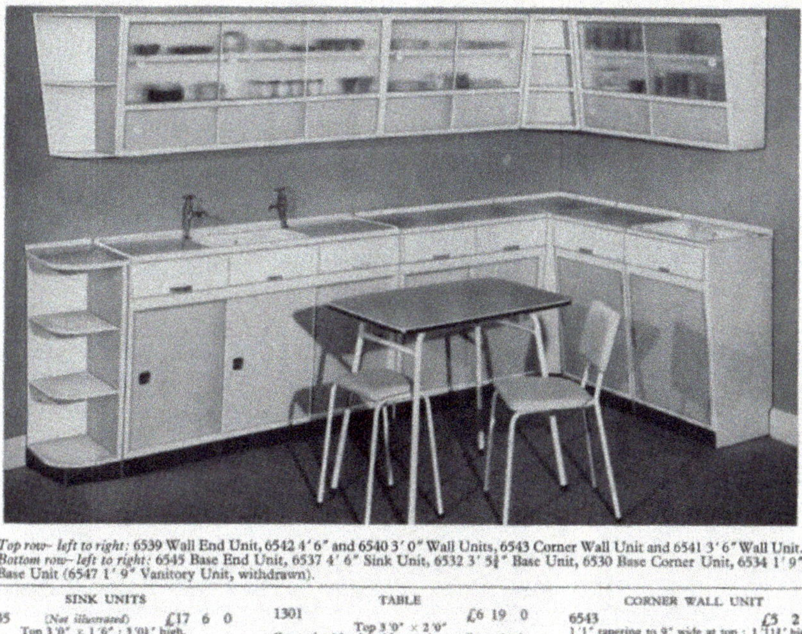

Top row– left to right: 6539 Wall End Unit, 6542 4′ 6″ and 6540 3′ 0″ Wall Units, 6543 Corner Wall Unit and 6541 3′ 6″ Wall Unit.
Bottom row– left to right: 6545 Base End Unit, 6537 4′ 6″ Sink Unit, 6532 3′ 5¼″ Base Unit, 6530 Base Corner Unit, 6534 1′ 9″ Base Unit (6547 1′ 9″ Vanitory Unit, withdrawn).

SINK UNITS

6535	(*Not illustrated*)	£17 6 0

Top 3′0″ × 1′6″ : 3′0¼″ high.

6536	(*Illustrated on page 122*)	£18 17 6

Top 3′0¼″ × 1′6¼″ : 3′0¼″ high.
Single drainers: reversible for left or right-hand units. Fitted with one drawer and shelf in cupboard.

6537		£25 5 0

Top 4′6″ × 1′6″ : 3′0¼″ high.
Double drainer. Fitted with two drawers and shelf in cupboard.

TABLE

1301		£6 19 0

Top 3′0″ × 2′0″
Covered with plain blue, red or yellow plastic material.

CHAIR

1302		£2 18 6

STOOL

1303		£1 18 0

Upholstered back and seats covered with plain blue, red or yellow plastic material. White stove enamelled tubular frames.

CORNER WALL UNIT

6543		£5 2 0

1′1″ tapering to 9″ wide at top : 1′11¼″ high : 6¼″ deep.

BASE CORNER UNIT

6530		£3 7 6

Top 1′7″ × 1′7″ : 3′1″ high.

123

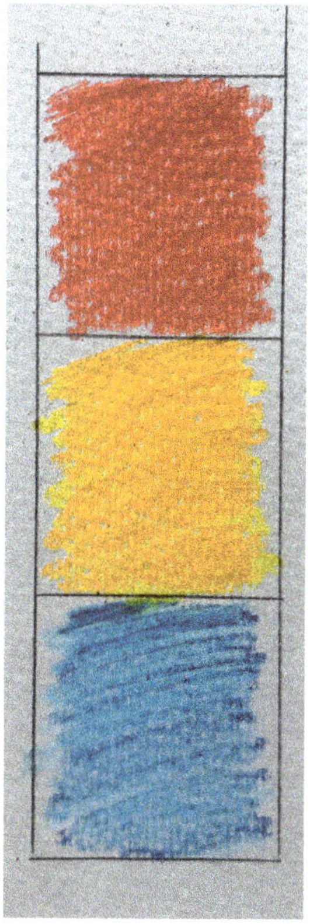

The Lebus Napoli kitchen range was designed to provide a sleek, streamlined integrated kitchen. In essence, this was a fitted kitchen.

The outside of the units was white, with walnut-grained melamine plinths and cabinet fronts. The splash of modern colour came with the choices for the cabinets' sliding doors: mushroom grey, lemon yellow, copper, turquoise, baby blue, red and yellow ochre.

In addition, there was the Napoli range of kitchen furniture. This furniture was the epitome of the modern fitted kitchen because not only could the base units in this range be fitted closely around cookers and affixed to the wall, but the availability of a specific unit in which to set and fix a sink and draining board brought integration to the kitchen. Lebus even supplied the sink and draining board, made of white vitreous enamel. Modular, matching wall units, a tall 'broom' cupboard, integrated corner units (base and for the wall) and seamless worktops completed the sleek, modern fitted kitchen. The units were white with black plinths and charcoal-grey Formica worktops; the colour-burst was in the choice of the cabinet doors – red, yellow or baby blue.

Lebus offered the Gayday range of kitchen tables, chairs and compact storage units for bedsits, studios and kitchenettes. Constructed from modern materials, these came with hard-wearing plastic tabletops and cabinet surfaces, and wipe-able plastic seat coverings. In white teamed with bright modern colours of red, yellow or blue, suites were either of tubular metal frames coated in enamel white or in the more traditional style of wood and painted white.

By the mid-sixties Lebus offered a lot of furniture – over 600 separate pieces in all. Unlike some furniture manufacturers that specialised in producing furniture for just one room, concentrating on manufacturing only bedroom or dining ranges or individual suites, Lebus was making any and all furniture required for the home. It was doing so because, on the one hand, it was 'the largest furniture factory in the world' and, on the other, it needed to secure revenues over and above its investments. The market was saturated with Lebus. The firm was working at full capacity and yet it was just about breaking even.

There was fierce competition in the furniture industry, with an estimated 1,500 firms vying for business. Manufacturers had a choice of raw materials to work with including chipboard and melamine. Fashions were trending and consumers had a wealth of choice. Oak furniture stained a medium to dark colour was falling out of fashion. The interchangeable oak bedroom range, a staple amongst Lebus's offerings and a best-seller for many years, had been falling out of favour with the buying public. What had once kept the business soaring above its competitors was now weighing it down. Lebus witnessed the stock of its competitors filling the spaces it once occupied in the windows of independent retailers. It had to concede to the unenviable fact that customers were indeed no longer *as in love* with Lebus furniture as they once had been.

As Lebus looked around at contemporaneous furniture firms, the company took hope and inspiration from the fact that many had come through difficult patches, experienced similar difficulties and yet bounced back into profit. Moreover, there were companies whose fortunes had been turned around through the gamble of launching brand-new furniture products – E. Gomme with its G-Plan range was a prime example.

Looking briefly into Lebus's main competitors

E. Gomme shared similarities with Lebus. The business was started by a sole trader, Ebenezer Gomme, and had produced high-end, quality furniture products since the turn of the century. In the mid-fifties it launched a new brand of furniture designed for the modern age. The G-Plan brand launched in 1953 and grew in popularity such that it overshadowed Lebus's Link furniture brand of 1957. The company's fortunes waned for a period in the mid-fifties. When Donald Gomme left, the business became a public company, and sales had picked up significantly by the end of the decade and the start of the sixties. The designs of Danish-born Ib Kofod-Larsen were a factor in this change of fortune. His G-Plan Danish range of teak furniture caused something of a 'revolution' with the furniture-buying public, and the product was still selling in volume well into the seventies.

Ercol shared the fact that the business was established in the UK by an, in this case Italian, immigrant and was manufacturing solid wood furniture using beech and elm. It had perfected the art of steam bending wood to make sleek furniture and offered finishes that were shades lighter than the veneers favoured by Lebus. Ercol's products were pricier by comparison to Lebus but were a popular choice to consumers.

Parker Knoll was a long-established company with a reputation for quality upholstered sofas and chairs, and much like Lebus, the company drew on its wartime manufacturing experiences and applied its engineering knowledge to furniture. Its trump cards were the recliner chair and the chrome-framed, black-leather swivel chair. The company's reputation had grown through the sixties such that Parker Knoll was regarded as the best of the rest, and its upholstered pieces were offered in an adventurous array of coloured fabrics for a buying public embracing mix-and-match interior styling.

Stag, a Nottingham-based manufacturer, had similarities with Lebus – it manufactured machine-made, wood-veneered cabinet and upholstered furniture for the dining room and bedroom, aimed at the mass market. The hiring of married couple John and Sylvia Reid (architects by profession) as designers proved a masterstroke. The 'C' range bedroom suite launched in 1953 – boxy in appearance, with recess handles, and offered in a choice of lighter oak or darker walnut – was embraced by consumers. However, it was their teak dining-room furniture, the 'S' suite, with its oval dining table and sideboard set on satin polished steel legs which enchanted the furniture-buying public.

Merrow Associates was a brand-new company set up in 1965 by an ambitious young designer called Richard Young. With Danish-inspired designs, they offered high-end pieces – sideboards, cabinets and tables made with highly polished rosewood, glass and steel.

Investigate the Europa Challenge

Europa furniture is made by the firm that was one of Britain's oldest and has now turned itself into Europe's most modern. The furniture first appeared just two years ago and was quickly recognised as transforming the entire British scene.

Because, of all Britain's furniture firms, only Europa is able to issue this Challenge: show us any other furniture that looks as beautiful, that's made with the same degree of care, that you can buy at anything like the price. It can't be done.

Investigate the Europa Challenge. There's a 36-page two-part booklet. It tells you furniture secrets, the dozens of things to look at. Look close, look hard, we say. At Europa designs for bedrooms, livingrooms, sitting-rooms. With chairs and sofas, for instance, see how we challenged ourselves to make them not only the most comfortable but also the most beautiful. With exciting new shapes and fabrics. And interesting new ways of shaping your living area.

The San Remo sofa units and matching chair in this picture are a case in point. They're how to get as much or as little sofa as you want and shaped just the way you want. As traditional two-armed sofas, or filling a whole wall if you put two units side by side, or *curved* (Curved in different ways. Because you've 1-seater or 2-seater or 3-seater units to link with the corner unit.)

Check for ideas that *work*, we also say. The San Remo corner unit has got its shape right, fits into a corner beautifully. (Corner units are meant to fit into corners but don't always, you'll be told.)

Go on looking. The more you look, the more you realise that Europa is everything it's cracked up to be.

Photograph: Capitol Hill, Rome. Europa wall units: base units from £20.0.0; other units from £7.10.0. Coffee table, £12.10.0. Terranova recliner chair, from £55.0.0. San Remo corner group — two 2-seater sofa units linked by corner unit — from £130.0.0. (San Remo sofa units: 1-seater unit — always with one arm — from £27.0.0; 2-seater unit from £36.0.0; 3-seater from £51.0.0; each arm from £6.0.0; corner unit from £46.0.0.) Armchair, from £31.0.0.

FREE For your free copy of "The Europa Challenge" and the name of your nearest Authorised Europa Stockist (only 1 shop in 10 is authorised to sell it), write today to Dept. H.G.5, Europa Furniture Limited, London, N.17.

Name
(Mr./Mrs./Miss) Block letters, please

Address

A magazine advertisement: Investigate the Europa challenge.

Based on what it saw in the industry as a whole, Lebus took the bold decision in 1967 to reinvent itself and launch a brand-new furniture range in which it would place all its investments.

Looking into 1967 – Europa

After a £1.8 million spend on restructuring and reinvention, in the Autumn of 1967 Lebus launched the Europa brand, designed by Cyril Rostgaard.

Rostgaard said: 'it was not the intention to manufacture furniture so avant-garde that it bore no resemblance to what had been done before: there is no question of being adventurous in that sense – we shall not be making furniture which is going to be suspended by wires from the ceiling!' (*Cabinet Maker and Retail Furniture*, 28 October 1966)

Lebus had invested £500,000 in 'robot-like' machinery sourced from Germany – in that regard it was ahead of its rivals. The firm closed all its provincial showrooms, reduced the sales team to just 26 representatives and paired back its list of stockists to a mere 1,350 – a move which caused a degree of resentment amongst the rest of Lebus's loyal independent retailers.

Europa, priced at around 20 percent cheaper than G-Plan, was pitched squarely in the middle of the market: middle-income housewives aged 18 to 35, who were only ten percent of the population but bought 30 percent of furniture.

Kenneth Dean (of Pearl and Dean fame), who had recently helped market G-Plan from losses to profitability, now worked for Lebus. Europa furniture was in some of Europe's capital cities. Dean's marketing strap-line was: 'The "Europa" challenge: show us any other furniture that looks as beautiful, that's made with the same degree of care that you can buy at anything like the price. It can't be done!'

Europa headboard recently for sale on an online auction site.

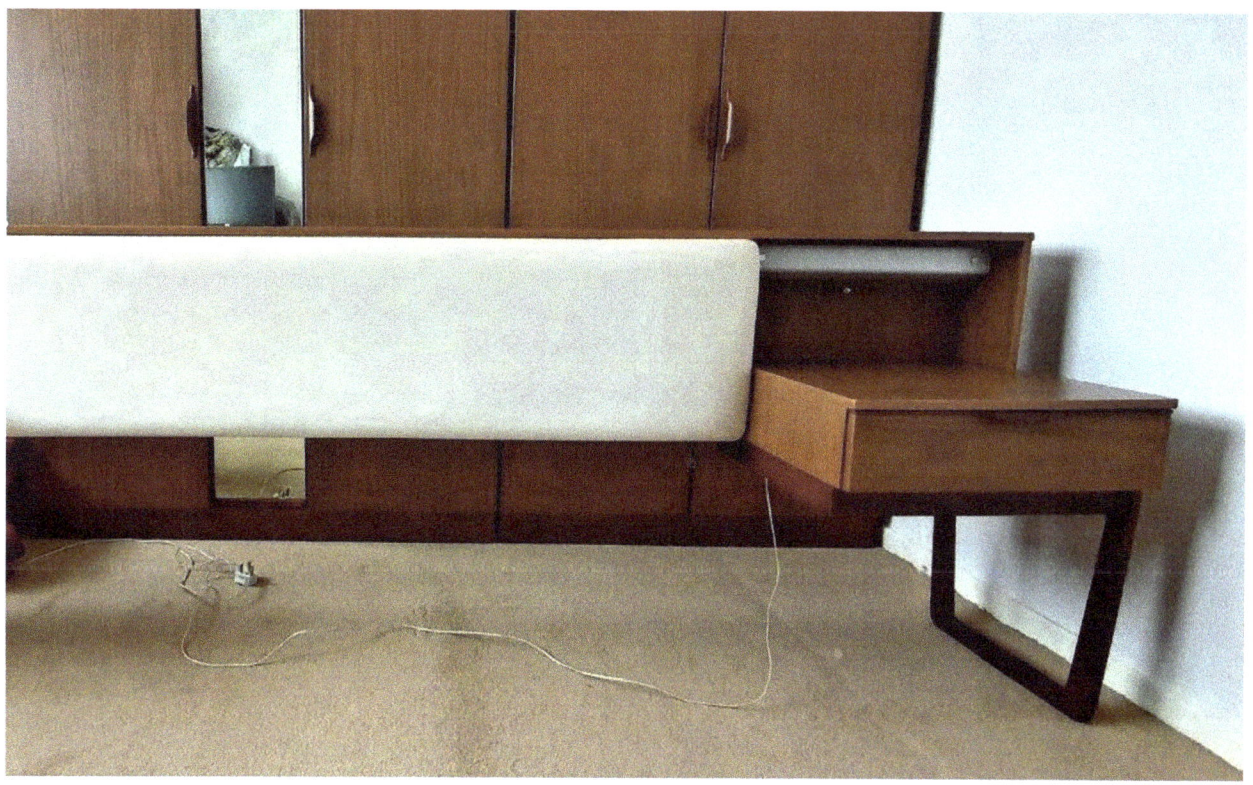

Europa bedroom furniture displayed in a mock-up bedroom setting. The versatile tub chair is featured in this scene. The bedroom range included wardrobes in various sizes, dressing tables in various designs and headboard.

Alternate bedroom set-up with different headboard. Some units were available without the sleigh legs and have been grouped to create the impression of a fitted bedroom.

Europa was showcased at the Ideal Home Exhibition at Olympia in the spring of 1968. Lebus needed the furniture-buying public to love it.

There were 40 different pieces in the Europa range, each with its own catalogue number, including both upholstered and cabinet furniture for the bedroom, dining area and lounge.

The 'tub' chair (produced by the upholstery unit, which remained at Woodley, Reading) was the first furniture piece of the Europa brand to be sale-ready, in the spring of 1967.

The tub chairs were upholstered in polyether foam, covered in a knitted stretch fabric with reversible cushion and zip cover, and with a swivel pedestal base of mild steel finished with satin chrome.

The body of a typical chest of nine drawers was constructed from a combination of chipboard covered with a simulated teak veneer (bought in ready prepared and subsequently glued on site). There were just three drawer sizes, and all drawers fitted any holes of the same size as a result of the close tolerances achieved through a production line of 'robot-like' machines at Tottenham Hale.

BRAGANZA . . .

. . . is the name of this interesting chesterfield group. Interesting because there are 2-seater sofas (shown here) as well as the usual 3-seater illustrated on the right. This suggests a whole new approach to your sitting area. With two sofas rather than one. Put them at right angles or facing each other depending on the shape of your room . . . either way, it looks very cosy. That goes for the designs themselves: low slung (only 2' 1" high) and chunky (2' 7" deep) but rounded on the inside and with deep squishy cushions. NB: cushions unzip for extra-easy cleaning.

8581 Armchair, 3' 3" x 2' 1" x 2' 7". From £39.10.0.
8582 2-seater sofa, 5' 3" x 2' 1" x 2' 7". From £56.0.0.
8583 3-seater sofa, 7' 3" x 2' 1" x 2' 7". From £76.0.0.

2-seater sofa and two chairs from £135.0.0.
3-seater sofa and two chairs from £155.0.0.

Extendable dining table and chairs, and tall sideboard.

CANDY-FLOSS COLOURS MORPHED INTO NEON BOLD

Europa sideboards came in various lengths and drawer and cupboard combinations.

This Europa sideboard has been up-cycled with paint and pattern by Gemma. Ernest Silvestri recently had the same model for sale in its original condition.
(Image of Ernest's sideboard by Suzy Downes)

These modular units had the flexibility of being placed in various combinations. (Image courtesy of Mark at JustBeauHome, eBay)

CANDY-FLOSS COLOURS MORPHED INTO NEON BOLD

The 'sleigh' base frames were of solid teak timber as well as the scalloped handles. Some sets of drawers were offered with alternate low bases and some items were modular – facilitating flexible arrangements.

Initial demand for Europa had been good and, by the middle of 1968, Lebus appeared to be winning a battle to reverse the pattern of loss making, with hopes raised to meet a long-term target of 15 percent return on the capital injection. However, this proved to be overly optimistic and despite a gallant effort, the imbalance between costs and revenue caught up with Lebus. Total losses were announced for the 52-week period ending 31 October 1969 of £1,010,117 (*Weekly Herald*, 29 January 1970). The cabinet-making side of the business collapsed in spring 1970 with devastating effect to employees, to the independent retailers who also made their living by selling Lebus furniture, and to the industry as a whole.

Lebus was able to salvage its upholstery arm and consolidated the business to continue the production of upholstered furniture from its base in Woodley, Reading.

Europa cabinet pieces came in a varied range of choices.
Lidia and Niko from Elverum Workshop made this cool arrangement.

Still Loving Lebus: Lebus Upholstery

Silver Anniversary at the Woodley plant in 1975

The year 1975 was special for Lebus – it celebrated 25 years in Woodley, Reading. The local paper had a four-page pull-out ('Lebus Silver Anniversary: Celebrating 25 Years of Upholstery Production at Woodley', *Reading Post*, 23 July 1975). The year was indeed a milestone – a time for both looking back over the last half-century, as well as looking forward.

Of course, upholstery production at Lebus went way back, initially occurring at the Tabernacle Street premises in London's East End, before a few years at Tottenham Hale during World War Two. After the closure of the cabinet-making plant in Tottenham Hale, and whilst Lebus concentrated mainly on upholstered products (since the Reading plant was set up this way), the requirements for the production of a number of Europa cabinet furniture pieces were also accommodated. This was on a minimal scale as compared to Tottenham Hale.

Rostgaard transferred to Woodley and utilised his design skills on upholstery (as well as a few cabinet pieces) and was elevated to the board as design director.

The *Reading Post* article was keen to stress the fact that a community that had known its Woodley plant as an upholstered furniture manufacturer should be aware that the company still supplied 'furniture for every room in your home'.

In 1975, Lebus Upholstery added its own versions of the free-standing units for the bedroom which had been trending since the mid-sixties to the market mix. By offering units in each range in various sizes, the illusion of the bespoke fitted room could be achieved by the consumer. The raw material was chipboard with a veneer of simulated wood or white melamine. Purchases were likely delivered flat-packed for home assembly. In 1975 a white melamine and teak finished suite comprising the latest four-drawer, knee-hole dressing table and 'his' and 'hers' wardrobes with mirror cost £193 with VAT.

The autumnal hues brown, beige, yellow ochre, orange and oatmeal were the most popular choices for three-piece suites of the mid-seventies. The leather-look was also very much on trend. Tubular steel furniture, popular from the mid-seventies onwards, was also in the mix.

What might be lurking behind the sofa…?

In 1975, with a turnover of around £15 million per annum, 465 employees and a sizeable fleet of 50 delivery vans, the future looked set for Lebus Upholstery. However, the company knew as well as any other UK furniture manufacturer of the time that the future is never that predictable.

Just a few years on, and the company's finances were under increasing pressure. Oliver and Anthony decided, after what must have been an excruciating tussle between emotion and

Model Numbers	Width	Depth	Height
4181/L Single Unit Left Arm Facing	32½"	36"	32"
4181/N Single Unit No Arms	29"	36"	32"
4181/T Shaped Table Melamine Top	40"	40"	15"
4181/R Single Unit Right Arm Facing	32½"	36"	32"

Europa

Milan

Take one look at the Milan and you're half-way there.
Test the soft, deeply filled suite and you'll know why Milan is one of the most sought after suites around. It's plush. It's sumptuously comfortable. And it embodies all the very best in European design. Finished in tough Boccara vinyl, the Milan is available in curved corner units or conventional suite.
Whichever you choose, you'll be getting a magnificent piece of furniture.

Model Numbers	Width	Depth	Height
3571/3 3 Piece Suite			
3571 Chair	40"	40"	31"
3573 Sofa	80½"	40"	31"

Illustrated 3571/3 in Boccara Vinyl 843/4/A Left and 3571/L.N.N.R. in 843/4/G Right.

Milan Registered Design No. 960630.
See page 20 for details of alternative covers.

Model Numbers	Width	Depth	Height
3571/L Single Unit Left Arm Facing	32"	40"	31"
3571/R Single Unit Right Arm Facing	32"	40"	31"
3571/N Single Unit No Arms	37"	39"	31"
3579 Rondo Pouffe	Diameter 40"		Height 14"

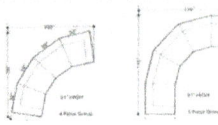

Seventies style: Lebus upholstered suites.

Top: Upholstery workshop at Tabernacle Street before World War One.

Middle: Upholstery conveyor belt at Woodley, Reading, c.1960.

Bottom: Lebus Upholstery today.

mentation, to sell out, thus ending a 140-year family association with the business.

The twilight years, 1979–2005

In July 1979 PMA Holdings bought the business. Malcolm Meredith had built up a group of furniture businesses including Gower Furniture and Bridgecraft Upholstery. The industry was facing difficult trading conditions, however, and the 1980–1981 recession saw a further drop in demand for furniture. PMA Holdings went into receivership in 1981.

Imports of European furniture – which was cheaper than British made – had increased throughout the seventies after the United Kingdom joined the Common Market in 1973. By now, furniture retail outlets ran along supermarket lines. They became bigger, were located out of town and had ample parking, such that it was possible to go and choose a range of flat-packed furniture to take home in a car or van. Queensway and MFI were prominent examples – the latter was regularly advertising in newspapers and on TV, and always seemed to have a sale on!

The receiver sold the Lebus trade name in 1982 to the Christie-Tyler Group, which, like PMA, owned a number of furniture manufacturers. However, Christie-Tyler also became a victim of the changing shape of furniture retailing. Following the demise of two of its major retail customers, Alders and Courts, Christie-Tyler also went into receivership in 2005.

British furniture manufacturers were now competing with the likes of IKEA. With Scandinavian origins as far back as the immediately post-war era, the company opened its first UK superstore in 1989. Its marketing strategy included free catalogues containing (more or less) every item it offered – from flat-packed furniture to plastic-handled cutlery sets. As a successful, global brand with a marketing model based around catalogues, it is ironic to think back to the parallels between Lebus and IKEA.

Saved by a customer, 2005–2012

Even then, Lebus was saved. In 2005 it was purchased by Henk Van Der Veen. He had been a customer of Lebus and had his own furniture stores in Eire. For the next seven years Henk Van Der Veen oversaw the survival of the company. In 2012 he successfully established a new management structure and Lebus Upholstery owes its survival to him.

One of the largest upholstered furniture manufacturers in the UK, 2012–2021

John Wakeman, director of sales, joined in 2014: 'Lebus Upholstery produces in excess of 1,800 three-piece suites per week. We employ over 500 people and turnover has grown to nearly £50 million per annum', he proudly told the author.

Speaking in the week the business reconvened (after the national lockdown of 2020 imposed by the government in response to the COVID-19 pandemic), Wakeman said: 'We have reopened the factory to one of the largest order books in our history. The stores that have opened so far have seen business really booming for them. The future for Lebus Upholstery looks very positive indeed'.

Now operating from a purpose-built plant in Scunthorpe, Lebus Upholstery has returned to its roots – being 25 miles south of Hull, where Louis Lebus arrived from Wroclaw in the 1840s and began cabinet making.

I'm reminded of a reflection made by Roland Phillips on his retirement (he began a 36-year career with Harris Lebus in 1920 as a sales representative covering northern territories): 'Scunthorpe, whose name was still in small type on the map I left in my office in Tottenham Hale, … is today [mid-fifties] a small town with a population approaching 60,000.'

I am also struck by a statement Wakeman made to the author, perhaps without necessarily appreciating its poignancy: 'The new management has grown the business to make the company one of the *largest* (upholstered furniture) manufacturers in the UK'.

Employee Ownership Trust – Lebus Upholstery

In July 2021 came the news that the business had become employee owned through an Employee Ownership Trust (EOT). Karl Walker is the managing director and Henk Van Der Veen is company director. This is a momentous development for a business which has always put people first. The workforce community has been, and always will be, the beating heart of the business.

Such a wonderful way to close this part of the Lebus story.

List of Main Sources

Books, articles and archives

A History of Harris Lebus 1840–1947, Louis Sol Lebus, 1965, unpublished

The Cabinet Maker and Complete House Furnisher (various dates)

The Development and Structure of the Furniture Industry, J.L. Oliver

Furnishing The World: The East London furniture trade 1830–1980, Pat Kirkham, Rodney Mace and Julia Porter, 1987

'How Lebus Turned Round', in *Management Today*, July 1968

Lebus furniture catalogues:
'English-made office and library furniture' 1907, 'Dessins D'Ameublements / Mobel-Vorlagen' 1909, July 1912, 1913, May 1926, September 1934, September 1936, July 1937, January 1939, March 1939, Spring 1953, Spring 1954, 1965 and 1966

The Lebus Log, in-house magazines

The Times online archives

Tottenham and Edmonton Weekly Herald

1900 House – book to accompany channel 4 series, Mark McCrum and Mathew Sturgis

1940 House – book to accompany channel 4 series, Juliet Gardiner

Semi-detached London, Alan A. Jackson, 2nd edition, 1991, Wild Swan Publications Ltd

The G-Plan Revolution: A Celebration of British popular furniture of the 1950s and 1960s, Basil Hyman and Steven Braggs, Booth Clibborn Editions

Sixtiestyle: Home Decoration and Furnishings from the 1960s, Middlesex University Press

Reminiscences gathered by Deborah Hedgecock and Hazel Whitehouse, Bruce Castle Museum (Haringey Archive and Museum Service) with Coombes Croft Library Reminiscence Group, 2007

Online

https://www.retrowow.co.uk/retro_style/furniture/parker_knoll.html

https://www.homesandantiques.com/antiques/collecting-guides-antiques/design-icons/the-best-of-mid-century-modern-design/

https://wbh1.co.uk/2020/02/15/furnishaflat1905/

http://www.moyak.com/papers/history-housing.html

https://www.findmypast.com/1939register/the-1930s-home

https://www.historyextra.com/period/20th-century/a-decade-of-domesticity-how-the-1950s-made-the-modern-home/

https://theconversation.com/amp/houses-through-time-some-homes-can-reflect-a-century-of-social-change-114782

https://purehost.bath.ac.uk/ws/portalfiles/portal/187924632/ROBIN_PAKES_TRADITION_AND_MODERNITY_IN_BATH_BETWEEN_THE_WARS.pdf

http://artdecostyle.ca/art-deco-style-blog/art-deco-colours

https://bigchill.com/us/blog/7-reasons-why-1950s-homes-rocked/

https://www.spoonflower.com/tags/1950s

https://blog.retroplanet.com/1950s-decorating-style/

https://blog.retroplanet.com/1960s-decorating-style/

https://blog.retroplanet.com/1970s-decorating-style/

https://www.christies.com/features/The-A-Z-of-furniture-A-glossary-7548-1.aspx

https://www.housebeautiful.com/uk/renovate/design/news/amp104/homes-through-the-ages/

http://www.antiquebox.org/walnut-and-burr-walnut/

http://www.vintageretro.co.uk/g-plan-fresco-versus-lebus-europa-late-1960s-contest-g-plan-won-easily/